T0393275

E-BOOKS AND 'REAL BOOKS'

On any given day, millions of people will read e-books. Yet many of us will do so while holding them apart from 'real books'. The fact that a book can be worthy – of our time, money, respect, even love – without being 'real' is a fascinating paradox of twenty-first-century reading. Drawing on original data from a longitudinal study, Laura Dietz investigates how movement between conceptions of e-books as *ersatz*, digital proxy, and incomplete books serves readers in unexpected ways. The cultural value of e-books remains an area of intense debate in publishing studies. Exploring the legitimacy of e-books in terms of their 'realness' and 'bookness', Dietz enriches our understanding of what e-books are, while also opening up new ways of thinking about how we imagine, how we use, and what we want from books of every kind. This title is also available as Open Access on Cambridge Core.

LAURA DIETZ is Lecturer in Publishing at University College London. She speaks and publishes widely on reading, authorship, and digital literary culture, serving on related prize, festival, and conference committees, editorial boards, and the Board of Directors of the Society for the History of Authorship, Reading and Publishing.

'Given the complicated nature of e-books, and the fact that the digital landscape and publishing industry change frequently, this is not a topic that many scholars are brave enough to tackle – but that is also why it is needed. Laura Dietz's rich scholarly engagement and far-reaching data survey make this essential reading for those looking to understand book publishing in the twenty-first century.'

Rachel Noorda, Associate Professor and Director of Book Publishing, Portland State University

'A nuanced survey of readerly perceptions around ebooks, this is a study that respects the complexities of engaging with the material and shows appreciation for the deeply contextual nature of the arguments concerned, dispelling notions of a rigid binary set up by metaphors around "the death of the book" or "book wars". This is an informative and insightful contribution to scholarly field of publishing studies.'

Simon Rowberry, Lecturer in Publishing, University College London

E-BOOKS AND 'REAL BOOKS'

Digital Reading and the Experience of Bookness

LAURA DIETZ

University College London

CAMBRIDGE
UNIVERSITY PRESS

Shaftesbury Road, Cambridge CB2 8EA, United Kingdom

One Liberty Plaza, 20th Floor, New York, NY 10006, USA

477 Williamstown Road, Port Melbourne, VIC 3207, Australia

314–321, 3rd Floor, Plot 3, Splendor Forum, Jasola District Centre, New Delhi – 110025, India

103 Penang Road, #05-06/07, Visioncrest Commercial, Singapore 238467

Cambridge University Press is part of Cambridge University Press & Assessment,
a department of the University of Cambridge.

We share the University's mission to contribute to society through the pursuit of
education, learning and research at the highest international levels of excellence.

www.cambridge.org
Information on this title: www.cambridge.org/9781009490764

DOI: 10.1017/9781009490795

First published 2025

A catalogue record for this publication is available from the British Library.

Library of Congress Cataloging-in-Publication Data
NAMES: Dietz, Laura, author.
TITLE: E-books and 'real books' : digital reading and the experience of bookness / Laura Dietz,
University College London.
DESCRIPTION: New York : Cambridge University Press, 2024. |
Includes bibliographical references and index.
IDENTIFIERS: LCCN 2024025144 (print) | LCCN 2024025145 (ebook) | ISBN 9781009490764
(hardback) | ISBN 9781009490771 (paperback) | ISBN 9781009490795 (epub)
SUBJECTS: LCSH: Electronic books. | Books and reading–History–21st century. |
Reading, Psychology of.
CLASSIFICATION: LCC Z1033.E43 D54 2024 (print) | LCC Z1033.E43 (ebook) |
DDC 028–dc23/eng/20240710
LC record available at https://lccn.loc.gov/2024025144
LC ebook record available at https://lccn.loc.gov/2024025145

ISBN 978-1-009-49076-4 Hardback

For Bryan Dietz
Fellow of Bell Labs, IEEE Life Member,
and my dad

For Bryan Dietz
Fellow of Bell Labs, IEEE Life Member,
and my dad

Contents

List of Figures   *page* viii
Acknowledgements   x

Introduction   1

1   Bookness   14

2   Paratexts and First Impressions: Taking a Chance
on an E-book   35

3   Ownership and Permanence: E-book Transactions   61

4   Materiality, Convenience, and Customisation:
E-books and the Act of Reading   93

5   Reading Lives and Reading Identities: Genre,
Audience, and Being a Reader of E-books   133

Coda   185

Appendix: Definitions   194
Notes   197
Index   247

Figures

1.1 Rocket eBook, © Mark Richards. Courtesy the Computer History Museum (www.computerhistory.org/revolution/mobile-computing/18/319/1721). *page* 2

1.2 Revised communications circuit, Ray Murray and Squires, 'The Digital Publishing Communications Circuit' (Published under a Creative Commons Attribution-No Derivatives licence (https://creativecommons.org/licenses/by-nd/4.0/)). 7

1.1 Active Book prototype (Courtesy the Centre for Computing History, exhibit reference ID CH53902). 25

1.2 'Yes' responses to 'do you consider e-books to be real books?' by age. 29

2.1 Eastgate Systems, Inc. packaging of Sarah Smith's 'King of Space' (1991) (Courtesy the Electronic Literature Lab, https://scalar.usc.edu/works/rebooting-electronic-literature/photos-of-sarah-smiths-king-of-space). 38

2.2 'When you choose print, what are your reasons?' (All readers, all years). 49

2.3 'When you choose digital, what are your reasons?' (E-book readers only, all years). 51

2.4 Publication status of last e-book downloaded. 55

3.1 Sources of e-books. 68

3.2 Sources of e-books: library, by year. 69

3.3 Reasons for choosing print: 'better for keeping as part of a personal library', by age. 83

4.1 Reasons for choosing print: 'a print book is more enjoyable to handle and use', by age. 97

4.2 Reasons for choosing digital: 'a reading device is more enjoyable to handle and use', by age. 101

4.3 Reasons for choosing digital: 'a reading device is more enjoyable to handle and use', by year. 103

4.4 Reasons for choosing digital: 'convenience' factors. 107

4.5 Reasons for choosing digital: 'easier to obtain', by year. 108

4.6 Reasons for choosing print: 'easier to read', by age. 114

4.7 Reasons for choosing print: 'easier to read', by age, print-only readers versus e-book readers. 115

4.8 Reasons for choosing digital: 'easier to read', by age. 115

5.1 Reasons for choosing digital: 'better for privacy – no one can see what I'm reading', by age. 137

5.2 Reasons for choosing print: 'I would describe myself as a bibliophile', by year. 169

5.3 Reasons for choosing print: 'I would describe myself as a bibliophile', by age. 170

5.4 Reasons for choosing print: 'I would describe myself as a bibliophile', by source of print books. 171

Acknowledgements

Thousands of people have been willing to talk to me about reading. Their generosity made this book possible, and the experiences they've shared have made this the most fascinating, inspiring conversation I could possibly have hoped to join. I'm deeply grateful to them all.

Thanks are inadequate for all the scholarly support and astute suggestions that have strengthened the book. I'm particularly indebted to friends and colleagues at University College London (UCL), Anglia Ruskin University (ARU), the Society for the History of Authorship, Reading and Publishing, and elsewhere. Naming just Tiffani Angus, Francesca Benatti, Kathi Inman Berens, Nick Canty, Ryan Cordell, Alexandra Dane, Matthew Day, Beth Driscoll, Astrid Ensslin, Judy Forshaw, Caron Freeborn, Danielle Fuller, Alan Galey, Dene Grigar, Vince Haig, Esmond Harmsworth, Leah Henrickson, Tanya Horeck, Timothy Jarvis, Mareike Jenner, Edmund King, Matt Kirschenbaum, Una McCormack, Helen Marshall, Simone Murray, Eben Muse, Corinna Norrick-Rühl, Colette Paul, Julie Rak, Melanie Ramdarshan Bold, Katharine Reeve, DeNel Rehberg Sedo, Rebecca Roach, Matthew Rubery, Sydney Shep, Tyler Shores, Claire Squires, Ann Steiner, Jon Stone, Emma Sweeney, Leah Tether, Bronwen Thomas, Shafquat Towheed, Claire Warwick, Millicent Weber, Kim Wilkins, Caroline Wintersgill, and Tory Young represents vast understatement. I'm especially grateful to the people of the UCL Centre for Publishing, including Daniel Boswell, Caroline Davis, Joanna Longden, and Simon Rowberry, and, above all, to Samantha Rayner, who has been with this project from the earliest inklings of research questions. The fact that there is anything to read here is a testament to her steadfast kindness, and to what pure, clear-eyed, bulletproof curiosity about books and how we study them can inspire students to do.

At Cambridge University Press, Bethany Thomas has shaped and guided this book from enhancing the proposal through every stage of editing and production. My heartfelt thanks to her and to Adam Hooper, Emma Goff-Leggett, George Laver, Heidi Mulvey, Aiswarya Narayanan, the manuscript reviewers who were so generous with their time and expertise, and the whole of the remarkable team at CUP.

Special thanks are due to the Centre for Computing History, the Computer History Museum, and the Electronic Literature Lab for the kind help with access and photo permissions, and as always for their work in maintaining indispensable collections.

I am infinitely grateful to my family, for their support and also the years of book talk and the examples, counterarguments, fresh leads, and big ideas shared over dinner tables and video calls; Dad's lore of the early days of desktop publishing is only one example. To my mom, Jeannie, my dad, Bryan, and to Shelby, Eanna, Jack, Catherine, Martine, Martin, Phil, Mandy, Niamh, Arun, Jill: thank you.

The greatest debt is, as usual, the one closest to home. E, C, B, you are everything. Sharing that bookstore café table was the best move I've ever made.

Introduction

Today, many millions will spend time reading an e-book. All will have excellent reasons for using digital formats. Some will read on screens because no other option is given: perhaps students whose lecturers assign digitised textbooks, or Kindle Unlimited patrons sitting down with a new novel that has no print edition. Others will have had a choice. If asked why, on that day and for that book, they opted for digital rather than print, readers will cite a familiar array of factors: speed of access, searchable text, and so on. They will explain how their personal requirements and circumstances make e-books the right choice at certain times. But many will do all of this while holding e-books at arm's-length. E-books will be described as part of their reading lives; even an indispensable part. Yet they will remain distinct from 'proper books' and 'actual books'.[1] Readers may qualify that 'in many ways *I prefer real books*, but e-books take up much less space in the house'.[2] They may explain that 'the convenience of e-readers for travel is amazing. I can carry a huge library in my handbag. However *I still prefer real books*'[3] (also demonstrating how a library can be devoid of 'real' books, yet still valued and still a library). Or they may spell out that 'digital reading is a nice convenience, but I hope it doesn't ever *replace real books*'.[4] These readers can't be written off as snobs, luddites, or unbending print absolutists; their reservations can't be dismissed as hatred of technology or fear of change. E-books are frequently worth their time, their money, their respect, even their love. The fact that a book can be worthy without being real is the fascinating quandary of e-reading in the twenty-first century, and the subject of this book. What does it mean – for ourselves as readers and for our understanding of what a book can be – to devote the hours of our lives to books that aren't real books?

I'm not an e-book evangelist (though, like everyone who reads them, I'm sometimes called upon to play the e-book apologist when defending my reading to someone who considers it illegitimate or second-rate). I'm better described as someone fascinated by e-books and the people who read

Figure I.1   Rocket eBook, © Mark Richards. Courtesy the Computer History Museum.
www.computerhistory.org/revolution/mobile-computing/18/319/1721

them. This is not because it was love at first sight. I had commonplace
opportunities to explore experiments in electronic publishing and squandered
nearly all of them. Growing up, we had a family address book desktop-
published using a GE TermiNet 1200[5] (when my father first became
interested in desktop publishing in the 1970s, relevant reference books, such
as Brian Kernighan and P. J. Plauger's *Software Tools*,[6] were sometimes sold
with UNIX source code on an accompanying spool of magnetic tape). In my
grade school library, CD ROM encyclopaedias sat next to the microfiche
readers, and I found microfiche at least as intuitive and vastly more fun. I had
a dim awareness of digital holdings in university library collections: things
that weren't webpages but one would nevertheless read on screen (specifically, the screen of a humming dorm-computer-lab Macintosh Performa, or at
best the candy-coloured clamshell of an iBook G3). But I have no memory of
ever reading one myself, nor feeling any warmth or wariness or hostility
towards these artefacts, nor having any opinion of any kind. Every encounter
with the digital book hit the wall of my indifference and lack of imagination,
until the Rocket eBook (Figure I.1).

In 1998, I was working as a research analyst at a small consulting firm in
Los Altos, and my boss asked me to write up a quick report on a soon-to-
be-released product.[7] She handed me a 5 by 7¾ inch block of bluish-grey
plastic, bigger on one edge like a dough scraper (or, observers would later
note, a wedge-shaped first-generation Kindle).[8] You could manually rotate
the display to grip the bulky side in your left or right hand. It came with a
stylus and a backlit LED screen. You hooked it up to your computer with
a cable, next to your PalmPilot dock, to download books: the micro-
selection included *Alice in Wonderland* and a handful of Agatha Christie
novels. The physical object had the visual and tactile appeal of an electricity meter. I was entranced. I held it in my hands (both hands, because it

weighed almost a pound and a half), elated by the possibilities and correspondingly impatient when the device I held realised so few of them, and blurted out that this would change everything. The Rocket eBook itself didn't last long enough to change much of anything,[9] and it would be nearly a decade before the Kindle, and the abundant cut-price bestsellers in Amazon's Kindle Store, made e-readers ubiquitous. But to me, that artefact felt like a step towards the realisation of a dream from so many stories: a personal book, one with a deceptively stable outside but contents that became whatever you desired in the moment. Like 'the idea of a talking book' (or talking scroll), something featured in literature since antiquity and that 'captured the popular imagination long before the technology came along' to make it a reality,[10] the idea of a mutable personal book evoked Lucy Pevensie in Narnia, reading her dreams and fears in the pages of Coriakin's magic book, or at the very least Arthur Dent extracting semi-useful information from his handheld Hitchhiker's Guide to the Galaxy.[11] A book about anything you wanted, or everything you wanted, and changing alongside you.

I didn't begin to ask about e-books and 'real books' until 2013. That set of questions grew from a study on the legitimacy and reputation of e-books and e-novels, which gathered data on reading and publishing in a format that had finally, after many false starts, burst into the mainstream. The question robbing publishers of sleep in the early 2010s was whether – or for the more pessimistic, when – e-book sales would overwhelm print. (The e-book plateau, where digital and print appeared to have settled into a rough equilibrium, only emerged later in the decade.) But for authors, the question of how to make a living in the e-book era ran alongside another question: how to be an author when the 'book' did not always, and might never, exist on paper. As one of my students put it, in questions after a graduate seminar on publishing technologies, 'but does an e-book *count*?' That characteristically insightful student asked from a writer's perspective – whether a digital-only publication was capable of delivering the kind of royalties, rights income, status, prestige (including eligibility for literary prizes), professional advancement, and/or personal satisfaction as print – without neglecting the participation of agents, publishers, distributors, retailers, and, ultimately (in every sense), readers in a process where consensus between people turns collections of words from manuscripts into books. What would it take for an e-book to *count* like a print book, to enjoy the same status, and deliver to its author the same rewards? Her question was enormous, and my answer painfully small – something I set out to remedy.

My initial hypothesis was that if it were possible for an e-book to *count*, it would be for specific e-books in specific contexts: that there would be something distinctive about those books, those publishers, or those readers. I found something quite different. It remained the case that e- and print were not equivalent, and there was (and is) no immediate prospect of them becoming so. It remained the case that there is a dramatic range of opinion: many nuanced and interacting stances, too complex to be divided into neat sides. But it was not a matter of some people accepting e-books as real books as a condition of embracing e-reading and/or e-publishing. Instead, it proved possible for some (again, not all) readers to consider e-books as something separate from 'real books', but to embrace them anyway.

Something else emerged from the data. Participants frequently used the word 'real'.[12] Readers explain that they 'prefer real books but ebooks are very convenient', that they 'tend to prefer real books to ebooks', and share many variations on 'I just prefer the real [print] thing'.[13] But what readers never used – not once in the dataset – was the word 'fake'. (Equally absent were related terms such as 'impostor', 'fraud' and 'sham'; 'hoax', 'cheat', and 'forgery'; and also 'unreal'.) E-books were, by some, condemned as 'impersonal', or 'sterile',[14] but not as fake.

In extended conversations about e-books, something else emerges. While a single statement about e-books or audiobooks may sound definitive – splitting books into digital versus 'actual', or 'proper', or 'the real thing' – over the course of a longer dialogue, it was not unusual for e-books to be excluded from 'actual' at one point but welcomed in at another. Even a medium of exchange as rigid as a survey offered space for this mutability. In three examples from a single survey year, 2022, participants raise realness unprompted in free-text responses – saying 'For some reason, *books* feel more '*real*'. Everything was digital in the pandemic, so reading a physical book became a way of reconnecting to a reality' or 'I'm a book snob … prefer *the real thing*: how it feels, smells, looks' or 'I prefer *real books* [to e-books]' – but went on, a few questions later, to answer 'do you consider e-books to be real books?' with *yes*.

Many excellent books and scholarly papers concentrate on the definition of 'book' (as I'll discuss in Chapter 1) and the place of digital books inside or outside that category. This book will not. The discussion here is informed and enriched by that literature, but does not aspire to advance that particular debate. My focus is not on the dividing line between books and not-books, but rather the nature, the uses, and the counterintuitive appeal of this territory of the unreal book: not real but not fake, still 'book', but of a new and intriguing kind. This book examines the paradox of mass adoption without mass acceptance: the phenomenon of e-book readers for whom 'the opposite of "e-book" is sometimes "p-book", but often *real book*'.[15] It explores the way in which readers finesse definitions of book-ness when they describe their range of experiences with digital books, as when 'older books, hard to find books I have in book form for personal library',[16] a division between print books as books 'in book form' and e-books as books but in some other form. It is about the space inside 'book' while outside 'actual book'; all the different permutations of 'no, but' that coexist with 'yes, and'. It's concerned with the space we make for ourselves as readers when we seize control of *book* and make it mean what we want, when we want. . .even if sometimes what we want is to deny our own agency, or that change is taking place at all. Exploring that space deepens our understanding of e-books, a major component of modern reading and hence a force in cultural, educational, economic, and political life. But it also opens up new ways of thinking about how we imagine, how we use, and what we want from books of every kind – and how this is expanding as book technologies evolve.

Methods

To explore this territory, and examine the phenomenon of mass readership of unreal books, I'll investigate how realness and bookness as forms of legitimacy are conceptualised, constituted, and experienced by contempor-ary readers. To do so, I'll analyse data on readers' choices, priorities, requirements, beliefs, and values relating to e-books, not as abstract questions but as they interrelate in actual reading lives. Data is drawn in the first instance from surveys, focus groups, and interviews with readers and writers. The survey ($n = 1,732$) was conducted yearly from 2014 to 2017 and again from 2020 to 2022. Additional material, including journalism, social media posts, author websites, and Amazon terms and conditions, was sought out to further investigate questions and themes identified in the surveys, focus groups, and interviews,[17] and interpreted using qualitative content analysis.[18] In this synthesis, I enlist methods from publishing studies, book history, and digital humanities. Media studies, particularly media archaeology and platform studies, and digital literary studies support my efforts.[19] I draw inspiration from studies that go where the readers are, from Janice Radway's interviews with forty-two romance readers in a midwestern town to the READ-IT project's groundbreaking qualitative data aggregation,[20] and as always from the interdisciplinary approaches of scholars such as Johanna Drucker, Lisa Gitelman, Matthew Kirschenbaum, Simone Murray, and Leah Price.

E-books and e-reading are extraordinarily contentious subjects, inspiring hyperbolic rhetoric and defensive position-taking among defenders and detractors alike.[21] The vocabulary of legitimacy is aggressively deployed not only by e-book retailers such as Amazon and Apple but also by anti-e-book commentators, giving rise to headlines such as 'How real books have trumped ebooks', 'Real books are back. E-book sales plunge nearly 20%', and 'Rise and Fall of the Kindle: how Real Books are Fighting Back'.[22] In a commercial environment where realness is treated as a commodity, it's all the more vital that new research on the cultural value of e-books draws on empirical evidence – and of more than one kind. Anne Mangen describes questions regarding differences between paper and screen reading experiences as 'properly empirical questions', despite a shortage of empirical studies and of contact between disciplines on such studies, though some progress has been made.[23] However, Ben Davies, Christina Lupton, and Johanne Gormsen Schmidt note the prevalence of 'empirical studies of reading in the present moment that might be accused of downplaying the cultural, historical, and spatial particularity of the inter-action between text and reader'.[24] Jonathan Rose pinpoints the temptations of speculation in the absence of data, noting the misrepresentations that result when scholars 'dogmatise enormously about the sociology of reading without bothering to study actual readers', while Christine Pawley stresses the importance of ethnographic and other qualitative methods to preserve the historical and spatial dimensions of individual acts of reading, and skirt the trap of distorting generalisation.[25] Danielle Fuller and DeNel Rehberg Sedo note how qualitative methods, widely used in book history and reading studies, are themselves under scrutiny, particularly the semi-structured interviews often hailed as the gold standard: researchers justifiably ask whether established data coding practices aimed at 'identifying similarities and repetitions' fail because this 'merely reproduces what we already know about the social world' and propose 'postqualitative' alternative approaches, such as diffraction analysis, that recognise 'instability of meaning'[26] and embrace multiple interpretations of data.[27] To subject data validity to scrutiny, I used a mixed methods study (in convergent parallel form, where multiple categories of data collected at the same time allowed me to confront and examine contradictions as they emerged) to triangulate on more robust findings.[28] But the more important component is, following the example of researchers above, working to remain open-minded. I wish to put forward my interpretations in the hope that they will be critiqued and questioned, and that debate can lead to new interpretations.

Scope

Three areas of concentration will help keep discussion in a book-sized, rather than library-sized, space: focus on readers, particular attention to novels, and one decade in time.

Out of all the possible (and fascinating) points of focus on the digital communications circuit, I've chosen one: readers.[29] My reason is their unique position regarding legitimacy. Readers are no longer routinely imagined as dead ends, as they were in some twentieth- and pre-twentieth-century models depicting readers as the last link in a linear chain, 'passive receptors' of material conceived and shaped by authors, editors, booksellers, and other actors 'above' the reader in every sense.[30] But their onward contribution (captured in contemporary models such as Ray Murray and Squires's update of Darnton's communication circuit[31] by dotted lines; see Figure I.2) is more flexible and optional than that of other

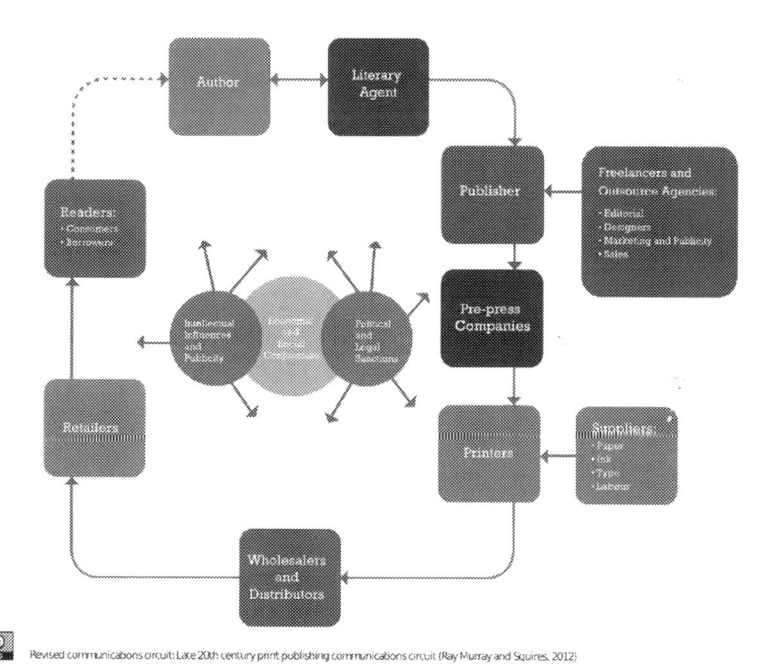

Figure I.2   Revised communications circuit, Ray Murray and Squires, 'The Digital Publishing Communications Circuit'[32] (Published under a Creative Commons Attribution-No Derivatives licence (https://creativecommons.org/licenses/by-nd/4.0/)).

participants: they do not have to take any further action, and the circuit will not come to a halt if they do not.

They are the only participants who do not hold as a primary concern how the work will be passed on to the next participant, and how the next participant will be convinced that the work *is* a book, and a book of quality. Their requirements (or lack of requirements) shape the efforts of those 'upstream' who seek to please them, yet their definitions of legitimacy can be more personal and individual, even idiosyncratic. This makes readers' experiences of book realness fascinating but elusive; at times veiled even to ourselves. The complexities of this form of legitimacy, and how we constitute it, won't reveal themselves without dedicated investigation.

An extraordinary range of artefacts and humanistic knowledge objects have been placed at some point, by their creators or by commentators and scholars, in the category of 'e-book'.[33] But in terms of trade publishing, novels are the largest single subcategory, making up such a large proportion of commercial e-book sales that any movement in the adult trade fiction sector shifts the entire e-book market. By 2015, two-thirds of e-books sold in the US with ISBN were adult fiction, a category that at the time claimed only a quarter of print book sales (and only a third of print sales before the start of the e-book revolution).[34] While data gathered at the height of the COVID-19 pandemic must be interpreted with caution, given how temporary conditions (bookshop closures, paper shortages, changing reading patterns under lockdown, etc.) affected different territories at different times, in the UK, in 2022, adult fiction accounted for nearly 80 per cent of e-book purchases.[35] Since 2015, the size of the e-novel market has become more difficult to quantify as an increasing share has been taken by Amazon, which does not share detailed sales figures, and self-publishing, for which there are no detailed sales figures centrally compiled, but the predominance of adult fiction for these publishers[36] suggests that the dominance of the novel has only increased.

Self-evidently, not all books are the same. Whether grouped by commercial category (cookery, travel, etc.), by genre (history, memoir, romance, etc.), by audience (children's), by setting ('beach reads', etc.), or by other logics, no two classifications will have the same usages, communities, or traditions. But e-novels are rarely grouped together and studied as a category despite distinctive characteristics that link as strongly to the history of the novel as the history of the e-book. Novels have a unique history in electronic publishing, a unique commercial environment (e.g. on key distribution platforms such as Kindle Unlimited and Wattpad) and, as I'll discuss in later chapters, sometimes perform differently from other kinds of text in studies of e-reading immersion, transportation, and comprehension. It's essential to consider where e-novels differ from other forms and where they do not, lest characteristics unique to this commercially dominant category be mistaken for characteristics of e-books as a whole.

Finally, the project examines attitudes towards e-book realness over time. The decade covered, 2013–23, is arbitrary (chosen for its placement in my own research life rather than any retrospective selection) yet fortuitously turbulent. The 2010s were already a time of enormous change in the e-book environment. The years 2014–17, when initial surveys were conducted, spanned developments from the United States Department of Justice ruling that Apple conspired with Hachette, HarperCollins, Macmillan, Penguin, and Simon & Schuster to fix e-book prices, the drastic rise in average price for mainstream-published e-books,[37] the explosion in the availability of low-priced or free-to-reader fiction in the form of self-published novels (often via Amazon) and pirated copies, the launch of Kindle Unlimited, and the shift from Kindle reading to tablet and smartphone reading. All of these developments contributed to the most significant change, the plateau of e-reading and shift of e-book sales from mainstream commercial publishers to Amazon and self-publishing.[38] The only thing that might make the 2010s seem like an uneventful decade for reading is comparison to the 2020s. This book was initially due for submission to the publisher in early 2021. But by mid-2020, it was undeniable that reading, digital reading in particular, would continue to be so profoundly affected by physical confinement, loss of access to personal book collections and ordinary sources of print books, scrambled routines and relationships to time, increased consumption of news, and isolation and anxiety, that it was necessary to ask how relationships to books and reading might be permanently changed by the crisis.[39] Would the pandemic be, as Bronwen Thomas asked in November 2020, the moment when digital reading came of age?[40] When the experience of digital reading as the default (for the many rather than the few) brought platforms and audiences to maturity? More pessimistically, I questioned whether the shared experience of digital as a life raft, keeping reading and shared experiences of literature afloat would really show the strengths of digital as an invaluable component to be retained – much less cherished – when conditions improved. It seemed equally likely that digital would become, to those privileged readers returning to a buffet of reading options, the government cheese of literature: a last resort to be shunned until the next crisis.[41] The span of 2020–22, when the second round of

yearly surveys were conducted, captured at one end the first of the
COVID-19 lockdowns and at the other the early months of the war in
Ukraine. Gathering longitudinal data in these years offered the potential
for identifying change, or lack of change, at times when access to books
and reasons for reading were in particularly violent flux.

Contribution

Research to date has demonstrated that e-book legitimacy is both complex
and contested: only partially understood, but still recognised as relevant
and important. Examinations of e-book materiality[42] intersect with
debates on the realness of digital artefacts, and activate longstanding
controversies surrounding the evolving metaphor of the book.[43] But it
had not previously been established that readers share any assumption that
bookness (or any other form of legitimacy) is consistently an important
factor in e-book desirability, utility, market value, or cultural value.
However fervent the bookness messages from retailers (or however fervent
the resistance from anti-e-book voices), readers remain 'active agents' who
can 'resist the codes implicit in the text'.[44]

The value of e-books – how and whether they *count* – matters to anyone
who cares about the value of books. The potential of digital publishing to
transform the processes by which worth is constituted and communicated
is long recognised. Even predigital proposals for specific mechanised
reading technologies, such as Bob Brown's 1930 Readies and Vannevar
Bush's 1945 Memex, confronted the issue of value: when pioneers speculated as to how new reading functionalities would change readers' relationship to texts, this included how readers would evaluate and esteem texts
(and in Brown's case, argue that mechanised reading represented an
existential, and long overdue, threat to print).[45] Before the earliest device
prototypes were built, researchers acknowledged the capacity for disruption and proposed ways in which any future move to mass e-reading could
transform the status of books and reading. The new ubiquity of e-books
makes it possible, and essential, to continue to bring these long-standing
explorations of e-book cultural value from the hypothetical to the concrete.
Legitimacy in the form of realness is only one aspect of cultural value, but
for e-books it is a fundamental aspect, crystallising the central question of
whether e-books can be classed with books and partake of the book's
cultural status and privileged cultural position. 'The book', as Galey
reminds us, 'is never just an ideal object in isolation, but always contextualised by the systems that surround it, whether those systems are social or
mechanical'.[46] Examining e-books within these systems, the data I have

collected to date indicate that legitimacy in the form of realness or bookness remains highly relevant for readers. However, conceptions of realness and bookness are flexible and context-specific. While realness and bookness are widely recognised as desirable qualities, many uses to which readers put their e-books make realness, and the responsibility and weight that come with it, unnecessary or actually undesirable. Further, the moiety of unrealness is as important as the unrealness itself, with three main categories of unrealness emerging as most prominent: e-book as *ersatz book*, as digital proxy, and as incomplete book. Individual readers move between conceptions, demonstrating willingness to adopt different ideas of realness (and by extension different stances regarding the nature and cultural value of e-books) depending on their needs in the moment, and what they require from a given e-book at a particular time.

Book Structure

The chapters to come are organised chronologically, examining conceptions of bookness before following readers through the stages of discovering, obtaining, reading, and keeping a digital book.

Chapter 1, 'Bookness', uses book history and digital humanities approaches to open discussion of the evolving metaphor of the book. This chapter reviews existing scholarship on the bookness of physical books, the realness of electronic texts, the complexities of e-book paratext, and realness as it relates to literary status, progressing to personal definitions of book realness and analysing original survey data on whether and why readers consider an e-book a real book.

The next four chapters follow a reader's journey, examining bookness and realness as they are constituted – and used to further the reader's purposes – at different stages. Chapter 2, 'Paratexts and First Impressions: Taking a Chance on an E-book', investigates first encounters with e-books and the process by which readers evaluate a given work on screen. It examines how trust is established and legitimacy constituted in practice, considering realness and bookness in terms of a given e-book's status as cultural product and cultural object. It further applies Genette's paratextual theory to the negotiation of status between reader, author, and publisher. Chapter 3, 'Ownership and Permanence: E-book Transactions', explores how, but also why, readers who have decided to take a leap of faith with their chosen e-book will obtain it, contrasting the motivations for purchase (or conditional licence purchase), loan, and piracy. It draws on legal scholarship, book history, and fan studies to explore how bookness and realness in the form of meaningful ownership may be constructed (should the reader wish it) even in the absence of traditional forms, and when readers may prefer temporary, informal, or actually illegal uses to permanent and authorised ones. It concludes with debates on the rights of the reader, the fraught question of e-book control, and readers' experiences of conflict with corporate entities over ownership of their collections. Chapter 4, 'Materiality, Convenience, and Customisation: E-books and the Act of Reading', looks at the comparatively brief period when the book is not anticipated or recalled, but experienced. Contrasting devices and platforms, it considers what kinds of pleasure readers seek from an e-book (in different settings, and at different times), and the ways in which an e-book does or does not deliver such satisfactions. Examining aspects such as tactile dimensions of embodied reading, the role of the material object, convenience and access, optimisation and customisation, and narrative immersion, it contextualises original findings with recent empirical research on screen reading and offer insights on how, where, and when intimacy, sense of achievement, and the feeling of being 'lost in a book' can be found in e-reading. Chapter 5, 'Reading Lives and Reading Identities: Genre, Audience, and Being a Reader of E-books', brings the reader's journey full circle, investigating how e-books, once read, are shared or not shared, displayed or not displayed, and made a cherished part of the reader's personal history or barred from such status. Working with theories from legal studies and psychology (on the definitions and uses of embarrassment, guilt, and shame), it considers how and why readers reconcile e-book reading with personal definitions of bookishness. It examines, in particular, privacy, including narratives of furtive reading, and public declarations of book-love. Investigating bibliophilia as both an identity and a set of bookish practices and values, it considers what it means to be a book lover in the digital era and report on how readers form, strengthen, and express relationships to digital texts. The Coda draws together realness, bookness, and the e-book reader's journey to offer perspectives on e-book legitimacy, worth, and cultural value, and outline implications for all participants in the communications circuit.

This book aims to begin to map the no man's land between e-books and 'real books'. This begins with acknowledging that it exists. In my study, some respondents have found fault with themselves for experiencing complexity. Apologising for the 'emotive', for the 'little voice' causing trouble, one explained:

> Mine is an emotive answer [to the question of e-book realness] not based on logic. Logic tells me that the actual format is fairly irrelevant and that all cultural product develops and changes over time…and so it should. The conception, construction and realisation of a written product far outweighs

what media it is produced in / accessed. So I guess I consider an e book to be a real book. . .but some little voice is still saying, "It's not though, is it?' Which is wholly irrational but there it is.

This book argues that such a stance is far from irrational. The space between bookness and 'real book'-ness is made together. There is much to be discovered by, instead of apologising for the contradictions, confronting the ambiguity and examining how and why we maintain it. In asking why it is we read books that aren't real books, it makes sense to ask who gains when we keep this area grey.

CHAPTER I

Bookness

'I also get [e-books] while reading an actual book, to allow me to read when I forget to bring my book.'

(Survey 2020)

'I read both books and on my kindle.'

(Survey 2020)

'I think it's snobbery to say that only print books are "real".'

(Survey 2022)

The question of whether digital books deserve full status as 'books' – and equality with print – has dogged e-books since their inception. It's inspired illuminating debate on the bookness of books alongside painful and rancorous position-taking.[1] Readers scarred by the 'book wars'[2] and exasperated by the 'either/or logic [that] has plagued discussion of all things digital and literary since the early 1990s "death of the book" debates began'[3] are now negotiating e-book realness on their own terms. This chapter uses book history and digital humanities approaches to situate e-books' liminal 'book but not *real* book' status within historic and contemporary conceptualisations. Addressing long-standing debates on materiality and longevity, it progresses through aspects of legitimacy – the realness of digital objects, bookness as historically defined for physical books, and genre boundaries of literary texts traditionally presented in physical book form – on its way to investigating readers' responses when asked whether and why they consider e-books real.

The legitimacy of e-books is the central focus of only a few studies, but the question of what makes an e-book an e-book, rather than some other sort of artefact, lives in some way inside every study of the e-book yet conducted, as a necessary step in defining the corpus to be considered. It draws particularly on rich existing scholarship on the evolving metaphor of the book.

The Metaphor of the Book

The question of 'what is a book' may be an old one, but it can be asked not as 'a tiresome postmodern game with words' but rather as 'an inquiry that is highly relevant to many facets of how a phenomenon acquires "cultural value"'.[4] In the twenty-first century, the question is more urgent, not less: as Caroline Koegler and Corinna Norrick-Rühl explain in *Are Books Still 'Different'?: Literature as Culture and Commodity in a Digital Age*, 'digitisation not only affects the structural conditions of the book market and the legal status of books but also book marketing and even how "books" themselves may be adequately understood'.[5] Inquiries that approach books as concepts, containers, cultural transactions, information architectures,[6] and other forms are in simultaneous use, and fruitful advances in the discussion often emerge from contrast.[7]

As 'the word "book" refers to two distinct concepts...an empirically measurable object [and] a powerful and comprehensive type of metaphor',[8] scholars have immense discretion over whether to frame bookness as something e-books can or cannot ever have. They can place emphasis on 'common features'[9] that e-books share with print books, or instead direct focus towards features that e-books lack. Attention to aspects such as fixedness,[10] embodiedness,[11] or romance,[12] foregrounds viewpoints from which e-books cannot easily be included in the category of book, while focus on aspects such as information seeking[13] and reader communities[14] foregrounds uses of books where digital can genuinely participate, if differently from print. Historical approaches (including platform studies and some schools of English literature criticism) have frequently contrasted the era of digital book adoption with previous format shifts (e.g. scroll to codex,[15] manuscript to print,[16] artisan production to industrial production,[17] or hardcover to paperback) and signposted the ways in which the definition of book has in the past expanded to embrace new forms. This emphasis foregrounds how the definition of book could (even if they judge that it has not yet) embrace the e-book. In contrast, sociological and cultural studies approaches, in examining the roles books play in book cultures and reading lives,[18] have tended to stress the ways in which e-books do not play the same roles or occupy the same position, hence foregrounding aspects of book status that currently, and may enduringly, exclude e-books. This is not to say that history and sociology or history and cultural studies are in any way in opposition: Westin's 'Loss of Culture: New media forms and the translation from analogue to digital books', for example, is the work of an archaeologist/historian approaching the question via critical heritage studies and Callon's sociology of translation.[19] In 'Ebookness', Rowberry argued that e-books are better understood as a service than as a product, drawing on platform studies and book history to investigate the porous borders of a form where 'not all digital books are ebooks, but all ebooks are digital'.[20] He identified three platform layers of e-books as technology, text, and service infrastructure, and examined ways in which e-book conventions sacrifice functionality for the sake of bookish allusions and fidelity to print traditions: e-bookness as tethered to bookness.

The Bookness of Physical Books

Philip Smith claims to have 'coined the term "bookness"' (in quotation marks) in the 1970s; inspired, in appropriately literary fashion, by questions on the 'horseness of horses' in *Ulysses*.[21] But in truth, the term has been originated many times over: remade in different settings and for different purposes, generally without reference to coinages that came before. Smith defined bookness against textness, describing a particular physical object (specifically, a 'hinged multi-planar vehicle or substrate on which texts...may be written, drawn, reproduced, printed or assembled') to exclude non-codex texts (such as *Bleak House* projected on a wall or *Mansfield Park* painted on a fan)[22] but include blank books, illegible books, and unopenable books, and hence demarcate the territory for book art as a subfield of fine art. But at roughly the same time, Donald Roy Howard was using the term in the context of literary studies, employing bookness in the 1976 *The Idea of the Canterbury Tales* as an 'opposing qualit[y]' to 'voiceness'.[23] There, bookness encompassed aspects of status deriving from rarity, expense, and impressive materiality, the book as an 'object of veneration...a thing with dignity, magic, and the power to inspire awe'.[24] Later scholarly uses variously defined bookness against scrollness (in the sense of a physical scroll or a scrolling webpage), emphasising the manner of navigation through a text organised as a codex,[25] against audioness,[26] or against other dimensions of print. Non-scholarly uses were and are even more various, deploying bookness to describe anything or anyone book-related[27] (such as a personal blog by someone who likes reading or a Pinterest board of *Game of Thrones* memes) or simply as a play on words (as with the New York Public Library's 'Twelve Days of Bookness' or a bookbinding workshop entitled 'Mind Your Own Bookness!').[28] Whether it is called bookness or not, the concept of bookness is woven through debates on books in every era where books have existed: a concept left unnamed where deemed too basic and fundamental to require mention. It is ultimately a term without defined lineage and without fixed meaning: too scattered to serve as jargon, and perhaps too playful (or too often playfully used) to find a secure home in scholarly discourse. In each usage, it is defined anew.

The two fields where bookness has something approaching a critical heritage are book arts and digital humanities, largely due to the enormous influence of Johanna Drucker's work in both. In *The Century of Artists' Books*, first published in 1994, Drucker sought ways to examine a book's book-ness (with a hyphen but, significantly, without quotation marks) as 'its identity as a set of aesthetic functions, cultural operations, formal conceptions, and metaphysical spaces',[29] a project she continues to pursue for e-books as well as print and artists' books.[30] Even in these fields, where bookness has a comparatively coherent suite of potential meanings, Drucker's functions, operations, conceptions, and spaces offer a broad canvas for scholars such as Hayles, Kirschenbaum, and Galey to explore bookness from different angles.[31] As book artist and academic Amaranth Borsuk puts it, 'from the vantage point of the twenty-first century, our own codex book has been normalised to such a degree that we question the "bookness" of anything that challenges our expected reading experience, with little regard for the fact that reading in one direction rather than another, scanning text silently, and putting a title and an author's name on a book's cover are all learned behaviours'.[32]

The Realness of Electronic Texts

Since the 1980s, when scholars were in the early stages of grappling with hypertext fictions and other digital-first literary forms, the wider debate on the nature and realness of digital artefacts has moved substantially away from visions of the electronic as either super-real (what Baudrillard described as 'hyperreal') or sub-real; Bolter and Grusin's work on the nature of digital remediations was a key turning point in challenging conceptions of the digital as inherently less real.[33] Input to the debate on digital realness has been forensic as well as theoretical: while realness and materiality are in no way synonymous, 'tangible, fungible, visible existence'[34] of the kind observable in the physical world can serve as powerful evidence in an argument for real existence, and discussions of e-book realness are frequently developed with reference to digital materiality.

Technical advances in the understanding of materiality at the nanoscale level have made it increasingly difficult to intellectually defend a position of the digital as literally intangible (a position eloquently countered by theorists such as Paul and Blanchette).[35] At the same time, the digital has remained to an extent 'popularly construed as intangible, invisible, ephemeral, unstable, and virtual'[36] and 'even the most astute and exacting critics of cyberculture tend to signal a certain ambivalence about the bodies that electronic texts have, judging at least from the frequency with which the word *material* appears between scare quotes. . .logic is logic, but material is "material"'.[37] Shep observed that 'the idea that digital objects should be reconceptualised as material, rather than virtual, has been the subject of considerable scholarly investigation in the humanities', noting McGann (2001), Hayles (2002), and Drucker (2003) as key figures.[38] Gitelman's investigations dramatically advanced the debate, addressing the full range of digital texts (including problematic forms at the margin of working definitions of 'text') in *Always Already New: Media, History, and the Data of Culture* (2006), but focussing more specifically on documents as understood in print contexts versus digital contexts in *Paper Knowledge: Towards a Media History of Documents* (2014). Hayler, in *Challenging the Phenomena of Technology: Embodiment, Expertise, and Evolved Knowledge* (2015), argued that 'e-reading remains the best possible example today of talking about an encompassing definition of technology' and uses e-books as an entry point to examination of technology 'not as a class of objects, but as a class of phenomenological experience' where the only constant is adaptation, and our knowledge of the book (or any) artefact evolves in tandem with the artefact's knowledge of us.[39] For e-books, investigations of materiality have developed various systems for understanding materiality and identified various forms. These systems, however, are more often cooperative than mutually exclusive, and build and augment more often than they compete.

Kirschenbaum's 2008 *Mechanisms: New Media and the Forensic Imagination* is a milestone text, influential in fields including media theory, technology studies, and game studies as well as book history and publishing studies. Kirschenbaum applied archivist Kenneth Thibodeau's 'tripartite model of defining digital objects'[40] on physical, logical, and conceptual levels to differentiate between forensic and formal materiality. Forensic materiality 'rests upon the potential for individualization inherent in matter'[41] and recognises the full range of physical traces, visible and invisible, of so-called 'virtual' artefacts such as files and software; with it, Kirschenbaum dismantled the myth of the identical copy as well as myth of intangibility. Formal materiality recognises the 'imposition of multiple relational computational states on a data set or digital object' and the way that the object becomes different when put to use by different actors at different stages, articulating a 'relative or just-in-time dimension of materiality'[42] for digital objects such as image files or, as Kirschenbaum specifically investigated later in the book, works of literature such as William Gibson's *Agrippa* or Michael Joyce's *Afternoon: a story*. Drucker built on Kirschenbaum's forensic and formal categories, folding in Blanchette's distributed materiality and its apparatus for examination of 'co-dependent, layered contingencies' of storage, software, hardware, networks, and other components as she established her concept of the performative dimension in 'Performative Materiality and Theoretical Approaches to Interface' (2013).[43] Performative materiality acknowledges that 'the materiality of the system . . . bears only a probabilistic relation to the event of production, which always occurs only in real time and is distinct in each instance' and that 'what something *is* has to be understood in terms of what it *does*, how it works within machinic, systemic, and cultural domains'.[44] This 'contingent' materiality is wholly compatible with Kirschenbaum's and Blanchette's theories, but is antagonistic to 'literal materiality' that takes a mechanistic approach and 'presumes objects of perception are self-identical and observer-independent'.[45]

Explicit considerations of e-book realness are rare, but highly significant where they appear. 'HCI-Book? Perspectives on E-Book Research, 2006-2008' drew together key questions and areas of inquiry as identified by participants in the Implementing New Knowledge Environments (INKE) project.[46] Though it ranged far beyond e-books into the wider territory of electronic resources, such as scholarly databases and hypertext literature less governed by the metaphor of the book, it included in its capacious overview many of the most important debates and controversies surrounding 'new forms of electronic-reader book-ishness'.[47] It examined the book, as book-object and book-metaphor, in terms of features such as tangibility, browsability, searchability, referenceability, and hybridity, offering a model for less binary consideration of print and digital affordances. It also highlighted the critical role of magnitude, of a book being 'more than can be consumed in a single visual event' in distinguishing an electronic book from other forms of electronic text.[48] Galey's 'The Enkindling Reciter: E-Books in the Bibliographic Imagination' (2012), further explored not only the possibilities but also the limits of a forensic approach to e-book studies, noting that while study of the full suite of material inscriptions is necessary for the understanding of any given e-book, it is not in itself sufficient.

The 'interplay of social and technical forces' requires the reader never be excluded from analysis.[49] Galey found that 'e-books may have. . .no absolute Real that serves to anchor the evidence of our senses. The reason is simple: e-books, like all digital texts, require us to interpret phenomena not directly observable by the senses. . .digital objects never speak for themselves; someone always speaks for them'.[50] Gooding, Terras, and Warwick (the latter a contributor to the INKE project as well) addressed realness in 'The Myth of the New: Mass Digitization, Distant Reading, and the Future of the Book' (2013),[51] pushing debates on the realness of an individual work of literature in digital form into deeper, more complex territory revealed by distant reading[52] and the realness of literary corpora 'impossible for humans to engage with' without automated tools or reconstitution into their original separate texts, and highlighting both the stridency and entrenchment of unexamined claims where little data exists.[53]

The Complexities of E-book Paratext

Digital presentation has been a factor for e-books since the first books were digitised, but the application of Genette's paratextual theory[54] to mainstream e-books is in its early days. Paratextual theory is most often applied in literary studies, but since 2000 has been imported into fields from history and philosophy to film studies and information studies, and applied to film, webpages, games, and other digital or part-digital content,[55] extending its influence far beyond the books that were Genette's deliberately exclusive original subject of study.[56] It is regularly applied in scholarship in and around the digital humanities, as with Tether's investigation into the rendering of paratexts of digitised medieval manuscripts (2013) and Cooper's examination of how digital editions of medieval manuscripts can create new epitexts (2015), and to interactive electronic literature such as hypertext works.[57] Yet its application to mainstream commercial e-books, of the kind found on Amazon bestseller lists, lags behind: in early 2013, Birke and Christ concluded that there was no existing scholarly literature.[58] Since 2013, scholarship on the topic has gathered pace. That year saw Birke and Christ's cluster of articles on digital paratext in *Narrative*, 2014, one of the first edited collections specifically on paratext for digital texts from Desrochers and Apollon, and 2016 one of the first short-form monographs specifically on e-novel paratext, an extension of Ellen McCracken's 2013 *Narrative* paper on 'transitional' electronic literature (fittingly, from the pioneering Palgrave Pivot, which is challenging the definition of what 'counts' as an academic book).[59] Digital paratext has been represented in a number of important papers in book history and the book sector of platform studies (as a key thread, if not the stated subject of the paper) including Galey's aforementioned 'The Enkindling Reciter' (2012) and Rowberry's 'Ebookness' (2017).[60] More recent work on non-e-book forms of born-digital fiction and poetry, such as Leavenworth's 'The Paratext of Fan Fiction' (2015), Shanmugapriya, Menon, and Campbell's 'An introduction to the functioning process of embedded paratext of digital literature: Technoeikon of digital poetry' (2019), Skare's 'The paratext of digital documents' (2021), and Ensslin's *Pre-web Digital Publishing and the Lore of Electronic Literature* (2022) further informs e-book paratextual studies, and, increasingly, new works on literary paratext, such as Batchelor's *Translation and Paratexts* (2018),[61] incorporate analysis of e-book-specific aspects not as an afterthought but as a substantial component necessary to understand the reception of any new book released in both print and digital formats.

Literary Status

Recent scholarship on status in the literary field acknowledges the impact of digital formats; many studies define their scope to exclude e-books, or e-only books, expressly because status is constituted and communicated differently away from print. However, other studies embrace the complexity and include e-books, including e-only, as central and essential. Bourdieu's *The Rules of Art: Genesis and Structure of the Literary Field*[62] continues to serve as a foundational text for examination of literary cultural capital in the digital era, supplying a sociologist's vocabulary for analysis of the sociology of books[63] and the socialisation of texts.[64] Thompson, writing in 2012, noted the influence of Amazon in the beginning of the disintermediation of sales reps and chain bookshop buyers, one example of the sidelining of some traditional gatekeepers and tastemakers.[65] Early twenty-first-century examination of novels' literary status and reputation by scholars including English and Squires often excluded digital, for, as Squires wrote in 2007, 'electronic literature [had] yet to make any major impact on the market'.[66] But their work is directly applied to born-digital literary work and online literary networks by scholars such as Hungerford. In *Making Literature Now* (2016), Hungerford used case studies of digital projects such as *McSweeney's Internet Tendency* and the game/novel *The Silent History* to investigate the roles of '"neglected agents" of cultural formation' in online settings.[67] More recent studies of how literary status is negotiated in what Murray calls the digital literary sphere,[68] such as in online components of literary and writers' festivals,[69] on Wattpad,[70] on Bookstagram,[71] in Goodreads ratings,[72] and through celebrity book clubs,[73] continue to generate data on and deepen understanding of how legitimacy is constituted for both print-first and e-only e-books. It is worth pausing, however, to highlight that in capturing authentic experiences from readers' encounters with festivals, emerging platforms for writing, reviewing, and sharing fiction, and new forms of the book group, these studies inevitably showcase the most popular genre of e-book: the e-novel, a form not studied as often as its central position in popular digital reading would suggest.

E-novels: Latecomers to the Party

E-novel reading has, in a generation, grown from a niche activity to a fixture of cultural and intellectual life. It stands as a commonplace means (and for e-only novels, the only means) of accessing works of long-form fiction. But its journey to prominence was not smooth. Though novels are now the most popular category of e-books, the practice of reading fiction off the printed page (in something of a parallel with the repeated false dawns of handheld e-reading devices) was a story of advance followed by retreat, 'discovery' and forgetting, leading to limited recognition in publishing history. Brown's Readies, suitably for a technology touted in a modernist literary magazine, promised in its initial batch of texts short works by Gertrude Stein, William Carlos Williams, and Ezra Pound (though the machine-readable micronised versions never materialised),[74] speaking to Brown's confidence that experimental literature would find its artistic match in experimental reading platforms. Rubery's work on projected books, where personal bedside projectors put reading on ceilings for hospitalised soldiers (and later a wider range of patients) during and after World War II, shows how screen reading intended to offer entertainment and distraction was heavily weighted towards novels, as well as how the scheme, which faltered after television became a ward fixture, is nearly forgotten by history.[75] But other early conceptions of the electronic book were more obviously heirs of Bush's research-organising Memex[76] than Brown's literature-sharing Readies. The first identified use of the term "'electronic book'" described the 1960s' 'proto-internet information sharing network' PLATO (Programmed Logic for Automatic Teaching Operations) and its slides-on-demand system for university students, while its contemporary the 'electronic "book"' announced by the U.S. National Science Foundation debuted search functionality with the scintillating page turner *An Electronic Index to Chemical Patents.*[77] The digital reading environment was for decades afterwards dominated by educational, reference, and technical titles,[78] where the benefits of searchability were most obvious. And pragmatically, eye-watering prices for both hardware and texts could be most easily justified for enduring, frequently consulted resources; one pioneering handheld device, Franklin Electronics' 1989 Bookman, which more closely resembled a pocket calculator than a paperback book, offered the Bible in three lines of text at a time.[79]

When novel-length fiction began to reappear, it was enmeshed with gaming. As Kirschenbaum and Werner explain, Pinsky, Hales, and Mataga's 1984 *Mindwheel,* the first identifiable work marketed as an 'electronic novel' (from publishers optimistic enough to trademark the term) was a 'hybrid book/digital artefact' that told its story across an adventure game on disk and prose in a clothbound volume, and was only subtly differentiated from disk/book packages sold under the label of computer games.[80] *Mindwheel* was accessible only to those who could afford a (then ruinously expensive) home computer. Other early digital fiction projects had audiences limited not only by access to computers but also by access to membership networks or academic and artistic communities. Pre-Web, early hypertext fictions of the 1980s were often accessed via dial-up bulletin board systems (as with Malloy's *Uncle Roger,* released via The WELL), or read as well as created on proprietary software such as Intermedia, HyperCard, and Storyspace (such as Joyce's 1987 *Afternoon, a story*).[81] *Afternoon, a story* was not available for purchase by the public on CD ROM until 1990[82] and Project Gutenberg did not publish its first free e-novels until the 1990s.[83] Though some early commercial e-novel experiments, such as Penguin's 1993 release of Peter James's *The Host* on floppy disk as well as in print,[84] were capable of achieving significant sales (12,000, according to James),[85] only a tiny fraction of new novels were made available in electronic format. Users of early 1990s e-reading devices (including the Rocket eBook) could choose from a minute selection that often relied heavily on Project Gutenberg's embryonic stock of public domain classics. Readership of electronic novels expanded considerably in 2007 with the launch of both Amazon's Kindle e-reader and Amazon's aggressively marketed catalogue of low-priced recent-release titles, and again in 2010 with Apple's April launch of the iPad, preloaded with the iBooks app, and June launch of iBooks for iPhone and iPod Touch.[86] But it is only since late 2010 that e-books, e-novels and otherwise, expanded beyond 1–4 per cent of the commercial book business, and then only in certain Anglophone markets.

As a small segment, e-novels garnered only moderate levels of academic interest, and scepticism regarding the future of e-novels was justified. Technodeterminist predictions had held that once the technology existed, audiences would simply materialise. Coover's much discussed 1992 *New York Times Book Review* essay 'The End of Books' posited a future where print would lose readership, and therefore relevance, because of its own limitations in presenting the new hot commodity: interactive fiction.[87] Successive waves, including hypertext experiments of the 1980s, commercially available handheld e-readers in the 1990s, and pre-Kindle e-ink reading devices of the early 2000s, were in their time heralded as harbingers of a new era where digital reading would become the norm and print reading rare or extinct.[88] With a similar cycle of inflated expectations followed by disillusionment, high-profile experiments in fiction for a mass audience distributed through the internet, such as Stephen King's digital novella *Riding the Bullet* and serial novel *The Plant*, both released in 2000, failed to prove either profitable or influential.[89] After so many disappointments, it was not unreasonable to adopt a wait-and-see approach, or simply to predict that the Kindle, the Sony Reader, and the Nook would go the way of the Rocket eBook, the Data Discman, and the Active Book (the latter demonstrating how neither creator credentials nor corporate investment were reliable harbingers of success) (Figure 1.1).[90] (Many further examples likely remain forgotten, leaving not even a prototype in a computer museum or promotional video on YouTube: as Tenen observes, closed system obsolescence and Digital Millennium Copyright Act roadblocks to scholarly access mean that 'platform makers may...embed instruments of censorship or surveillance into cultural works, in a way that makes them physically resistant to interpretation or critique' and 'we know less about the history of electronic publishing than we do about the premodern book'.)[91] Since 2011, scholarship has responded to begin to give commercial e-books and e-reading the attention they merit, but there were and are shortages in terms of longitudinal studies[92] and data gathering on key topics in times of rapid change.

Selling Realness

Rhetoric of realness pervades public discussion of e-books. Wide variation in how the term is used only serves to underscore its ubiquity. Like bookness, realness is a fixture of the debate, and a fixture treated as valuable: it is vied for, contested, and worth contesting. Realness is a form of legitimacy foregrounded by e-book distributors as they attempt to

Figure 1.1   Active Book prototype, courtesy the Centre for Computing History (exhibit reference ID CH53902).

address (and resolve to their advantage) my student's question: whether an e-book *counts*. Drucker noted in 2003 how the most inflated millennium marketing claims promising 'the expanded book, the super-book, the hyper-book' deflated along with the companies that made them, fading from use as (sometimes visionary) devices and platforms failed to win audiences or deliver on their bold promises.[93] Realness is now more often framed in terms of equality with, not superiority to, print. E-reading device and e-book retailers are not only emphatic but also careful in their use of the word 'real' in marketing messages and product descriptions, deploying it strategically to describe discrete aspects of e-books as well as the books themselves. One example is how, when announcing the device launch of the second-generation Kindle, Amazon promoted its display technology as using 'real ink', but on an 'electronic paper display' that 'looks and reads like real paper', presenting the device as a hybrid incorporating real and facsimile elements.[94] In contrast, Amazon has over its years in the market overwhelmingly framed the digital products one can read on their Kindles as 'books',[95] not bracketed by professions of 'real' or 'like real', or even, in most cases, a letter 'e' or other indications of their digital format. Exceptions are rare and, consequently, arresting, as in a launch speech where Jeff Bezos followed numerous references to e-books as books with a boast that 'if you want, Kindle 2 will even read to you – something new we added *that a book could never do*'[96] [emphasis mine] (whether this constituted a Freudian slip, revealing Bezos's real opinion of e-books, is an intriguing question, but a single line from the founder does not by itself override the company's almost uniformly consistent message).

This attempted positioning of e-books as real books is a strategic commercial decision. Nicholas Carr classed the Kindle's projection of 'bookness [as] essentially a marketing tactic, a way to make traditional book readers comfortable with e-books', recognisably part of Amazon's 'existential commitment to the idea of literature' that Striphas earlier identified as the 'ethos of bookishness' that Amazon 'cultivated through...paraphernalia touting the wonder of books and reading' as part of a larger business strategy.[97] As Murray points out, 'in the Amazon world, whether or not we actively purchase any given title, we are being constantly sold the flattering image of ourselves as bibliophiles – literary connoisseurs belonging to an almost secret society of book lovers, replete with its own lingo, rituals, and enthusiasms'[98] – a campaign more obviously forwarded by selling e-books as books than as some other kind of product.[99] Retailers of print books are similarly motivated, commandeering 'real' as a synonym for print when they advertise 'A Real Bookshop for the Real World', or 'There's nothing like a real book & nothing like a real bookshop!', or simply 'Buy Real Books Online'[100] (this last from an online purveyor of print books) – all selling, in Murray's dual sense of *retailing* and *promoting,* bookishness as well as their books. As Price says of realness as sold by Amazon, or by the New York Public Library (touting the 'real-life librarians' who grace your wedding hire of the space), 'there's no point in specifying that something is "real" unless someone suspects that it's fake'.[101]

Given the commercial and commentariat atmosphere in which they buy, read, and share books, it's supremely unsurprising that participants in my own surveys, focus groups, and interviews also frequently use *real* as a synonym for *print*. Discussion was punctuated with variations on 'I tend to prefer real books to e-books', 'I prefer a real book', or 'I just prefer the real thing'.[102] References to print books as 'actual BOOKS', '(actual) books', or 'proper, print books' contrast sharply with references to e-books as 'some imaginary thing on screen'.[103] Descriptions of print books as real books went unremarked upon in focus groups: these were not flashpoints for debate, or an invitation to discuss the value of e-books. They were treated as valid shorthand, a mutually understood way to differentiate print from digital. Of the many possible constructions participants could have used to distinguish between the two, such as 'e-book vs print book', 'e-book vs book' or even 'e-book vs BOOK-book' (using contrastive focus reduplication to emphasise that one is referring to the 'real', true, or default mode rather than a variation, for example, 'I had a JOB-job once. [a "real" 9-to-5 office job, as opposed to an academic job]'),[104] the construction many used was, effectively, 'e-book vs real book'. Even e-reading enthusiasts sometimes praise the Kindle experience as 'it feels like I'm reading a real book' or state that e-books 'are getting better and better' and hence increasingly 'resemble books' (to the latter, a more sceptical peer replied 'why do you not just get a book then?').[105]

However, this shorthand of 'e-book vs real book' sat alongside other uses of the word 'real'. Realness in the sense of 'legitimate' genres enjoying high prestige (say, in a debate on the status of science fiction, criticising 'elitist' views as '"it's sci fi, it doesn't count as real books"', or a dismissal of 'self-helpy type books' as 'while helpful and interesting, don't feel like real books anyway'), or in the sense of mainstream published as opposed to self-published books, mingles in the discussion with realness in the sense of a print object.[106] The ability, in a real-time focus group or interview, to ask a participant to expand upon a given use of the word *real* is invaluable for teasing out potential layering of meanings; where written survey responses are ambiguous, they remain so.

However, written responses are more precise than verbal ones in flagging distinctions between real and 'real', and using scare quotes in a sense similar to the 'material' ambivalence discussed by Gitelman.[107] If scare quotes (which I didn't use in my survey questions) are typically 'used to alert readers that a term is used in a nonstandard (or slang), ironic, or other special sense' to 'imply "This is not my term" or "This is not how the term is usually applied"'[108] the point at which they appear in survey results is telling. While the word *real*, used to denote a print book, appears frequently in free-text responses across all years of the survey (as with the ubiquitous 'I prefer a real book'), *'real'* is almost entirely absent from 2014 until the final questions of 2022. The scare quotes suddenly appear in responses to the new question discussed subsequently, where they exemplify the 'this is not my term' function, and add a further layer of meaning in the many free-text responses where they feature.

Asking Readers: 'Do You Consider E-books to Be Real Books?'

The most direct way to investigate the question is, of course, to ask it.

Surveys on reading occasionally ask directly about attitudes towards e-book realness. Results vary widely, and appear predictably sensitive to the wording of the question, not least in terms of use of scare quotes. One 2017 survey of US book and magazine readers ($n = 1{,}020$), asking about 'consumer attitudes' regarding books and e-books found that 20% completely or somewhat agreed with the statement 'e-books are not real books'[109] – evoking spontaneous free-text responses in my own surveys such as the 2020 'I don't really see e-books as books'. However, a survey of US book readers in the same year ($n = 451$), asking 'if you choose a print version of a book instead of an e-book, what are the reasons for purchasing a print book?', found that 55% agreed with the statement 'I want to read a "real" book again'[110] – evoking instead the non-spontaneous free-text responses in my 2022 survey, directly responding to the 'why?' question, such as '[e-books] are "real" in that they exist to be seen and discussed in the world'.

These tantalising, but frustratingly brief, glimpses offer some hint as to the nuances of the question. I wanted to find out more about readers' reasons, as well as how such views correlated with book buying, book usage, and other attitudes towards print and digital reading. In 2022, I added to the end of the survey 'Do you consider e-books to be real books?', followed by 'why?' There was no 'don't know' or 'not sure' option, or 'strongly' versus 'somewhat' degrees of agreement: instead of asking participants to express the nuances of the question via a Likert scale, I wanted to ask them (appreciating that this is more time-consuming) to explore those nuances in their own words. (And, as discussed subsequently, several used the free-text to explain that 'the real answer is "yes and no"'.) Despite its placement at the end of the survey, when one might expect a few weary respondents to drop out, 99.1% of the 2022 respondents completed the question.[111] Of those 228 individuals who gave a 'yes or no' answer, 196 generously included a free-text response to 'why?'

Of the 228 responses, five out of six (83.3%) agreed that they consider e-books to be real books. (A figure that's remarkably close to the 80% seen in the 2017 survey of US book and magazine readers mentioned earlier,

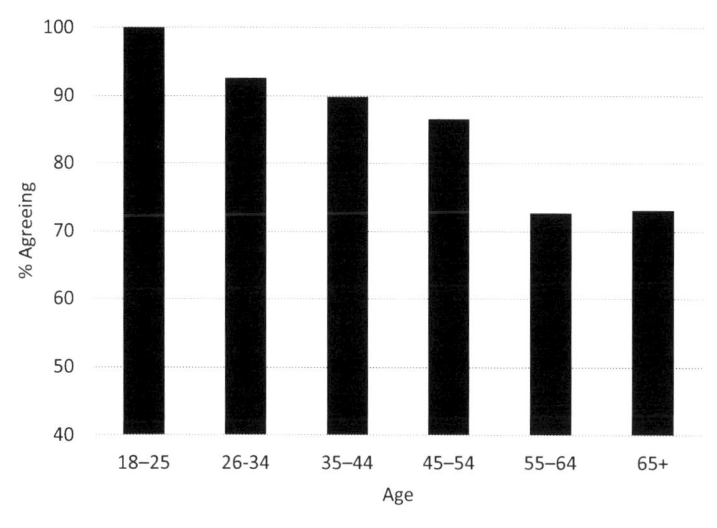

Figure 1.2 'Yes' responses to 'do you consider e-books to real books?' by age.

asking about the *real* instead of the *'real'.*) The younger the respondent, the more likely they were to agree, though this sat on the cusp of statistical significance ($p = 0.05$): less than three-quarters of those aged 55 and older (72.8%) said that they consider e-books to be real books, compared with 89.1% of those younger than 55 – and all of those younger than 26 (Figure 1.2).[112]

UK residents were somewhat less likely to consider e-books real books: 77.3% agreed, versus 91.6% of those resident elsewhere in the world. Gender identity was not a significant factor.[113]

Agreement did not depend on devices used for reading e-books, sources of e-books, genres of e-books read (with the exception of a slight connection to non-fiction e-book reading), or indeed to genres and sources of print books (with the exception of a slight connection to receiving print novels as gifts). But it did depend, strongly, on whether respondents had recently read e-books. Almost all respondents who had read at least one e-book in the past twelve months agreed (92.7%), compared with fewer than six in ten others (58.7%).[114] It is striking that even among those who don't read e-books, a majority agrees: clearly, considering e-books real is not enough to make you read them, nor is considering them unreal enough to stop you. However, *reasons* for choosing electronic formats over print proved irrelevant: those who choose e-books because they find them easier to obtain, faster to obtain, better value, and so on were not significantly more or less likely to agree. The same is true for most, but not all, reasons for choosing print: because they find it better for keeping as part of a personal library, for example, or because they prefer to support independent bookshops, or because they find print better for sharing or giving as a gift (notable, as it marks attitudes towards the bookness of e-books as outside the bibliophilic cluster of values discussed in Chapter 3). The exceptions were reasons that have to do with experience of the material object. Those who particularly value holding a physical codex and reading from a printed page are less likely to consider e-books to be real books: respondents who choose print because it's more enjoyable to handle and use (78.8% vs 95.2% of others),[115] and those who choose print books because they are easier to read (72.4% vs 91.5%).[116] This singling out of one specific kind of book experience is something I'll return to in Chapter 5, on reading and rereading. But it's notable that for those who consider e-books as enjoyable to handle as print, and as easy to read as print, agreement on realness approaches 100%.

Why Are (or Aren't) E-books Real Books?

Even at the end of a fairly long survey, when respondents gave their free-text answers to 'why?', they gave responses that were reflective, wry, funny, insightful, impassioned. Especially impassioned: nothing I have ever asked in the service of publishing studies research has made people so angry with me. The question proved inherently inflammatory, poking at the old wounds of the 'e-book wars', aggravating both for reviving a tired controversy and for the tired controversy it revives. My choice to force answers into binary yes/no paths was itself potentially vexing. But the question was also posed at an unintentionally infuriating point. Placement was not random: the question was inserted at the very end of the survey to prevent priming respondents and affecting their answers to the year-on-year questions. But an unintended consequence of that placement was provocation. Almost three-quarters (72.1%) of 2022 respondents were e-book readers, and had just spent some minutes answering questions about their thoughts, feelings, and values about reading...only to reach a final question that, in its bland neutrality, seems to accept the premise that at least some people may see those books as less. From there, it is a short leap of bookish logic to accepting that if their books are less, their reading is less, and they themselves are less. If one were looking to design a question to antagonise book lovers, this would not be a bad start.

Responses ranged from full paragraphs – mini-manifestos, potted personal histories, fleshed-out arguments about materiality and tradition and affect – to a single character ('?', as eloquent in its succinctness as many longer answers challenging the premise of the question). Six overarching themes emerged. Four – equivalence, materiality, ownership, and utility – weave through arguments for and against e-book realness, arguments I'll revisit through the chapters to come. But two – certainty and elitism/ableism – do not accept the premise of the question, and explain why some respondents judge that inviting in even the possibility of doubt as to the realness of e-books is dangerous, exclusionary, insulting, and foolish.

Certainty

E-book realness is something many respondents are very, very sure about. An e-book is a real book, as several respondents put it in the same words, 'because it is' (or 'because they are?' or 'because they are!', with every variation in punctuation passing a different judgement on what it means to ask). Variations of 'books are books', 'the book is a book', 'a book is a book', and so on were among the most common free-text responses, as were variations on 'reading is reading'. In short, 'of course they're real :)'. Some perform mystification, countering with 'it's right there in the name' or 'I mean, of course, definitionally e-books are books', archly adopting a stance where application of the word 'book' resolves all questions. Other respondents reach one step beyond 'because they are' to say 'because they are actual books': *actual* serving to add nuance, demarcating within the territory of *books* a further zone of notional books, in which e-books are in danger of being relegated. As it was put in my favourite response (to this and, indeed, every survey question I've ever posed): 'Because they're actually fucking books. Who gives a shit if it's on a digital or physical format. Them bitch ass letters still show up in the same god damn order. Sorry for the language, I'm lit.'

'Who gives a shit' eloquently encapsulates a body of responses that questioned the necessity of the question. In contrast to those who found the question dangerous and wrong – on which see subsequently – these respondents treated the question as nonsensical, ridiculous, or irrelevant. Saying that they are 'not sure quite what this question is getting at', they ask 'why not?' and 'why would you think they are not real books?', explaining that they 'don't understand how they wouldn't be real' or 'sorry – I find the idea that e-books might be considered anything other than "real" baffling'. Or, as noted earlier, they might shut the question down with a crushingly simple '?'. Their bemusement could be summed up by 'because they are? What a weird question'.

Others, however, elected to explain *how* they came by their certainty, couching their response with 'as a print technician', or 'I studied cyborg theory', or '(and I used to design printed books for a living)'. These calls to expertise fold in legitimacy in another way (arguably, a defensive one that presupposes that one's credentials may at any moment be checked) but represent a step down in terms of strength of belief. In describing their journeys towards the conclusion, they accede that a journey was necessary; that it was possible to believe, and necessary to consider, arguments against e-book realness, and that these arguments could have swayed them were it not for their personal education and expertise. Such seeking is a far cry from 'because they are!'

Strength of belief takes another step down in responses that set boundaries on realness: setting '[their] criteria for what constitutes a book' and explaining when e-books meet them and when they don't. Respondents qualify that 'yes, they are real *on one level* (i.e. supplying the reading material)' or 'well, they are books, *in the sense of* the word definitions as they evolve' or '*as far as* content yes. *But* you can't browse the shelf and check the blurb in a kindle which removes much of the anticipatory pleasure' [emphasis mine in each case]. And certainty dissolves for respondents who defied the intentionally binary framing of the question and detailed the ambivalence in which they're suspended. 'Difficult question', 'the real answer is "yes and no"', and 'phew. That's a hard one,' are followed by exclusions such as lacking a feeling of ownership (discussed in greater detail in Chapter 3), or contexts such as 'If someone asks if I've read a book and I read the e-book, I say yes. In that instance, book = story. But when I hear the phrase "real book," I think of something tangible—a particular physical object', or a story of how their views changed over time. The 'that's a hard one' response contains just such a narrative: 'Maybe 3 years ago, I would've said no. In some cases, ebooks in my present environment have felt like a lifesaver', the three years in question being 2019 to 2022, and the 'present environment' being the start of the COVID-19 era. The intensely personal nature of the question is grounded in feeling by the respondent quoted in the introduction: 'Mine is an emotive answer not based on logic...So I guess I consider an e book to be a real book...but some little voice is still saying, "It's not though, is it?"' Layer upon layer of uncertainty couches the realness of the e-book in equivocal terms, dependent on the reader, the author, the place in time (like a realness that's performative in a way analogous to Drucker's performative materiality, a realness that 'occurs only in real time and is distinct in each instance'),[117] and sometimes on 'some little voice'.

Others, not to be outdone, went straight to the nature of reality, asking versions of 'what is real?' and 'what's not real?' As one put it, '"Real" is a kind of arbitrary and personally defined label. For me, [e-books] satisfy almost all of my criteria for what constitutes a book; but I would rarely call them "real", 'cause I don't think in those terms' – ploughing into Bolter and Grusin's conceptions of remediation[118] and right through into mediation in the Hegelian sense. It's worth noting, however, that questioning the nature of reality did not equate to accepting e-books as either real or not real (or indeed that real, or 'real', means whatever an individual wants it to mean). 'What is real?' was given as a reason for why e-books are real books, but 'what exactly is "real", anyway?' was given as a reason for why they're not.

Elitism and Ableism

There was no such ambiguity in responses focussed on the justice of the question. Respondents raising issues of elitism and ableism were firm, certain, and disgusted. Numerous respondents noted accessibility as a critical affordance of digital books, including classing them as 'narrative or informative text in the same way braille books might be' (and neatly equating equivocation on the legitimacy of digital reading with equivocation on the legitimacy of reading braille). Some spoke to the experience of hypothetical others ('some disabled people'), others to their own, as with 'I loved reading a book as a child but as I've got older health has made holding a book more difficult and listening is better on the eyes'. And there is no arguing with 'the argument about what constitutes real reading is very annoying for those of us with disabilities who have less choice of how we read': it's not theoretically annoying, it is actively and currently annoying – for which I make a heartfelt apology to this and to every other respondent whom I hurt or offended with the question. 'Hurt' is not an overstatement: while some called questioning digital realness 'snobbery' or 'privileging materiality over accessibility', one equated it with questioning the legitimacy and value of a person, explaining that 'defining a "book" strictly by the dead trees is like defining a "human" as having a penis. Reductive and incorrect'. Multiple respondents agreed that they 'don't like the arguments made about why they are not real books – they tend to be elitist or ableist', that 'only classing physical books as "real books" feels outdated and ableist' and that 'this is also very ableist...Implying that [e-books] are somehow less valid is not okay'; evoking what people who are blind face when confronted with messages that they are 'not reading in the same sense as other people' because their books are audiobooks.[119]

Conclusion

Real or 'real'? If unreal, unreal in what way? The complexity of readers' conceptions of the realness of e-books demonstrates how strands of the metaphor of the book, the bookness of physical books, the realness of electronic texts, and the particularities of paratext and literary status for digital works interweave. Envisioning e-book realness as a form of legitimacy, a collective process mediated by individuals,[120] the voices of these particular individuals can be heard moving through Drucker's functions, operations, conceptions, and spaces of bookness, pursuing 'what something *is*...understood in terms of what it *does*, how it works within machinic, systemic, and cultural domains'[121] – contingent and relative materiality,[122] and contingent and relative bookness to go with it. The next step is to follow readers into those domains, and from the abstract to the concrete, to ask what e-books *do* in the context of their own lives. For what uses is realness an asset or a requirement? In what settings is it inessential, or even an impediment? Progressing through stages of discovering, obtaining, reading, retaining, displaying, and (sometimes) loving a digital book, the next chapters consider how the e-book genres we read, the devices we read on, the bookshops and libraries and collections and illegal download sites we patronise, and above all our reasons for choosing e-books and print books interrelate, and suggest ways in which how we think of our books shifts in sync with what we want from our books. To return to Galey, 'e-books may have...no absolute Real that serves to anchor the evidence of our senses' and 'digital objects never speak for themselves; someone always speaks for them'.[123] The coming chapters listen as readers do that speaking.

CHAPTER 2

Paratexts and First Impressions
Taking a Chance on an E-book

'[e-books are real because] In publishing, all books are ebooks before the files are sent to the printers.'

(Survey 2022)

'Actually I also judge the cover [of an e-book], even though it's not like a printed one ... if I see one that obviously has been badly done on Photoshop or something like that I'm going to go, "No, just no. No way. I don't trust it."'

(FG 4 participant 2)

'[an e-book is real] Because it's pretty much the exact same as a physical book except I can read them in the dark!'

(Survey 2022)

'[an e-book is not real because] not the same product.'

(Survey 2022)

A reader enters a bookshop. Not a physical bookshop, with a fixed location and a finite stock selected to appeal to a defined clientele; the reader isn't weaving between shelves of signed first editions in Toppings of Ely, or ziggurats of business bestsellers in Hudson Books at Logan International Airport. Instead, it's a bookshop of two dimensions, contained on a glowing screen. It's infinitely thin and, thanks to the millions of titles on offer, for all intents and purposes infinitely wide. Bits of book flash across the interface: gifs of cover images, blurbs 'From the Back Cover', page counts and colophons, an arrow to click to 'Look Inside'. Whether these fragments relate to any print binding is not easy to determine. Personalised suggestions jostle with sponsored products, while ratings and rankings and recommendations (genuine and fake) swoop and dive into their field of view. The reader is not naïve: they know that none of this landed at the top of their screen by accident. But how they sift through the information on offer, how they weigh up evidence in evaluating books and authors, and how they make a judgement on what is worth their time and (sometimes) money speak to what counts in deciding whether a given book *counts*. And for e-books, when, and whether, realness is required.

This chapter investigates first encounters with e-books and the processes by which readers evaluate a given work. It examines how trust is established and legitimacy constituted in practice, considering realness and bookness in terms of a given e-book's status as cultural product and cultural object, and the ways in which e-book legitimacy can hinge on relationship to a print edition or to traditional mainstream publishing. It analyses the reader's rationales of realness on the theme of equivalence, contrasting conceptions of an e-book as real because 'bits and ink – there's no difference', and unreal because they are 'not the same product'.[1] Finally, it considers the digital proxy and the *ersatz* book as two discrete types of e-book unrealness.

In making a judgement as to the legitimacy of a given e-book, prospective readers confront separate but entangled stigmas: not only the lower status of digital books, a 'format deemed lacking in cultural value',[2] but also the lower status of self-publishing. Examining how readers interrogate an e-book requires also examining how creators present that book: how publishers and authors (and publisher/authors) work to anticipate readers' questions, attempt to allay their fears, and collaborate to constitute credibility. Paratextual theory offers the tools for such investigation.

Paratext: 'Threshold of Interpretation'

Paratext is 'what enables a text to become a book and to be offered as such to its readers and, more generally, to the public'.[3] If there is an element of audacity in putting forward a zip file of data and describing it as a book, Genette reminds us that there is an element of audacity in putting forward any text and describing it as a book. No matter how traditional, conventional, or even derivative a text might be in some ways, without 'productions, such as an author's name, a title, a preface, illustrations' (though paratextual elements range much further than this), it is not yet 'endowed with significance' as a book.[4] Paratext is what creators use to not only '*present*' but also '*make present*, to ensure a text's presence in the world, its "reception" and consumption in the form (nowadays, at least) of a book' [emphasis his].[5] It is 'the fringe of the printed text which in reality controls one's whole reading of the text',[6] embracing a wide array of elements that adjoin the text, and offer instruction and context that guide the reading of that text. Examples range from chapter titles to book titles, cover design to advertising copy, personal inscriptions to Woolf's (initially) private reflections in her diary on the process of creating *Jacob's Room*. Paratext can convey a work's status bluntly, as with the word 'classic' printed above the title of a novel, or quietly, as with printing the same novel in a small and inexpensive format that, by its very economy and plainness, declares itself a student-friendly edition of a canonical text.[7] Genette developed his concept of paratext in the 1980s, exploring some aspects in *Palimpsestes* (1982, first translated into English in 1997) before a more comprehensive treatment in *Seuils* (*Paratexts*) (1987, translated into German in 1989 and English in 1997).[8] He refined his ideas in a time when e-books were obscure, almost a curiosity, yet they have found new life in the examination of book-objects hatched generations later. Paratext's very utility and versatility has made Corinna Norrick-Rühl question whether it should be described as 'theory' at all, suggesting that it might instead be viewed as somewhere between theory and toolkit.[9] But whether theory or kit, paratext is ideal for exploring contemporary questions of legitimacy and reputation, offering a means, comprehensible between academic disciplines, for discussion of fluid as well as fixed elements.

E-book Paratext: Crossing the Threshold on Screen

Paratext advances many agendas at once. For any work of literature, paratext is tasked with establishing value and worth, 'ensur[ing] for the text a destiny consistent with the author's purpose' by positioning it on multiple axes and anticipating the concerns of multiple audiences.[10] But paratext can't dictate; it can only negotiate. It is the 'zone of transition, but also *transaction*' where authors, publishers, and readers meet, 'a privileged place of a pragmatics and a strategy', and paratextual messages are not instruments of control [emphasis his].[11] 'A novel', as Genette put it, 'does not signify that "This book is a novel," a defining assertion that hardly lies within anyone's power, but rather "Please look on this book as a novel"'.[12] Paratext, for such a work of fiction, simultaneously labours to present it as a novel and as a good novel, to be evaluated according to the standards of the desired genres, traditions, audiences, and markets. The strain of serving multiple audiences can be particularly intense where publishers are attempting to take advantage of the possibilities of digital literature while pursing credibility in environments designed for print. An example is the 1990s interactive literature publisher Eastgate shipping floppy disks in packages 'safe for bookstores' (see Figure 2.1), with codex-like covers and spines, pitched to booksellers on the same kinds of in-person visits used by mainstream publishers for print books, and adopting 'establishment'

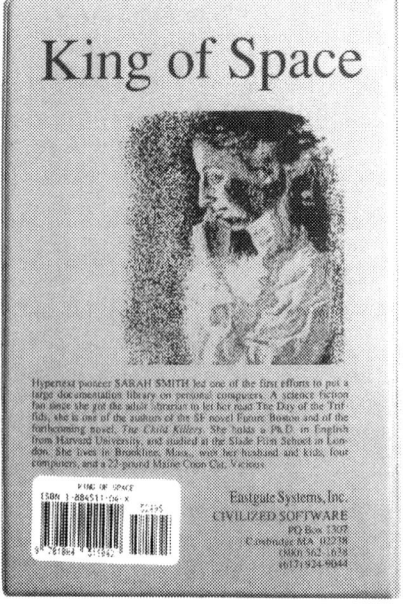

Figure 2.1   Eastgate Systems, Inc. packaging of Sarah Smith's 'King of Space' (1991). Courtesy the Electronic Literature Lab, https://scalar.usc.edu/works/rebooting-electronic-literature/photos-of-sarah-smiths-king-of-space

intellectual property policies aligned with the interests of university tenure committees and 'traditional bookselling' practice, despite the heavy financial burdens these imposed.[13] As Dene Grigar observes, 'the folio, which was made to resemble a book that could sit on a shelf, served as a breadcrumb leading from the late 20th Century print culture to the early 21st Century digital one'.[14]

A novel on screen must answer all the questions put to a novel in print, while also addressing concerns specific to digital novels. Foremost among these are concerns about the text's relationship to traditional mainstream publishing. Was it chosen? And if so, by whom? Key evidence of industry approval, and if so the degree of investment by members of that industry, is sought in existence in print. 'If it hasn't been backed by a publisher', as one focus group participant in my own study put it, 'instantly my mind goes to, "Well, why not?"'[15] Ultimately, the brutal question digital novels must answer is 'if the publisher wasn't willing to invest in it, why should I?'[16] How e-novels, and any e-books, respond via paratext – how authors try to encourage favourable interpretations, and how readers try to seek reliable information – reveals much about how the paratextual transaction actually functions for books on screen.

Proximity and Authority

Genette's grouping of elements into five key dimensions (spatial, temporal, substantial, pragmatic, and functional) brings to light patterns, commonalities in aims and tactics over time, and insights into the presentation and reception of texts in the real world. However, much scholarship to date has bypassed Genette's distinctions, implying that because his categories date from the era of print, and never had firm boundaries in the first place, engaging with them is fruitless.[17] Birke and Christ propose retiring most, if not all, of Genette's twentieth-century, text-based, deliberately flexible subcategories, arguing that 'context (or the universe of texts) moves so close to the text that "thresholds," paratextual elements that negotiate the space between text and context, become increasingly difficult to isolate and identify'.[18] Simply abandoning his distinctions, however, squanders a vocabulary ideally suited to discussion of textual boundaries; a vocabulary that is and always was open to evolution. The boundaries of 'multiform and tentacular' paratext are defined by Genette as subtle and mutable, inevitably taking different forms in different contexts and at different times.[19] McCracken's approach of 'augmentation and modification'[20] allows for nuance, and selective application of relevant subcategories, rather than a wholesale banishment of taxonomies informed by centuries of book history, and which frequently draw connections between contemporary paratextual strategies and related approaches from the print and manuscript eras. To do otherwise would sever e-books from the reading and publishing traditions from which they spring.

Discarding the spatial dimension is particularly dangerous, as proximity to the text can play a critical role in conveying to readers authorial intention: the intention without which an element is not paratext at all.

'Respectful Distance'

In the spatial dimension, Genette divides paratext into two broad categories: peritext and epitext. Although both 'surround and extend' the text, in a printed book, peritext is 'within the same volume': printed and bound with the words of the text itself.[21] A typical example is a cover, but more deeply embedded are types such as illustrations, epigraphs, chapter titles, and the author's name (and all that such a name evokes in terms of gender, nationality, class, etc.). Epitext, in contrast, is 'at a more respectful (or prudent) distance . . . located outside the book'.[22] An example could be a descriptive entry in a publisher's catalogue that seeks to place the book under a science, psychology, or self-help category, or an author biography that emphasises credentials, or simply demographics such as age. But epitext could just as easily be a recording of a public talk by the author, perhaps conveying some of the same information, verbally or visually. This distinction allows us to consider separately elements attached to and elements distanced from the text, and to examine the influence of elements bound in print but more loosely affiliated in digital format.

To be paratext, elements must be 'characterised by an authorial intention and assumption of responsibility', affirmed by either the author or the publisher whom they have empowered to distribute and represent the text.[23] Hence, a book review in a broadsheet is outside the boundaries, until such time as a quote is plucked from that review and placed in a press release (epitext) or printed on the back cover of a subsequent paperback edition (peritext). That which is not authorised remains metatext: commentary about a book, potentially influential, but not part of the transaction between reader and creator. Proximity matters, not least because classic paratextual theory comes from an era where the more closely bound an element was to the text, the safer it was to assume that it was indeed authorised. While discernment is always needed (deceptive paratext having a long tradition in print), epitext by its distanced nature demands a greater degree of scepticism and scrutiny. Readers typically confront epitext in the rush of the outside world, encountering some elements but not all (no one but an author's publicist or mother could realistically track every output), and continually sifting the authorised from the unauthorised. Print peritext, in contrast, comes from an object of finite size and at least some integrity, where additions may be discernible as additions (as with comments scribbled in the margin) and any bound element difficult to ignore. In effect, in Genette's view, any print peritext element, even a decorated end-paper, 'cannot *not*' be influential [emphasis his].[24]

Establishing Legitimacy: Digital Elements of the Peritext + Epitext = Paratext Equation

Much epitext is now digital for books in any format, as author websites and tweets, author-generated BookTok and Bookstagram content, publisher-generated book trailers on YouTube, recordings of public events, and online versions of press interviews invite readers to access the author (or at least their public authorial persona) digitally even if they are still accessing the text itself in print.[25] In my own study, participants' responses emphasise how integral personal research is to their book selection processes: by the time a book is in one's hands, 'you have an idea' of what to expect, because 'you've read about it already'.[26] Recommendations are very common, but personal investigation is even more so. But for e-books, digital epitext is, in some ways, at a less 'respectful distance' than is the case for print books. If downloading an e-book is quick and easy, Googling the author is even quicker and easier. For readers using tablets, smartphones, and personal computers, the two tasks – obtaining books and researching books – take place on the same device. Some models of e-readers can, with effort, still be kept offline, relying on USB cables to transfer titles from a separate connected device, but WiFi (such as Whispernet-branded connectivity, which Amazon once made central to its Kindle sales pitch) makes inviting the retail space into the device, browsing the bookshop via e-ink, the convenient default option. 'During the reading process one can easily tap a tablet's touchscreen to view comments, ratings, reviews, and author information and commentary without putting the device aside.'[27] For an e-book, digital epitext is, in a sense, attached to the physical object, akin to precarious peritext, and potentially filling the information gap left by peritext such as front matter that readers knowingly skip. Unlike print books, which regularly come into their possession by the design of others (as with gifts, or by chance, as with books left behind in holiday cottages),[28] sources of e-books are almost invariably prominent, even obtrusive. The e-books participants obtained came from identifiable sources: public libraries, Project Gutenberg, and university libraries most often, but sometimes an 'e-mail direct from author (PDF)' or a download from Pirate Bay.[29] Even a PDF found via Google search is downloaded from somewhere, and e-book gifts, rare as they are for these participants (only 4.0 per cent had received one in the past twelve months) are typically 'given' via a link to a website from which the recipient can download their present. (It is part of what makes an e-book collection a walled garden: little enters without the owner's permission, little is shared, and, aside from expiring loans and repossessed Orwell novels,[30] nothing ever truly leaves.)

Proximity matters because it, to a large extent, determines what elements readers use, and what elements readers trust. Closeness to the text still suggests (even if those signals are not accurate) that a given message is truly from the author or publisher and not from the device, and hence meaningful. Distance suggests that a given message is *not* from the author or publisher (and, if genuinely objective, meaningful in a different way). In terms of closeness, and suggestion of meaning, few paratextual elements are as prominent as a cover image.

Judging E-books by Their Detachable Covers

McCracken speculates that 'given this expanded network of epitexts for e-books, the front cover is perhaps less important now as a marketing device than it is for print books',[31] but data from my study suggest that it remains an element of paramount importance. These participants describe relying on it not only for information about the type of book but also for clues as to its status and trustworthiness. If anything, the cover may take on greater importance when some other signals of publisher investment, such as paper quality, are no longer available for consultation.

Covers are an eminently reasonable place for readers to start when forming their initial assessments of how much investment and expertise have gone into a particular book. Cover design represents daunting effort, whether by a demotic author or, in the case of a mainstream published book, the combined input of design teams, editors, and sales and marketing specialists[32] – even where images may be part or wholly AI generated, humans are still, at time of press, required to define the task, write the prompts, evaluate and refine the outputs, and shepherd the chosen design through the gauntlet of publisher and retailer approvals. Readers risk a bit of money and a great deal of time on their choice of book. Participants in my study frequently underscored that evidence of others' risk, what publishers have invested themselves, ranks alongside the demonstrable skill of the author and editor in determining whether a given novel is worth their own money and time.[33] They were sceptical of supposed difference, noting that 'there used to be this perception that an e-book cover worked in a different way to a print book cover...I'm not entirely sure if that's true', while reporting that in their own experience, 'when you transfer to e-books...that [cover] image still plays a role and also the blurb', and that they 'tend to judge the book by its cover no matter if it is print or digital'.[34] A 'badly done' or an 'unprofessional' cover, therefore, instantly destroys any possibility of trust in the book. Not only does it suggest self-publication but it also signals to them carelessness: a book where 'the cover looked really dodgy'[35] is expected to remain dodgy throughout. 'Cheap or unprofessional' covers 'badly done on Photoshop'[36] were perceived as both typical of self-published e-books and quite reasonable grounds for rejecting a title.

When participants discussed using covers as indicators of quality, it was not a matter of trusting covers but rather trusting their own experience with covers. They had faith in their ability to decode the paratextual messages authors and publishers have placed there, relying on mental models of a printed book for their information-seeking task much as experienced users of traditional libraries have been observed to apply mental models of traditional libraries to digital library searches.[37] A further complication comes from the difference between stable formats, such as PDF, and reflowable formats, such as .EPUB and Amazon's .AZW. Not only does reflow dynamically change aspects such as margins and line breaks (usually for the worse, from a design point of view) but the option of customisation also raises issues of discerning authorial responsibility.

Discerning Authority in an Adaptable Book-Object

Peritext is and always has been porous. Movement between categories of peritext, epitext, and metatext is expected and commonplace, for print as well as for digital books. A given element may move in and out, included in this edition, excluded in that, and perhaps eventually achieving its 'ultimate destiny': to 'catch up with its text' and become part of the text itself.[38] The only things that are unusual about promotion or demotion of elements in e-books are (a) the degree of reader involvement and (b) the degree to which adaptations are reversible and sometimes invisible. (However, Galey argues that the near-infinite fluidity imagined by some early theorists of the e-book is greatly overstated.)[39] Customisation at the point of purchase is not unknown for print. A manuscript owner in 1100 or a bookshop patron in 1720 could select their binding or indeed leave the pages in a stack held together with string. The modern reader can choose between hundreds of print editions of *Pride and Prejudice*, selecting paratext that emphasises the novel's status as a classic, or its central romance, or its various film adaptations, making a conscious decision to match the edition to their conception of and/or reading strategy for the text (or perhaps picking up whatever is closest, and accepting discordant paratext as the price of convenience). But for the e-book, peritext is not only 'flexible',[40] it is perpetually so, at the point of purchase and at almost any point beyond: 'fluidity marks the electronic text in contrast to the stationary nature of print on a page: adjustment of font-size, brightness, contrast, and landscape or portrait orientation'.[41] If one is a typical reader, making use of multiple modes and platforms (in my surveys, most respondents who read e-books at all had used two or more different devices for reading in the past twelve months) one may be simultaneously using a smartphone app for one book and a desktop browser window for another, or taking advantage of the 'save my place' feature on Kindle to swap between devices for the same text, and encountering it through two equally but differently personalised interfaces. There is not one personal version but the potential for a plethora of personal versions, appearing in sequence or simultaneously, optimised for different settings and situations. But assuming that customisation effectively obscures authorial intention, rendering any element useless as peritext (or even non-paratextual) is speculating ahead of the facts.

Precarious Authority

Genette designated a specific category of paratextual elements distributed in or immediately around the print object but not affixed to it.[42] A 'precarious peritext' is an element like a French 'please-insert' that, while created and authorised by the publisher, remains a slip of paper easily separated from the bound copy, unlike 'durable peritext' elements such as bindings and tables of contents.[43] While it would be on one level simple to reclassify all e-book peritext as precarious, that would ignore the way peritextual matter is actually stored in an e-book file, and the ways in which readers experience peritext on the level of an e-reading device.

Formatting as experienced by the reader can be highly adaptable for a reflowable e-book file, with elements such as font, margins, and line spacing adjustable via device or app settings, and elements such as pagination adjusting dynamically to accommodate setting changes. But these setting changes, stored in a local file, do not change the e-book file itself. (The settings are meant to endure over multiple reading sessions, but users of e-reading apps are all too familiar with the software crashes that return settings to default.) Opened and read on a dozen non-synced devices, the file could be experienced in a dozen guises. An e-book 'is simply a disguised zip archive',[44] containing a series of separate files where text, images, formatting, and so forth are stored discretely, to be interpreted and displayed by the interface software each time the e-book file is opened. It is a simple exercise to change file type for an unprotected .EPUB file and view or alter the constituent files, and only slightly more complicated to strip out Digital Rights Management and do the same for a protected .EPUB or .AZW file (as some participants in my study do, despite the fact that this violates terms and conditions from Amazon and some other retailers. Please see Chapter 4 for more on these participants' e-book customisation). But such alteration would not take place by accident. The reader would need to take a series of steps, such as downloading specialist software such as Calibre (and, if a coding novice, downloading detailed instructions) to make a permanent change. In this way, e-book peritext is, in fact, more durable than print peritext: while a file can become corrupted, it can only be intentionally, and not accidentally, dismembered or defaced.

Where e-books have conspicuously less integrity than print books is the invisibility of such permanent changes. Kirschenbaum notes how eighteenth-century legal scholar William Blackstone argued that legal records be kept exclusively on rag linen paper rather than leather, wood, or stone not because paper was durable, but because it was not durable: unlike robust surfaces that could be scoured clean, the paper document was 'fragile enough to readily expose any attempt to tamper with or change it'.[45] Many elements of print paratext can be forcibly removed, like a torn-off paperback cover or a razored-out colour plate. But such durables of print typically leave scars: a defaced and visibly diminished text with gaps, spaces where meaning should be, that invite a frustrated reader to go looking for what's been withheld. (The status of removable paper dust jackets, which were for much of the nineteenth century treated as disposable protective wrapping, but are today desirable elements of a new hardcover book and essential for that book's sale as an undamaged copy, highlights the importance of context in determining what leaves a gap and what does not.) The question is whether the removal of electronic paratextual elements (including elements that don't mimic print, like dynamic indexes) leaves scars and gaps, or whether, as Galey identifies in his case study of a digital edition of *The Sentimentalists* released with incorrect ContentID information, 'readers [of the corrupted version] would have no way of knowing that they have not, in a basic sense, read the same novel as other readers'.[46]

Short of such Calibre-enabled file-level tampering, what is mutable in the reflowable e-book is not the file but the interface: not only because it is customisable but also because it is perpetually remade. As a 'web page in a wrapper'[47] the e-book is read (much like a webpage where content and formatting instructions are distributed over a series of text .XML and image .JPG and .CSS stylesheet files) through mediating software that compiles input from various sources. Rather than storing the output each time, the software stores the data needed (including user settings and, if all goes well, the user's progress through the text) to make it afresh in the next session. In a sense, the version a reader is actually looking at on screen, generated from the instructions in .EPUB or .AZW files and associated settings and progress files, ceases to exist when the reader looks away: not only when they 'shut' the book (closing an application on their tablet or opening a different book on their e-ink reader) but also every time they turn the page. (Leading to the experience that has frustrated so many readers: flipping backwards in an e-book to check something on a previous page and discovering that the pagination has changed, and the words one was looking for have moved despite no changes to font or other settings. This phenomenon of wandering text is identified in some studies as a potential barrier to reading comprehension, retention, and/or immersion, interfering with a reader's ability to construct a cognitive map of the text.[48] For more on wandering text as part of the digital reading experience, see Chapter 4.) Kirschenbaum, examining Max Barry's 2011 novel *Machine Man*, where the author used a software development version control tool to both preserve all interim versions of the text and post these accumulated versions to his personal website, concludes that 'in this model the text becomes less an object or an artefact and more like an *event*' in a programming sense.[49] If that model can be extended to cover an .EPUB or .AZW file where the inner workings are less visible than Barry's but no less intricate, one might consider the reflowable e-book as experienced by the reader as an event rather than an artefact. If so, readers might be observing the early generations of an additional subcategory of paratext: event paratext. Such a type of paratext would contrast with and function separately from artefact paratext; potentially as a paratextual equivalent of Drucker's performative materiality, one that similarly 'always occurs only in real time and is distinct in each instance'.[50] This problematises present conceptions of digital paratext and opens the door for an expansion of paratextual theory. If there is such a thing as event paratext, and readers are viewing and responding to a set of paratextual signals that exist but only for a single viewing, the reflowable e-book is not real, and not real because it is a digital proxy: in this case, a digital proxy for a digital artefact. (And if the reader is conceptualising the e-book itself as a digital proxy for a print edition, doubly distanced.)

Proxy status, and subsequent unrealness, does not by itself stop paratext from functioning as paratext. Genette's categories embrace mediated categories, such as interviews, conversations and colloquia.[51] But it does emphasise the greatest problem with event paratext: discerning authorial intention.

Changes or additions made to a text without the author's or publisher's approval are not paratext. The challenge facing the reader is determining which aspects of the e-book they are viewing on screen are intended and which are accidental (e.g. in the case of a corrupted file such as the edition of *The Sentimentalists* examined by Galey) or imposed (e.g. in an e-book that includes promotions for other books overlaying the final pages, and it may be difficult to tell which were included by the publisher and which were generated by an e-retailer's algorithm). Mutability does not of itself make a particular aspect irrelevant, or even ambiguous. Font, a prime example of a feature controllable via user settings, can nonetheless be initially set by the publisher as part of the .EPUB or other e-book file (settings have for most of the Kindle's history changed on a book-by-book basis, but on some newer models and the Kindle app changing font for any book can change font for every book). Not every book has 'publisher font' as a menu option. But where that option does appear, the very existence of 'publisher font', even when not chosen, focuses the reader's attention, however briefly, on the publisher's original intentions: the invitation to alter is also an invitation to contemplate paratextual choices, highlighting them in a different, but far from trivial, way. (A sobering check on this new way of communicating with readers comes in the form of limited font libraries. Many e-reading devices are loaded with only a handful of popular fonts and, if presented with a file set for anything else, will default to the manufacturer's choice; in Galey's example replacing Joanna with Georgia on Kobo,[52] but on Amazon apps and Kindles typically reverting its own custom Bookerly font. This severely constricts publishers' options, much in the way that production process limits on colour, size, layout, and so on would constrict other design options on a print edition.)[53] This engagement could even, at least for some users, be considered ludic, a game-like interface where playful interaction is not a means to an end but part of the experience. Perpetual customisation, in some ways, exemplifies the transaction element of paratext, where authors and publishers do not and indeed cannot dictate, they can only meet readers on the threshold and make proposals, from which the negotiation may begin.

The invitation to customise, to join publishers and authors at the threshold, does not automatically make a text less important or desirable: these options are only promoted as features because retailers believe they add value to the product. But this form of customisation undermines claims to realness in two ways. One is that drawing attention to publisher-suggested settings foregrounds the idea of an original, valid version, true to the author's intentions, that the e-book-as-proxy emulates with greater or lesser fidelity: as one respondent put it, explaining why they consider e-books to be real books (but not without some qualification), 'I will confess that Kindle and even Google Books seem less like real books because their fonts and text sizes can be changed. I appreciate those options, but I still prefer to see whatever the author, designers and publishers intended'.[54] The second is that by selling proxyhood as a feature, retailers remind readers of the commercial value of unrealness. If 'an ebook is a shadow of a real book' or 'electronic materials feel like a copy, a pdf of the book', as two rationales for e-book unrealness put it, that shadow is cast by something: the 'copy' is still connected to the book, and gains value, and meaning, from that connection.

Immutable Impressions? The Case of Choosing for Reasons of Selection

The e-book's problems with reputation – the suspicion and uncertainty readers feel when trying to judge whether it is a 'proper book'[55] – impact its legitimacy. Results from one suite of questions from my survey, those on selection, offer further insights into ways that trust in print, and lack of trust in digital, is driven by beliefs rather than experience.

When it comes to one form of trust, faith in the selection of books available in a given format, print enjoys what appears to be an unearned advantage. Overall, 'better selection' is not an important motivator: only 13.3 per cent of all respondents choose print for this reason, making it among the least common reasons in the survey (Figure 2.2). (In my surveys, I asked about reasons for choosing print and digital not to identify affordances – these have been widely studied, from industry and academic perspectives, and exhaustively discussed in the popular press – but to look

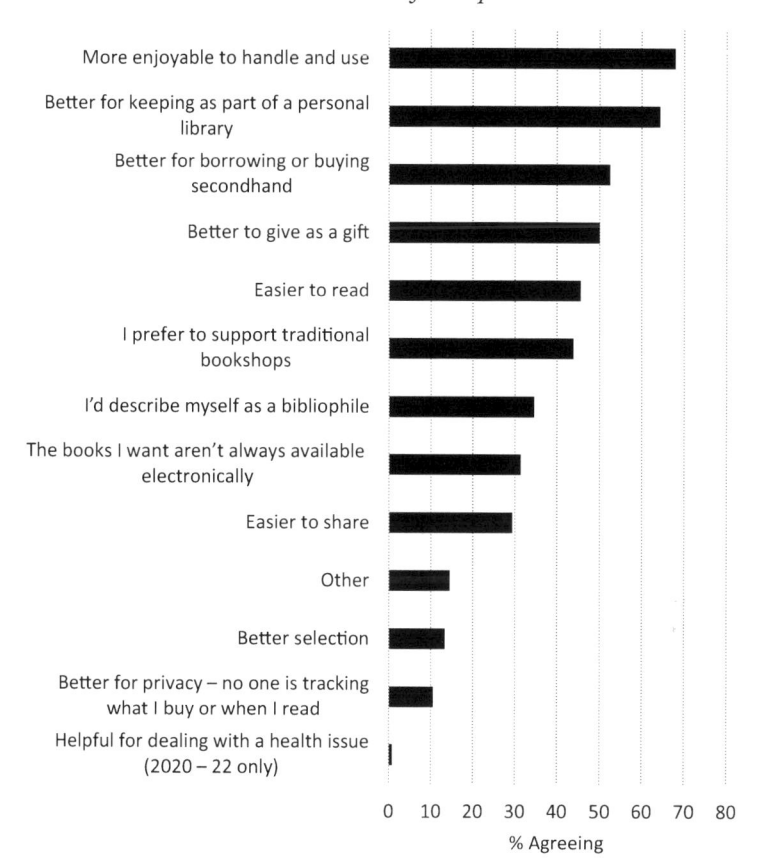

Figure 2.2 'When you choose print, what are your reasons?' (All readers, all years).

at their relative importance, and how they relate to book-reading and book-buying behaviour.)

What is interesting is the degree of disconnect from recent digital reading experience. For print selection (the only form of selection print-only readers were asked about), there is no difference between print-only readers and e-book readers. Those who agreed were somewhat more active consumers of print books, more likely to have obtained one in the past twelve months from Amazon, a library, and secondhand bookshops. However, other than an increased likelihood of having used Project Gutenberg in the past twelve months, there were no links to sources of e-books, e-book genre, or reading device usage. And there were no links at all to reasons for choosing e-books – even to choosing e-books for reasons of better selection. (In contrast, despite its relative unimportance as a motivator, choosing print for reasons of better selection is positively and significantly correlated with every other print motivator in the survey, other than choosing print because it is 'helpful for dealing with a health issue that can interfere with my reading', a question added for the 2020–22 surveys only.)

Digital Selection

The rise of digital self-publishing, combined with that of digital-original imprints (which retain the gatekeeping functions and many editorial processes of traditional publishing, only without print editions in the first instance), the number of books only available in digital form has increased exponentially.[56] At the same time, continuous digitisation efforts, in the form of collection-led initiatives from individual publishers as well as libraries, archives, and Google Books, and by independent actors such as Project Gutenberg,[57] have swelled the ranks of older print-original material available in digital form, and where original editions are out of print all but replacing print as the readily available option. Newly published books are now released with a digital-access policy in mind, and it's an unusual and conspicuous choice to sacrifice potential sales (and antagonise readers who rely on e-books for accessibility reasons) by releasing any book in print without an accompanying e-book edition.[58] But despite the near-universal availability of digital as an option for new books, and increasing availability of digital as an option for older works, readers in this survey are near-unanimous in their judgement that selection is *not* a reason to choose digital. A mere 4.8 per cent of e-book readers choose e-books for this reason, making it the least important motivator in the survey (Figure 2.3).

As some qualitative responses explicitly noted, 'better selection' does not necessarily mean 'wider selection'. A number of participants cited self-published books as a key source of material they wanted to read, and hence a key reason to choose digital reading.[59] Others, however, described self-publishing as the source of an oversupply of low-quality or otherwise uninteresting books that made it more difficult to find books they actually wanted: 'I don't have the stamina' or 'life's too short, I've got 17 unread novels already on my shelves without looking for bloody self-published books'.[60]

Examining the tiny group who choose e-books for better selection reveals a pattern similar to that of print: ties to values and preferences are considerably stronger than ties to behaviour. Links to sources of

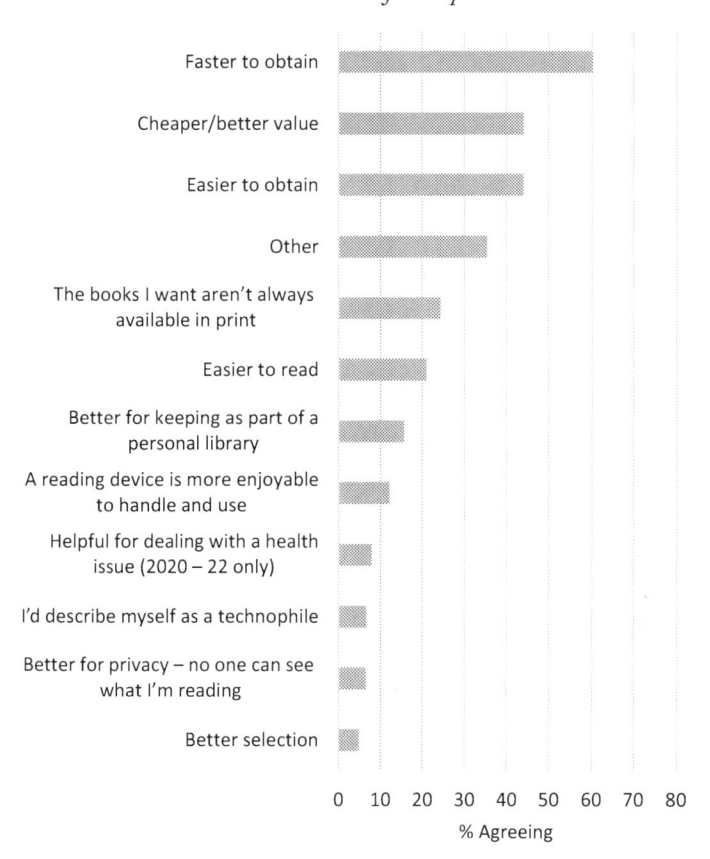

Figure 2.3 'When you choose digital, what are your reasons? (E-book readers only, all years).

e-books and types of e-reading devices used are negligible[61] – the last being particularly remarkable for the portion of data collected under pandemic conditions, when intermittent lockdowns temporarily disrupted access to print books and increased access to digital ones. But those who choose digital for reasons of selection could be described as all-around digital enthusiasts: more likely to share most reasons for choosing e-books, including the exceptionally e-bookish values of preferring digital for personal libraries and considering an e-reading device more enjoyable to handle and use.

In short, perceptions of good selection are linked to a general preference for, and enjoyment of, a given format, but largely disconnected from reading habits and purchasing/borrowing experience. A belief that print has better selection appears to be just that: a belief. And, more importantly, this advantage may be unassailable. If it is not based on evidence in the form of personal experience, but rather on sentiment, there may be no improvement creators or retailers can make to change minds. The impression is entrenched, just as belief in the low quality of self-published novels (which can be in print, but are overwhelmingly released as digital-only) is entrenched: if, as discussed later in this chapter, readers frequently mistake high-quality self-published books for traditionally published books, and only identify as self-published the poorest examples, there is little opportunity to revise judgements.

Self-publishing and the Elusive 'Book of Quality'

*'The difference between the e-book and print book is that [with a] print book you have packaging, so you already have some kind of preconception of what your experience should be. Sort of. . .what will be coming, in a way. With an e-book. . .you just have the cover, and then you go through, it's sort of **difficult to judge whether...it's actually a book of quality**, in a way? I mean, if it's from one of the Big Five, it's probably. . .more reliable in a way.*

(FG 2, respondent 1)

*'[A recently-read self-published book] had typos, it was clearly badly edited, **it just looked like self-published, which was awful**.'*

(Interview 1)

Self-publishing continues to contend with 'this horrible stigma'.[62] 'Vanity publishing'[63] may predate digital, but the explosion in self-publishing facilitated by digital delivery has cemented the link between the two in the market and in readers' minds. Participants acknowledge that quality can be found in self-published books ('self-published. . .could be amazing') and note the proud tradition of independent artists in many fields, comparing self-published fiction to avant-garde zines and punk aesthetics ('the Sex Pistols were far better when they were putting it out themselves').[64] But many still strongly associate self-publishing with low quality, with 'amazing' examples the exception rather than the rule. In interviews and focus groups, participants discussed self-publishing in response to specific questions but also spontaneously, raising it continually as they described their experiences of e-reading. Some are confident in their ability to identify self-published books at a glance ('you'd know the ones that are [self-published]'), and not simply due to quality issues such as poor copyediting (though 'thinking, they need to get a better copy editor'[65] is a common occurrence in their experiences of self-publishing). They describe a 'whiff' of fan fiction or a related 'whiff' of vanity publishing.[66] Telltale signs, for these participants, include not only typographical errors and other editorial gaffes but also simply 'something about them' and the presence of the 'odd':[67] aspects that are not blatantly incorrect, but are nonetheless out of step with what experienced readers expect (a further indication that readers are not isolated from the logic of the field[68] and their personal judgements are informed, though not controlled, by industry norms).

Participants want good books, and describe themselves as open to the idea of good books coming from many sources, not only in print and from mainstream commercial publishing. A number are active, enthusiastic readers of self-published books, particularly fiction. Some report that 'self published books are often only available as ebooks, so I buy those on ereader' or that some 'favourite' books are books obtained 'for free on Amazon'.[69] A number note fan fiction as particularly important, either as the genre that attracted them to digital reading or a genre they discovered through digital reading.[70] Even those who do not (or do not knowingly) read self-published books cite examples of self-published works they consider to be of outstanding quality, including print bestsellers that were initially self-published such as Andy Weir's *The Martian*.[71] Many stress that they do not dismiss self-published books out of hand (e.g. 'I'm not generally opposed to [self-published books]')[72] and some condemn such dismissal as snobbery,[73] of a kind detrimental to book culture, an outdated and ill-informed prejudice. However, their personal experiences of self-published works are frequently of books where 'the quality of writing and editing is not as good as traditionally published novels'.[74] Even where the 'ideas were really interesting' or 'content was fantastic', poor editing could render a book unreadable.[75] Intriguingly, given the confidence many expressed (as above) that they could identify a self-published work by its general oddness, several described experiences of haphazard professionalism, as with an excellent cover but poor editing, or of being caught out: 'I didn't realise [the book] was self-published until I started reading it and I thought, "This cannot possibly have gone through a reputable publisher."'[76] This makes it possible that many have read high-quality self-published books without realising it. Their general impression is that quality can be found in self-published books, but that it is 'harder to find', especially when past encounters of 'really awful' self-published books have 'put [them] off…it could be amazing, but it could be really, really dire'.[77] 'Pleasant surprises'[78] are, largely, surprises.

These experiences reinforce the negative perception of self-publishing as an author's 'last resort',[79] and the common assumption (acknowledged by participants as typical, even if they would not want to make such an assumption themselves) that 'this has probably been rejected by every publishing house in Britain...That's why it's self-published'.[80] As noted, the stamp of mainstream publishing signals to these participants' investment. Gatekeeping is widely considered to guarantee a certain (if not perfect) level of 'quality control' and to offer 'an indication of whether it's worth reading or not'.[81] Without such guarantees, personal recommendations are even more important, whether from friend networks for fan fiction or 'traditional mediums like newspaper columns and book reviews and things'.[82] The industry gatekeeper can be dispensed with, but not simply replaced in a one-to-one swap: some readers stress that for self-published works there is a 'higher standard of recommendation', where multiple endorsements are needed to provide the same level of trust: 'if it's a self-published book then you have to wait for three or four people to tell you that it's actually really good' instead of just one friend.[83]

This frames traditional publishing as a service to readers, with professional editors paid to 'jump in and go find things' because 'life's too short'[84] for readers to do so on their own time. This vocabulary of service may downplay an editor's power, but only highlights the overwhelming trust placed in editors: they will supply the best traditionally published material, but they will also find and elevate the best self-published material, as with 'so, you just think that if it is self-published, if it is good enough to be worth reading, a publisher will pick it up eventually'.[85] It leaves an uneasy balance, where the editor is an unquestioned expert, controlling what readers can see, but who is nonetheless effectively subordinate, someone to whom the reader can delegate work.

The enduring trust in professional judgement intersects with the lower perceived value of digital in the category of digital-only works that are not self-published. Digital-only releases by traditional publishers are again rare, with experiments from the 2010s, including Big Five imprints such as Penguin Random House's Hydra and Alibi and Avon Impulse[86] and series from highly respected literary magazines such as Ploughshares Solos,[87] largely augmented with print-on-demand options or quietly retired. Despite the fact that a digital-first or digital-only release from any of the above would have received the same editorial attention and is held to the same standard as any print release, digital-only remains, as a category, 'dubious'.[88] There is a suspicion that a book released only in digital form is by definition second-best: 'why would [the publisher] invest in print for other books but not this one?'[89] Explaining why they don't consider e-books to be real books, one respondent cuttingly laid out the enduring legitimacy gap for anything not released in print form with 'Obviously books that do not merit print publication...do not merit print publication'.[90] As another put it, 'e-only, in my head, I equate it with, like, films that go straight to DVD'[91] – a statement that, coming from a young adult, invoked the obsolete technology of an earlier generation to comment on the credibility of digital books for their own generation.

The question is how this perception of digital-only as a cheap option, suitable for second-rate books, plays into readers' perception of individual books ... and if readers know, or care, whether their e-books have print editions. I asked e-book readers about the print status of the last e-book they read. The options were 'Digital version of a print book (you could have chosen a printed copy)' and 'Digital original (there was no printed copy to choose)', but also 'Didn't check' and 'Don't remember'. If print status were irrelevant, one would expect a large number of answers in the latter categories. However, readers are in fact overwhelmingly aware of, and overwhelmingly remember, the print status of their e-books. Of the e-book readers who answered the question, nine out of ten (89.3 per cent) were confident that they had this information (Figure 2.4).

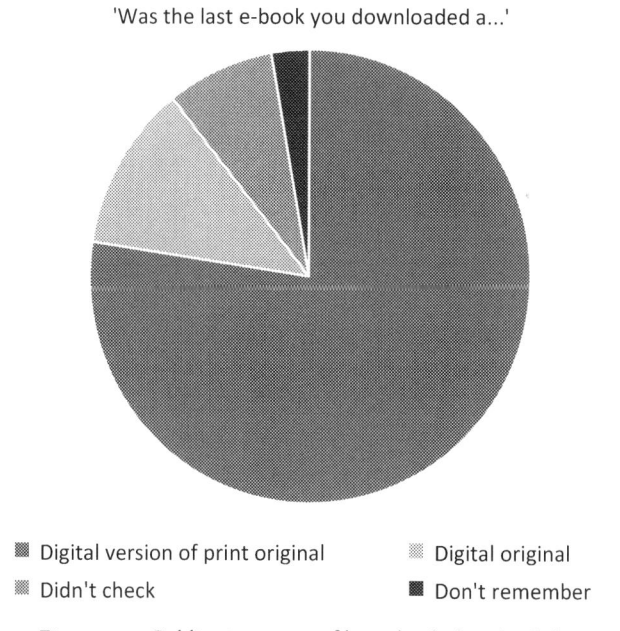

'Was the last e-book you downloaded a...'

- ▨ Digital version of print original
- ▨ Digital original
- ▨ Didn't check
- ■ Don't remember

Figure 2.4   Publication status of last e-book downloaded.

Only 7.9 per cent 'didn't check', indicating that readers almost invariably do check at some point in the process of obtaining a digital book. Of those who were confident that they did know, digital original was a rare choice. More than five out of every six (86.6 per cent) reported having read a 'digital version of a print original', where they could (at least in theory) have opted for a print copy. These proportions were largely stable over the course of the survey, meaning that the massive increase in digital reading, and turmoil in print book availability, during lockdown had little discernible effect.

This commitment to digital versions of print originals may not, however, be as powerful as it first appears. Readers' recollection of the print status of last e-book read depends not only on their memory but also on the accuracy of their original assessment of that print status. And as data indicate, sources of such information can be misleading.

Signalling Status: Digital-only, or Also in Print?

Publishers and author/publishers who cannot answer 'yes' to the reader question 'is this book in print?' face a grave obstacle. They must respond to another question – 'if it is not in print, why not?' – and if this second answer is not convincing, the text will not be viewed in the same light. Epitext offers authors a chance to answer with a narrative, telling a story that defines their digital-only or self-published work in terms of its relationship to print and in the context of a larger writing career and authorial identity. Authors may make extensive use of public authorial epitext, in the form of mediated interviews and articles, unmediated social media and personal websites, actively deceptive pseudo-allographic or crypto-authorial ploys, or a coordinated campaign using a variety of such approaches. Their narratives can align them with traditional mainstream publishing as 'proper' print authors who happen to be releasing one-offs for artistic reasons: for example, Richard Russo using interviews to defend use of the now-defunct digital publisher Byliner for his novella *Nate in Venice* as the only way to publish a novella as a standalone work, and hence to realise his vision.[92] Their narratives may also align them against traditional mainstream publishing. Such stories can present them as artists resisting a corrupt corporate oligarchy that exploits writers and fails readers, as with Polly Courtney using near-identical wording in interviews, articles, social media bios, and tweets to reinforce the message that she 'dumped' her Big Five publishers and now self-publishes for reasons of principle.[93] But authors can and do attempt to embed messages of legitimacy in the digital book-object, not via epitextual narrative but via what are in print peritextual elements: front matter, covers, and page design. For the former, this involves the arguably deceptive tactic (though, as noted above, paratext is often deliberately deceptive) of the single-author imprint.

Masquerading as 'Chosen'

Self-published authors have for decades been advised to evade rather than confront the self-publishing stigma by 'choos[ing] a publishing imprint name, to make your book sound more as if it has been published by a company rather than an individual'[94] – a tactic that predates e-books, and indeed computers. Blogging in 2011, author Lindsay Burokur described her choice not to conceal her status as the publisher of her own work as an iconoclastic and risky one, reporting that 'someone more experienced (and more successful) than I said that indie authors should create an imprint because (a) reviewers who say they won't take self-published fiction might consider work from small presses and (b) there are readers who refuse to try independent authors'.[95] She concluded, however, that despite the 'stigma associated with self-published books' she considered such a 'disguise' incompatible with her 'embrace' of the independent author mission and identity: 'I'm all for trying to make the packaging of my books professional, but I don't think it's in me to make up a press in an attempt to look like something I'm not'.[96] (In other posts, Burokur describes being approached by publishers, including Amazon's digital-only 47North imprint, but turning these down,[97] using authorial epitext to position herself as credentialed by, but in principled opposition to, mainstream publishing in a manner reminiscent of Polly Courtney.)

For a Kindle Direct Publishing author such as Lindsay Burokur, explicit differences between undisguised self-publishing and using a single-author imprint typically appear in only two places. One, falling outside peritext, is a 'Publisher' line on an Amazon product page. (This typically sits far below the first and second screen of content and requires scrolling to find: focus groups revealed that even committed e-book readers who regularly purchase from Amazon were sometimes surprised to learn from fellow participants that this section of an Amazon product page existed.) The other is the e-book front matter. Distinguishing between independent, small-press, single-author, and customers of pay-to-publish vanity publishing firms based only on a name is difficult even for industry insiders and experienced researchers, and for members of the public sometimes impossible: in the early 2010s, one data-gathering exercise produced by a self-described coalition of independent authors set itself the task of quantifying royalty income, author by author, in part to question whether self-publishing was truly less lucrative than traditional publishing for a typical author.[98] This required definitively categorising books by publication type. The project described a labour-intensive process of researching each imprint individually, hunting online for any clues regarding hundreds of obscure names, and on particularly complex cases giving up.[99] Even the layout of the front matter is less important electronically: if the typographical arrangement appeared haphazard, only some participants highlighted this as a sign that 'not as much care [has] gone into this as perhaps should'.[100] Others were ready to attribute mistakes to the e-reading device or app rather than the novel itself: a sharp contrast to their lack of patience with imperfect copyediting, where details on the level of unusual hyphenation were sufficient for participants to conclude that a piece 'wasn't done professionally'.[101] This willingness to effectively give the novel the benefit of the doubt suggests, for this one aspect, something like a level playing field: an arena where the skill of professional book designers does not confer advantage. But in an e-book, where the reader has little else to go on, front matter does at least promise an answer to pressing questions on relationship to traditional mainstream publishing.

Equivalence as Realness: 'Same' as the Benchmark for a Real Book

The enduring importance of relationship to a print edition in determinations of value and credibility is equally visible in determinations of realness. Across all the free-text answers on why e-books are, or aren't, real books, 'same' was one of the most frequently occurring words. 'Same words', 'same content', 'same book', and many variations on 'it's the same thing, just in a different format' featured in arguments for e-book realness, while the aforementioned 'not the same product' made a counterargument against. This theme of equivalence is entwined with those of utility (e-books offering the 'same experience', which I'll return to in Chapter 4) and materiality (e-books having the 'same content', discussed further in Chapter 5). But same *book*, same *thing*, speaks to an argument about the fundamental nature of an e-book – and not to the e-book's advantage. E-book designers' emulation of print,[102] even at the expense of functionality,[103] actively invites the comparison, while at the same time setting up unwinnable direct competition. Backing away from the 'super-book' dreams that showcased what digital could do that paper could not,[104] visions that made Coover so confident that the print novel would die of neglect,[105] creators are left in a contest where the best that can be hoped for is a draw. E-books are left not trying to out-book print books, but out-print print books. The result is lukewarm arguments for realness like 'same words and story. They are not as pretty to look at but while reading this doesn't really matter to me' (where the beauty of print books still makes them superior, but in ways not as important *while reading*') and 'because it's *pretty much the exact same* as a physical book except I can read them in the dark! I do prefer a physical book as they don't run out of battery and feel nicer' [emphasis mine] (where even the valued affordance of night-time reading is outweighed by battery life and 'feel' factors, e-books remaining the less-preferred option). Even among participants who agreed that they considered e-books to be real books, fidelity to a print edition could be set as a condition for realness, as with '[e-books are real books] if content is identical to the print version' – and if the 'content' (however defined), is not identical, the e-book is not real. 'Pretty much the exact same' is, ultimately, not the exact same – and in that head-to-head, e-books come off worse.

'Not the Same Product': the Ersatz Book

Participants in my study describe willingness to consider digital-only books as equal to also-print books, but in practice may not take in evidence that might make them reconsider their perception of e-books as a whole. In terms of trust, this suggests that e-books may be grouped together in a permanently lower category: ultimately and irretrievably lacking. That lack speaks directly to a state of bookness that e-books cannot attain, and links to forms of unrealness distinct from digital proxyhood, event para-text, and performative materiality.

In terms of this form of trust, the e-book most often functions for the readers in this study as an *ersatz book*. It is a substitute, and potentially a good one. The ersatz at best equals the original: it does not exceed and cannot supplant, and more than likely falls short. But fundamentally it is something different. It is 'like a book', nearly a book, potentially valuable and worthwhile, but not fully legitimate: it is 'just not the real thing'. But while the *ersatz book* is different from a book, it is also different from a digital proxy. These participants' experiences of e-book legitimacy, and multiple forms of unrealness, demonstrate two things. One, that unreal-ness is perfectly acceptable to some readers at some times: e-book readers do not choose digital books because they fall into a camp of believers who consider e-books always real, but because they are willing to read unreal things. And two, that different forms of unrealness can coexist.

Conclusion

Trust in a book takes a long time to build but only a moment to break. On this dimension, legitimacy and realness are deeply enmeshed with reputation, and a novel that is not available in print is, by many respondents, assumed to be of lower quality. Readers demonstrate understandable caution, retaining respect, even reverence, for the traditions of print. They subject e-books and e-novels to stringent investigation before even considering induction into their reading lives, or the designation of 'book'. That said, caution does not equal conservatism: these readers are in theory highly generous in their willingness to consider e-book bids for inclusion, and to learn new ways of evaluating texts in new formats even as they import old ways from their experiences with print. Readers demand professionalism but are willing to consider the possibility of excellence appearing in e-books with no industry pedigree, even if their own experience of self-published e-books has made them pessimistic. However, receptiveness in theory may not translate into receptiveness in practice, as readers' means of determining self-publishing status are unreliable. In evaluating individual e-books, readers negotiate with authors and publishers in some new and some familiar ways, continuing to draw on what in print are peritextual elements, particularly cover images and page-level design. This defies simplistic transfers of paratextual theory to e-books: it is not possible to ignore the spatial dimension and declare that peritext no longer exists, but neither is it realistic to assume that all peritextual elements are either visible or influential.

When it comes to first impressions and taking a chance, e-books are effectively unreal. In some ways, they function as *ersatz books*, perceived as lacking the certifying investment of the publishing industry or the sumptuous range of choice on offer in print (even if those judgements are not based on fact). But in terms of paratext, e-books and e-novels function as digital proxies of stable but incomprehensible 'disguised zip files' of data. Both forms of unrealness are at least sometimes acceptable. Readers demonstrate the ability to move between frames of reference regarding e-book realness, and hence between conceptions of the nature of an e-book. And as we examine in Chapter 3, on transactions, this movement can be purposeful, and very much under the reader's control.

CHAPTER 3

Ownership and Permanence
E-book Transactions

*'If I love a book, I need to **keep** a [print] copy. E books just don't give that feeling.'*

(Survey 2021)

*'I can **keep** [an e-book] with me at all times to read whenever I have a moment. My entire library is carried with me.'*

(Survey 2021)

The book is chosen. The reader, having fought their way through jungles of epitext and negotiated with the author as to the value of the selected text, is ready to obtain it. But obtain it how? For a print book, the decision is difficult enough: whether to borrow or buy; if buying, hardcover or paperback, new or used; comparison shopping for the chosen edition from competing retailers, and so on. For an e-book, a different landscape of options presents itself. Even among digital artefacts, e-books are elusive. Readers working in a commercial context dominated by Amazon, where the 'Buy Now' button typically means 'buy conditional use licence now', are for each book confronted afresh with questions of what 'buy', 'collect', or 'own' mean in practice.

This chapter explores how readers who have chosen an e-book decide on their next step, contrasting the motivations for purchase (or conditional licence purchase), loan, and piracy. It will draw on legal scholarship, book history, and fan studies to explore how bookness and realness in the form of meaningful ownership can be constituted if desired, acknowledging that bookness and realness may be unwanted when readers prefer temporary, unauthorised, or unambiguously illegal uses. It concludes with modern conceptions of the rights of the reader and the fraught question of e-book control, and readers' experiences of conflict with corporate entities over ownership of their collections.

The Legalities of E-book Ownership

When e-reading went from niche to mainstream, the new e-book market dragged authors, publishers, and readers into areas of intellectual property law rarely encountered in practice and not yet tested in the courts. Existing agreements between authors and publishers regarding who was licensed to reproduce, distribute, and sell works did not, in most cases, explicitly cover digital editions; conflict over such rights in older contracts has been the basis for numerous lawsuits and remains an area of disagreement.[1] (One example is the contentious and very public battle between Random House and the estate of William Styron; Styron's heirs eventually succeeded in clawing back digital rights and released the 2010 e-book edition of *Sophie's Choice* with Jane Friedman's Open Road Publishing venture.)[2] Existing case law regarding the rights and privileges of readers was equally inadequate to deal with the potential of digitisation, including storage and sharing of digital files and use of a given file across multiple devices.[3] Print-era customs served as foundations for some e-lending frameworks. A common example saw public libraries loaning to only one borrower at a time (as if it were a physical book sitting on a shelf), and loaning a given copy only a certain number of times (as if it were a physical book that would wear out and have to be replaced).[4] However nonsensical from a technical point of view, such agreements observed prior consensus on fair compensation and reasonable use, building on terms negotiated between libraries and publishers that weighed the needs of users and institutions against the commercial needs of authors and publishers, as well as preserving trust and cooperation between parties still mutually involved in the sale and use of print books. (With print still at that time accounting for the overwhelming majority of transactions, straining print partnerships for the sake of e-book opportunities was rarely deemed advantageous.) It is notable that the pilot study on library e-lending that followed the 2013 Sieghart Review, which agreed on the critical importance of compensating authors for each instance of borrowing, included as participants 'authors, publishers, agents, libraries and booksellers':[5] a list more representative of the creators and distributors of books than the buyers and borrowers of books, with librarians standing alone as, if not the voice of readers, at least guardians of readers' interests.[6] As I'll discuss later in the chapter, when readers consider rules regarding e-book use as unfair, they are disinclined to comply with those rules.

The approach of Project Gutenberg and Google, in contrast, exemplified the Silicon Valley ethos of 'move fast and break things': a 'build it first and ask for forgiveness later' policy familiar to other digital culture pioneers.[7] 'Backward-looking', far from being an insult, is an accurate description in this context of an approach building on tradition and prioritising existing relationships. 'Forward-looking' is not necessarily a compliment: as Google Books demonstrated in its rush to digitise over the objections of many authors and publishers, a future-oriented approach can be as mired in humdrum practicalities as a history-oriented one (as Project Gutenberg was reportedly shaped not only by a vision of access to literature but also the need for a value-for-money use of '$100,000,000 of computer time' on a University of Illinois mainframe,[8] and no more likely to be shaped by logic, justice, or even adherence to the law). Individual readers are similarly pulled between the past and future, informed by predigital practices and by emerging possibilities, and immersed in a larger cultural conversation on digital-era rights and responsibilities.

Examining three entities particularly influential in shaping modern perceptions regarding ownership of e-books demonstrates the variety, and flexibility, of stances on realness. The first is Project Gutenberg. The Project promises 'books for all and for free':[9] not stand-ins for books, or pale imitations of books, but books. Michael Hart's analogy of a 'Star Trek replicator'[10] suggests copies, but wondrous copies befitting a science fiction utopia: perfect, indistinguishable from and interchangeable with the original, entirely authentic and real (however much this promise collides with what Kirschenbaum calls the 'illusion [or call it a working model] of immaterial behaviour: identification without ambiguity, transmission without loss, repetition without originality').[11] When confronted with legal barriers to distributing real books, as when the edition on which they based their painstakingly constructed files of the works of Shakespeare did not enter the public domain as expected,[12] the Project did not change their stance that e-books are real books. Instead, they complied, taking down the files, and then lobbied to change the law (though plans for Hart to serve as Lawrence Lessig's plaintiff in the actual Supreme Court case against the Copyright Term Extension Act of 1998 broke down).[13] The second is Google Books. Google's contrasting response to legal challenges was to pivot to presenting e-books as sub-real. Despite early interest and significant investment in mass book digitisation, to the degree that 'the corporation's self-narrative places digital books at the company's inception',[14] when challenged, they recast their artefacts as 'snippets', things that are not books or meaningful parts of books (despite the fact that patient users can, through repeated searches, read large portions of a given book), and reframed the sharing of those artefacts as nothing more than harmless indexing.[15] The third is Amazon. The juggernaut of the e-book market, it has since the 1990s experimented with a wide and often contradictory range of approaches and narratives. And as discussed throughout this book – at length justified by Amazon's reach and influence – it sometimes describes its products to customers in ways that suggest books, real and ownable, and at other times in ways far short of real.

All three, however, have one aspect in common: by simply proceeding with what was suddenly technologically possible, and putting to one side the question of how this did or did not harmonise with existing legal frameworks and custom, these agents set an influential example of risk-taking and aggressive manoeuvring. In this period where the legal territory is broad and contested, readers' views are not necessarily informed by legal or regulatory realities. Readers' understanding of their rights as readers or owners is highly variable, often incorrect, and influenced by contradictory messages from self-interested retailers as well as folk wisdom, both on traditional rights of authors and on philosophies of free access and exchange common to digital culture.

Reading in Context: E-books in a Sea of Stolen Goods

The participants in my study are not unusual in describing a digital reading landscape that extends over many territories, each with its own legal environment and accepted norms, and with few if any signposts on the borders between. E-books rarely stand alone. They are read, frequently on the same devices, alongside journalism, commentary, crowdsourced reviews and Wikipedia entries, social media posts, and so on. Participants' e-books and other digital material come from a vast array of sources: some mainstream and some fringe; some adapted from print and some digital-original; some legal and some blatantly illegal; and many in a grey area somewhere in between, where readers may not know and may not care to inquire after status.

Much of participants' on-screen reading consists of free-to-the-user but not necessarily legal material, shared with explicit Creative Commons licensing or a less formal adherence to what Lawrence Lessig describes as 'the ideals of the Internet and cultural freedom'.[16] Fan fiction, spontaneously mentioned in the survey and focus groups by many participants, exemplifies the latter category.[17] Fan fiction thrives in both its original non-commercial territory and increasingly, after further transformations, in commercial arenas. Prominent examples of fan fiction reworked to remove identifiers include Anna Todd's *After* (discussed later in this book), Cassandra Clare's *The Mortal Instruments* series, and, of course, *Fifty Shades of Grey*.[18] Community standards regarding credit, attribution, and reuse, negotiated over decades in intersecting fandoms, are stretched to cover a vastly expanded audience as fan fiction is both made visible and corporatised by the entrance of actors such as Wattpad.[19] As legal scholar Aaron Schwabach explains, 'while there are some areas in which the law [regarding fan works] is unsettled, there are more in which it is settled but widely misunderstood by owners and fans alike'.[20] In my own study, participant responses highlight the degree to which even informed, experienced users can be unclear as to the legal status of what they are reading and sharing. They also demonstrate how good faith reliance on familiar terminology can spread misinformation. When participants describe fan fiction as 'not published, it's free', or its creators as 'writers' outside the category of 'actual published authors', one can see how such terms serve, in the context of the conversation, to draw useful distinctions between categories of works: commercial and non-commercial, authorised and non-authorised, and so on.[21] One can also see how easily describing published works as 'not published', or 'writers' as separate from, and by implication less than, 'actual published authors', could lead to unintentional violation of actual rights as creators and intellectual property owners.

For e-books, as with news (cited by many participants as a core type of screen reading, and often read on the same devices as e-books), unauthorised use is commonplace. The UK Intellectual Property Office finds that e-books, whether mainstream-published, self-published, or shared on free-to-user sites, are most often accessed legally, but piracy is on the rise. The Office estimated that in May 2022, 24% of Britons who read e-books had pirated at least one in the previous three months: deemed an 'average' infringement level, higher than audiobooks (22%) but lower than digital magazines (41%), and nearly double the pre-COVID figure of 13% in 2018.[22] But even with that sharp increase, the Office found that only 11% of e-book readers pirated all their recent books: the great majority still obtained either some (13%) or all (76%) of their recent books legally.[23] Results from the US are similar: the Immersive Media and Books 2020 report, by Rachel Noorda and Kathi Inman Berens and funded by OverDrive, the American Library Association, the Book Industry Study Group, and the Independent Book Publishers Association, found that while 14.4% of reader survey respondents engaged in some book piracy, piracy accounted for only a portion of the books they obtained, and that in the early COVID period book pirates actually bought more books (e-book, print book, and audiobook) than the general survey population.[24] Together, these figures indicate widespread flexibility: some readers who never pay, but more who sometimes pay, and are not averse to a spot of piracy in certain circumstances. For them, the decision is not whether to pirate, but when – and why.

'Pirated' or 'piracy' was offered in most years by my own survey respondents as a write-in source of e-books. Specific websites included the entertainment-focussed Pirate Bay,[25] which offers novel downloads alongside music, games, and software, but also more academic-focussed websites including AAARG[26], Sci-Hub, and Library Genesis, that offer unauthorised copies of peer-reviewed research papers, monographs, and various forms of scholarly texts[27] (and which have been used by AI developers to train Large Language Models without the authors' knowledge or consent).[28] Piracy did not rule out selective future purchases: some explained that they would later 'buy physical copies if book [is] good'.[29] Some participants in my study who acknowledged reading ambiguous or openly pirated material expressed mild sheepishness ('pirating…which is a bit bad…') or a need for secrecy ('given that this is sufficiently anonymous, I tend to pirate e-books to see if it's any good and then buy it if it's decent in hard copy'), but for the most part a calm acceptance of strategic piracy and no regrets ('sure, I'll buy [e-]books. But normally if it's hard to pirate').[30] (However, it is worth noting that they could have felt regret without expressing it, and that participants who did feel more conflicted may have kept quiet on the subject.)[31] When acknowledging that they are using material in ways prohibited by the site or author, they often express irritation rather than remorse, and dismiss restrictions as both futile and an unreasonable impediment to use, as in this exchange in focus group 4:

> P2: *'Yes, I know that some websites are learning about [manual copying of files] because I know fanficiton.net stopped doing that…they used to let you but now you can't copy and paste anything, they've got it protected. So they're sort of learning.'*
> P4: *'They make it tricky.'*
> P3: *'Isn't it still just publicly available though, so why do they need to lock it down?'*
> P4: *'It seems obnoxious given that some people want to read stuff offline.'*

The right for authors to control how their work is downloaded is here regarded as less important than the right of readers to access the material on their own terms, in the formats most convenient and comfortable for them. Authors such as fantasy novelists Maggie Stiefvater, Samantha Shannon, Tom Pollock, and Laura Lam describe a painful bind where online piracy, sufficiently widespread to devastate sales, is often carried out by devoted fans who consider downloading an illegal PDF harmless, or even 'free advertising' and a compliment to favourite authors.[32] Though there was some censure of the 'grey area' or open piracy behaviour of other readers, such as family members or nameless hypothetical strangers (as with 'my brother is Torrenting books', greeted by the group with a general sigh of dismay),[33] among participants in my study, there was little open scolding or judgement of pirates in their midst (notable, as there was at times scolding and judgement on other topics such as appreciation of book materiality, as discussed in Chapter 5) no matter how explicit the discussion of illegal use. The single instance in any focus group of censure directed at a person present was in focus group 1.

> P3: *I think pretty much everything I have on my Kindle I've just borrowed. Books that someone else downloaded and just gave me…'*
> P1: *'You can't download books illegally.'*
> P3: *'I didn't. I got it from someone else. I never touched the internet, from my point of view!'*

This saw the censure laughed off, and the subject immediately dropped as the group moved on. It is notable that, while joking, the participant's rationalisation of illegal downloads as a form of 'borrowing' didn't argue that the theft was trivial, but rather that the theft wasn't real theft. As law professors Michael Heller and James Salzman put it, ownership is a 'storytelling battle' between six fundamental narratives – first-in-time, possession, labour, attachment (not in the sense of emotion but in the sense of 'it's mine because it's attached to something that's mine'), self-ownership, and family – that a party can selectively assert depending on which story best serves their immediate interests.[34] 'Theft,' they explain, 'like ownership itself, is a legal conclusion, not an empirical fact'.[35]

Books Bought but Not Owned

Despite the prevalence of piracy and artful manual downloads, in my own study most of participants' digital reading consisted of e-books conventionally bought or borrowed. Terms and conditions, whether for major retailers, libraries, or free sources such as Project Gutenberg, further shape readers' understanding of what they should and should not do with a book (and, as discussed subsequently, misconceptions regarding terms may

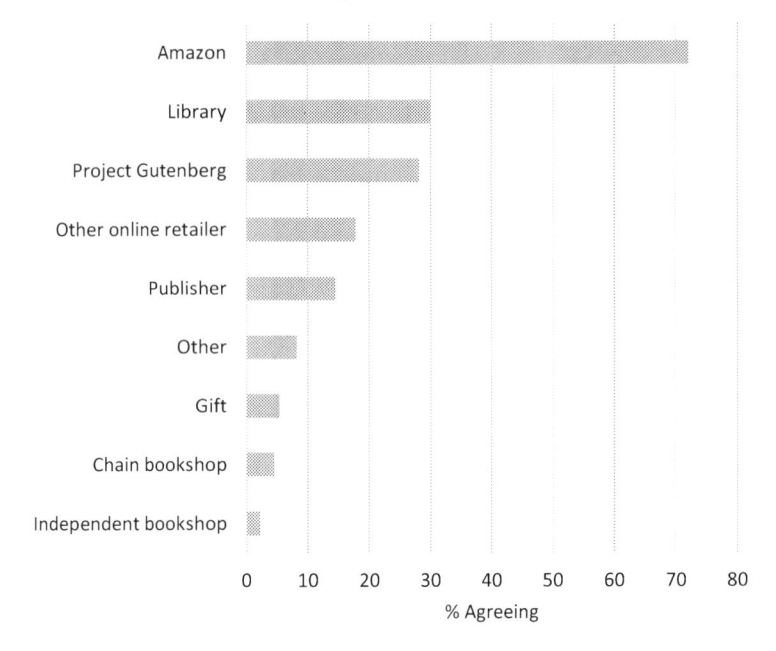

Figure 3.1   Sources of e-books.

mean that self-reported levels of unauthorised use underestimate the true scale). Amazon was the biggest source by a wide margin. Nearly three-quarters (72.0%) of e-book readers had obtained an e-book from Amazon in the past twelve months, more than twice the level for libraries (30.0%) and Project Gutenberg (28.2%) (Figure 3.1).

No other source was used by more than one in five readers. Most sources saw minimal change over the course of the survey: direct from publisher increased slightly (peaking in 2016 at 21.6%) while non-Amazon online retailers (peaking in 2016 at 29.5%) and Project Gutenberg (peaking in 2017 at 34.4%) rose slightly before falling back to original levels (though not in a pattern obviously linked to the pandemic), but most other changes were negligible. The exception was librar-ies. These saw a sharp increase, nearly doubling from 21.9% in 2014–17 to 41.2% in 2020–22, when so many readers shared the experience of 'did not go to a library in person for fifteen months, so e-book checkout was kind of a necessity'.[36] Usage predictably peaked in 2020 (44.1% in 2020,

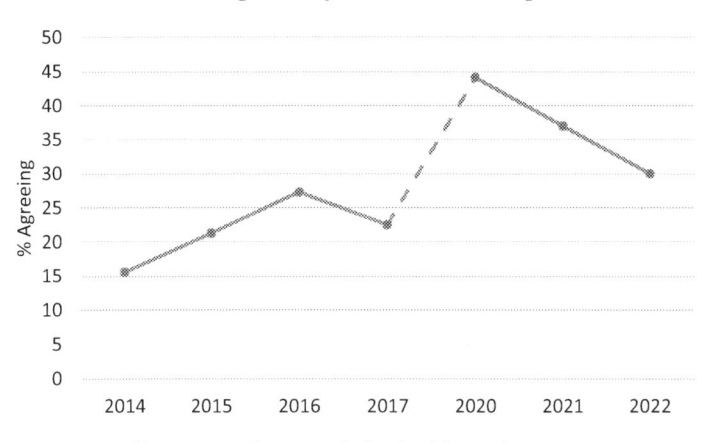

Figure 3.2   Sources of e-books: library, by year.

vs 41.3% in 2021, and 37.0% in 2022), but remained in 2022 still higher than before COVID-19 (Figure 3.2).

Increased pandemic demand was not without downsides: while many benefitted from enhanced collections, as with 'my library service expanded their eBook collection massively and got some great titles' (enhancements that were for many libraries temporary, and often linked to special, less costly licensing terms offered by publishers at the height of pandemic lockdowns) others found the competition for titles a barrier to reaching the books they wanted, explaining that 'due to ebook demand on libraries early in 2020 one of my library systems reduced the amount of ebooks you could loan/do holds on' or 'more people are accessing the public library's [sic] in my area, and the wait times for e-books are longer'.[37] As this book goes to print, it's not yet possible to predict whether library e-book loans will remain so popular. But the pandemic was for so many a chance to not only try e-books but also *rely* on e-books, as with 'when the libraries were closed, ebooks were what kept me going'.[38] For at least some, those who 'started using [e-books] more frequently because [they] got a library card and. . .now prefer ebooks to print because of the ease of reading them', or 'for a while, only ebooks were available from the library and that got [them] used to them so now. . .prefer them even though print through the library is back to being easy to get', the experience was good enough to convert them to regular e-reading.[39]

However, experience of buying from Amazon doesn't necessarily translate to full understanding of what one is actually purchasing, because

Amazon terms and conditions are confusing. Conditional use licenses such as Amazon's are not unusual for digital book retailers or sellers of digital goods in general. Its tight restrictions on what a user can do with an e-book (e.g. not only banning resale but also such actions as conversion to another file format) and reservation of the retailer's right to revoke access at any time are in many ways industry standard. But customers can be 'misled by the apparent disconnect between the message communicated by the Buy Now button and the limited set of rights contemplated by EULAs and terms of service' as Amazon, like other e-retailers, knowingly 'leverages the common understanding' of the purchase of goods.[40] Such leveraging includes use of the same front end terminology for physical and digital goods (like a physical book and an e-book) when the actual terms are quite different. Perzanowski and Hoofnagle's 2016 survey of digital consumers revealed that large majorities believed that clicking a Buy Now button conferred ownership of an e-book (86%), the right to keep an e-book (87%), and the right to read an e-book on other personal devices (81%), and significant minorities believed that it conferred the right to lend (48%), gift (38%), or bequeath (26%) e-books.[41] Whether or not e-retailers can be proved to be actively and intentionally misleading consumers for the sake of profit (as Perzanowski and Hoofnagle posit), e-retailers benefit from the confusion when customers think they are getting more for their money than they actually are. Heller and Salzman point out that far from being an outlier, Amazon is engaging in typical corporate practice when it includes 'strategic ambiguity' (as when an airline declines to clarify which of two passengers owns an armrest, or the wedge of space taken up when a seat is reclined) as part of its overall ownership design, 'a social engineering tool designed to steer your behaviour, invisibly and decisively'.[42] Perhaps the most influential signal is 'automaticness': with '1 click' the reader takes possession, when a loan is expired the book simply disappears from their virtual shelf. The ground rules are relegated to 'terms and conditions' areas: separate zones of small-print legal terminology, framed not as reasonable arguments that a rational person can and should master, but as baffling and impenetrable collections of words, useless for the purposes of communication and utterly inaccessible to the non-professional. This infantilisation of the e-book reader – choice removed, details unknowable – sends a message that there is no point in engaging with the existing terms: *you won't be able to understand them, and even if you did you have no power to negotiate*. The result is an idea that the only way to effectively navigate a transaction is by trial and error, proceeding when permitted and stopping only when blocked, treating anything that is technically possible as permissible: *if I wasn't allowed to do it, they would have stopped me.* In choosing obscurity, Amazon and other retailers have effectively released users from any feeling of obligation to consider what is ethical and why, or what might be the best way to approach a PDF of unknown provenance sitting on a dubious file sharing website; arguably, from any feeling of agency in the ongoing formation of ethics regarding e-book ownership and use.

In my own study, survey data and, particularly, focus group and interview data underscore the degree to which e-book readers are unsure about ownership. While some participants were well-informed about Amazon's terms and what they meant for readers, many others were not. Some were aware that they were in the dark (often expressing irritation at arcane terms), but others were unknowing holders and confident sharers of misconceptions. But whether or not they have accurate knowledge of conditional use licenses, participants were as a group dissatisfied with the forms of ownership offered, in the current environment, by e-books. Whatever was on offer, it was not enough. Some informed participants singled out objectionable terms and conditions, particularly that when retailers 'can take it away at any time', exchanging money for an e-book is 'like renting it' while 'print copy ensures you actually own the book; electronic means you are at the mercy of the electronic rights and device makers'.[43] They noted that they 'disagree with e-publishers' policies that restrict sharing of e-books/inheritance of e-books' or chose digital in a specific incidence only because there 'was a special deal for e-books that I'd get to keep a PDF version of. Not rent a license to'.[44]

Whether the limitations were legal or practical, the fault of the terms or the fault of a counterintuitive interface (e.g. even participants who, though they could legally loan an e-book file, did not necessarily know how to go about the awkward process of extracting and transferring the file), the limitations were deemed not just burdensome, but unacceptably so: offensive and unjust. What makes them unacceptable is comparison to print books. Perzanowski and Hoofnagle argue that 'buyer's "default behaviour" is based on the experience of buying physical media, and the assumptions from that context have carried over into the digital domain'.[45] My findings strongly support the idea that readers believe firmly, and feel deeply, that the affordances of print constitute their rights as book-readers: if one can do it with a print book, one should be entitled to do it with an e-book. This speaks to a fundamental belief that on at least one level, e-books have bookness: the rights of a book-reader apply.

Crucially, Perzanowski and Hoofnagle found that 'respondents in [their] study indicated that they would turn to streaming services and

BitTorrent if they were unable to engage in the uses typically associated with personal property ownership'.[46] My study's participants, in openly discussing their own book piracy, and not judging themselves or others for such breaches, suggest that this prediction is accurate.

Principled Resistance

Widespread and unrepentant piracy is not necessarily an indication that participants consider e-books to be unreal. Such a viewpoint would be one way to ease qualms about piracy (there is no crime in stealing something that is not real) but not the only way. Another response to the disconnect between what feels right and what is legal – the powerful shared conviction that readers should be allowed to enjoy the same rights of ownership with e-books as they do with print books – is to recast non-compliance as principled resistance.

Many participants expressed a sense that breaking bad rules is often justified and sometimes admirable, particularly when the actor or institution making the bad rules is not respected or liked. Amazon, accused by Perzanowski and Hoofnagle of manipulation and fraud, is singled out among retailers by a number of my participants (for more on the emotional dimension of dealings with Amazon, please see Chapter 5). For such readers, violating Amazon's terms can be cast as standing up to a bully: something done for self-respect as much as for any material gain. But even beyond a self-respecting citizen's response to unfair demands, indifference to terms can be cast as romantic: an expression of a more ardent readerly identity. If in nineteenth-century British novels 'the vulgar owning without reading epitomized by sofa-table books and dummy spines finds its antithesis in reading without buying . . . and even reading without owning (remember the hero of Ranthorpe freeloading at a bookstall)'[47] then the bookstall-loafing and reading-room-raiding hero of the Victorian period can perhaps find a counterpart in the PDF-ripping reader of today: similarly so enamoured of the text that obsession with ownership seems petty by comparison. (The theft of a treasure beyond price does at least demonstrate taste.) de Certeau was referring to defiance of a very different sort of authority when he described powerless-but-free readers as 'travellers' who 'move across lands that belong to someone else, like nomads poaching their way across fields they did not write, despoiling the wealth of Egypt to enjoy it for themselves': he spoke of resisting pressure to conform to official, sanctioned reading practices, not official, sanctioned file sharing regulations.[48] But readers can locate honour and dignity in poaching of the two separate kinds. Reading without owning can be righteous and even demonstrate a deeper, more principled commitment to books and reading. This offers a new perspective on digital book piracy. It validates some earlier findings on the scale of the phenomenon, including Perzanowski and Hoofnagle's, but challenges conclusions as to the motivations behind it, with major implications for authors and publishers seeking to curb illegal book downloads. This central role of affect, of feeling (connected, or righteous, or respected, or conversely feeling disconnected and disdained) further underscores the degree to which book ownership, for these participants, is bound up not only with practicalities but also with emotion. Acceptable levels of control are here subjective and personal, successful to the degree that they give the individual a sense of meaningful ownership, and overwhelmingly framed in relation to print books.

Ownership as Realness: Feeling, 'Safekeeping', and Reaping What Authors Sow

The ability to keep and control – alongside feelings associated with keeping and control – underpins many respondents' core reasons for regarding e-books as real or unreal. Ownership is one of the overarching themes emerging from free-text responses to the question in the 2022 survey. To some respondents, e-book was unreal 'because I don't own a physical copy'; realness was absolutely contingent on that tangible and traditional form of ownership. For others, lack of a print copy was more an issue of affect, or lack thereof: 'Don't feel like I own it in same way as a physical print book' or 'I don't feel as if I own e-books in the same way I do physical copies' (offering the possibility that the ownership still existed, but did not deliver the same satisfaction, a legal but not emotional reality). Lack of control over the book's destiny was another reason for unrealness, as with 'you can't look at it again, see it on a shelf, lend it to someone, discuss it with a friend. Feels like a much more private reading experience' or '[I don't feel as if I own it and] I used to like sharing books with family and friends': without the ability to lend and share, and experience emotions that lending and sharing inspire, the book is not real. Linked to this is the matter of permanence, and how 'Digital can disappear', both in the sense of a deleted file and of versioning and obsolescence. As one respondent explained, 'e-books will turn out to be more transient than the written word. Around the corner will be a new, unknown reading delivery system that we can't even dream of. Books, however, those things written down, or placed between covers for safe keeping, will outlive us all.' Here, ownership is not limited to the individual: 'safe keeping' spans generations, and e-books are unreal because they can't be kept for posterity in the same way as print.

However, ownership in another sense provides a powerful argument for e-book realness. As noted earlier, one of Heller and Salzman's six fundamental narratives of ownership is labour, 'the idea that labor justifies ownership – that you and you alone deserve to *reap what you sow*' [emphasis theirs].[49] A number of respondents consider e-books real because they 'know how much work goes into making both [e-books and print books]'. 'The same amount of work went in to create them as print books', another respondent argues, 'so why would they be any different?' In their estimation, realness hinges on the fact that 'it's a finished written text', specifically 'something someone has written'; 'a person wrote it, a person is reading it. It's a book' – it is the human involvement, the human effort, that makes it so. (A conception of realness that expands Foucault's author function to enfold additional responsibility as well as additional means to control a text,[50] with enormous implications for AI-authored books; as Leah Henrickson has established, it is entirely possible for readers unsure whether a machine, or its creator, can fulfil the author function, to conclude that a text was written by nobody.)[51] It's not only the author's effort at stake: editor and publisher investment (in the form of effort and expertise as well as money) make it possible to say that 'ebooks contain all that is required for a manuscript to become a book, ie. [sic] an edited text in the final version of record including the publisher's paratext'. Even though these are reader arguments in favour of e-book realness, the qualifiers – '*the same* amount of work', '*all* that is required' – demonstrate how fragile that status is. As discussed in Chapter 2, where 'books that do not merit print publication' are viewed with scepticism, and readers even sometimes ask 'if the publisher wasn't willing to invest in it [to the same extent as a print edition], why should I?',[52] mere suspicion that the 'amount of work' was not *the same*, or that *some* but not '*all* that is required' had been supplied, would be enough to place realness status in jeopardy.

Even with editor and publisher effort in the mix, the figure of the author looms larger still. When respondents explain that e-books are real 'because they are authored and written to be read', 'you are still reading the author's work', and 'the content that the writer came up with is still contained in the work, I don't think it matters whether it's printed on paper or an .epub file!', they are, in differently nuanced ways, asserting the right of any person to be rewarded for intellectual labour, confirming that 'any format which conveys the author's expression counts,' and refuting insinuations that what the author has created is less real when it is read on a device rather than paper. If it were, some authors would sow yet be left with nothing for anyone to reap. One respondent declared their self-interest: e-books are real 'because my book's coming out in e-book format ☺' – but the readers quoted earlier are very much on their side.

Print versus Digital: Different Tactics in the Pursuit of Control

Ownership matters, but it doesn't matter equally to all readers. When asked 'when you choose print, what are your reasons?' motivators linked to control are among the most important in my survey: keeping and collecting, but also borrowing and accessing (on one's own terms), as well as giving and passing on. There were differences between demographic groups, but patterns of book acquisition and access offered sharper contrasts: between those who borrow books and those who do not, between those who buy from various locations, between those who read different categories of books, and those who read on different platforms. There are particularly stark differences between those who read e-books and those who do not.

'Better for Borrowing or Buying Secondhand'

Fully half of respondents (53.0%) choose print because it is better for borrowing or buying secondhand, a proportion that increased significantly over the course of the survey (from 44.5% in 2014 to a peak of 60.4% in 2022). Older respondents and men[53] were less likely to agree. Intriguingly, there is no difference between e-book readers and print-only readers. But it's meaningful that the survey asked 'when you choose digital' and 'when you choose print', leaving open the possibility that each format will be best for different reasons at different times:[54] participants frequently explained that preference depends on context (e.g. 'if I am travelling, it's easier to have it on my kindle', or '[digital] easier for travel or in hospital').[55] While readers who value borrowing and buying secondhand were more likely to have obtained print books from every source in the survey, it was, unsurprisingly, exceptionally strongly correlated with recent history of borrowing and secondhand purchase.[56]

The pandemic affected patterns of book borrowing. In 2014–17, just under half of e-book-reading respondents (47.5%) had borrowed a print book from a library in the past twelve months, double the proportion (21.9%) who had borrowed an e-book from a library. At this point, the e-book borrowers were effectively a subset of print borrowers: using the library solely for digital was quite unusual, accounting for only 4.0% of e-book readers. This changed dramatically after lockdown and library closures. From 2020 to 2022, roughly the same number borrowed in print (44.3%) and digitally (41.2%) and fully 30.8% of those who borrowed from a library borrowed only e-books, not print.

Libraries, however, now have significant competition for e-book borrowing. Amazon launched Kindle Unlimited in the US in 2014 (with other markets following, sometimes years behind) and Prime Reading in 2017. From 2020, I began to ask about Amazon e-book loans separately from Amazon e-book purchases: two in ten of 2020–22 respondents (22.2%), obtained an e-book in the past twelve months as part of a Kindle Unlimited or Prime Reading membership. But the overlap between Amazon buyers and borrowers proved nearly complete. Only a quarter (27.3%) of Amazon e-book purchasers also borrow, but nearly all Amazon borrowers (90.8%) also purchase; a mere 2.0% of e-book readers in the survey fell into the rare category of those who borrow from Amazon but do not buy. While modest compared to Amazon purchases, and even library e-book loans, the Kindle Unlimited/Prime Reading figures dwarf those of other subscription services such as Scribd or 24symbols: fewer than one in twenty respondents (4.3%) had used them in the prior twelve months.

Focus group participants confirmed that borrowing digital books from libraries was often aggravating, leaving readers feeling controlled rather than in control, and, implicitly, of having a technologically simple process artificially complicated to serve the commercial needs of publishers and/or retailers, as when 'you used to be able to do some kind of jiggery-pokery [to load a public library e-book onto a Kindle in the UK] but they stopped it and you can't do it now'.[57] Some noted the ease of returning an e-book,[58] but checking that book out in the first place was often exasperating. As one participant put it, 'borrowing e-books is a real pain as well. I went through a phase of trying to do that, because I thought it was going to save me so much money. But it was really annoying to download them and get them on there'.[59] A quirk of Amazon lending made the hassle even more obnoxious: 'and when they disappear after the loaning period is gone, they leave behind a little notify [sic], "You used to have a book here but now you can't open it"'.[60] To lose a book, but be forced to keep a reminder, gave this reader the worst of both worlds: taunting ghost spines on a digital shelf, a memorial to inconvenience rather than reading pleasure.

Further, there are significant correlations between agreements with 'better for borrowing and buying secondhand' and almost every other motivator in the survey. The strongest correlations, with choosing print because it is easier to share and better for giving as a gift, speak to the importance to these readers of book exchange, but other sentiments, such as print books being more enjoyable to handle and use and identifying as a bibliophile, are more about preference than practicality: a grouping (which I will discuss again in later chapters) of bookish values.

Conferring Ownership: Gifts

The kinds of ownership these participants valued included control over not only a book's present but also its future: the ability to sell, to loan, to give as a gift, to bequeath. Ownership of a physical book includes the ability to determine the fate of one's own personal copy, and many respondents in my own study consider this affordance of print important. (And given Perzanowski and Hoofnagle's data about the significant minorities of customers who mistakenly believe that they already have rights to lend, gift, and bequeath e-books, this is likely an underestimate.) 'I'm a serial recommender', as one put it, and being a serial recommender (framed here as an identity, not just an activity) includes 'want[ing] to be able to give them a copy'.[61] Giving may be near-automatic, where 'most times' a reader will 'resell/swap or give [print novels] away after reading', or may be reserved for only the best of the best: '[If a novel is truly exceptional] I might buy a copy for someone [as a gift]'.[62] But either way, digital reading and print giving can coexist: '[despite having become] a consumer of mostly digital media...I enjoy receiving (and giving) print books as gifts, and treasure them when they arrive'.[63]

The importance of gift-giving to the book industry, and to book culture, is difficult to overstate. From a business perspective, the months leading up to Christmas account for an outsize proportion of annual sales and are vital for survival, as publishers and retailers market books not to readers but to customers who are buying for other readers (or would-be readers) in their lives.[64] The historian Stephen Nissenbaum goes so far as to credit (or condemn) book gifts as the foundation of modern Christmas traditions, calling booksellers and publishers the 'shock troops' on the 'cutting edge of a new commercial Christmas', with books (including 'Gift Book' anthologies tailored towards specific recipients, based on their demographics or interests) 'making up more than half of the earliest items advertised as Christmas gifts' in nineteenth-century America.[65] Though Amazon launched its first Kindle model in 2007, it was the 'Kindle Christmas' of 2010 when e-book sales expanded from a fraction of the book market to a major force: the gifts were not the books but the devices, and while print book sales peaked as was typical in the weeks leading up to Christmas, e-book sales peaked the week after, as Kindle recipients bought to stock their gifts.[66] Books are culturally important objects that can, at least if the book is sufficiently highbrow, confer cultural capital on both giver and recipient, and they are available for a strikingly lower price than many other forms of art.[67] But even the humblest literature has powers beyond its value in terms of capital, cultural or financial: as Natalie Zemon Davis demonstrated, the book as not just a 'commodity' but 'bearer of benefits and duties'.[68] Giving books fuses gift exchange with knowledge exchange, strengthening social bonds whether the present is in the form of priceless incunabula or 'vernacular literature' such as personal recipes.[69] Recognising 'the powerful tradition for understanding what a book was and what it embodied...a privileged object that resisted permanent appropriation'[70] acknowledges that it is something larger than one person, made to be shared and never fully relinquished even when given away. Book gifts were even centuries ago a perfect example of 'objects [that] carried with them something from their givers—Mauss called it a spirit animating the gift'[71] and retain a special ability to serve as 'a physical token of the emotional bond shared by the giver and recipient';[72] Nissenbaum puts 'the "commercialisation of sincerity"'[73] in a distancing extra set of quotes, but the publishing industry's success in promoting books as always-appropriate gifts, harnessing existing and authentic aspects of book exchange, is exactly that. Few if any other gift options offer such a combination of meaning, connection, high status, low cost, and, not at all trivially, ease of wrapping.[74] (This last affordance of print books was a key factor in the rise of Amazon: according to his biographer, Bezos selected books as his initial product in part because books were simple to package.)[75]

In my own survey, exactly half (50.0%) of respondents chose print because it is better for giving as a gift, with no significant difference between e-book readers and others. (Agreement was slightly stronger after the start of the pandemic, with 48.3% agreeing in 2014–17 and 52.2% agreeing in 2020–22.) This is less an indication that they prefer print for this purpose than an indication that they give books as gifts at all. Giving a specific e-book as a gift, as opposed to giving a generic gift voucher, remains awkward in many cases: on Amazon, for example, at time of press, gifts can only be redeemed in a customer's own country, and redemption links can't be resold.

Sharing Books via Exchange of Copies

Sharing books in the sense of loaning, giving, or bequeathing one's personal copy is a key consideration for ownership. It's not just 'ability to lend' but ability to 'share with children, family and friends',[76] with the loan, gift, or bequest of a book serving as a means of underscoring a book's importance to the giver. The exchange creates or strengthens a connection between giver and recipient, and can foster a special connection between book and recipient as well: 'I feel connected to books, and sometimes to the people who gave them to me'.[77] But it always also affirms the connection between book and giver.[78] This connection may or may not be public (and, if personally inscribed in a physical copy by the author, becomes part of the book's peritext).[79] If the gift is anonymous, the recipient might never know who bestowed that book. But the giver always knows, and respondents describe the gift of a book as deeply meaningful.

E-book loans between individuals are often technically impossible (one respondent lamented the retrenchment of schemes such as Lendle[80] and many criticised Amazon for impeding or blocking peer-to-peer loans) and are often described as, like e-book gifts, less meaningful or satisfying: the experience, like the book itself, is missing some pieces. As respondents noted, 'you lend out physical books. It's satisfying/enjoyable to share your reads in person with friends' and they specifically buy not only print copies but also, where possible, durable hardcover copies for some books 'so that [they] can then pass them on when [they're] done'.[81] Some noted the physical act of pressing a book into a friend's hands as a key element of the exchange, as with 'I like passing books on as well. I will be, like, [mimes handing a book to fellow participant with both hands, as if in a ceremony] "take this!"'[82] They described the experience as diminished by digital exchange – instead of 'I got this from my friend' the feeling was 'well this just got beamed to me, and it's from. . .somebody' – and joked about the inadequacy of making it 'more of a social thing' by ceremoniously handing over a USB stick.[83] But more often the experience is simply missed, when they identify a text they want to share but cannot, because they read it digitally in a format they cannot easily 'beam', pull down from a shelf and make the connection then and there: 'you're having conversations [about good books you want to loan], and you're like, oh, it's on my Kindle'.[84] To diminish or lose such an opportunity for connection can be seen as not just a personal issue, but a 'cultural' one that leaves society impoverished, as in this exchange in focus group 5:

P5: *'The crap thing is that you can't hand on a new book to friends.' ['yes' – sounds of agreement]*
P1: *'Yes, that's the biggest downside.'*
P5: *'I think this is an enormous sadness really.'*
P7: *'Yes, it's huge.'*
P5: *'It's a kind of cultural and social sadness because handing on a book is a pleasure.'*

Unsharability is precisely what makes e-books, to some respondents, not real books. If they 'used to like sharing books with family and friends',[85] and no longer do thanks to digital reading (one respondent's reason for not considering e-books to be real books), that exemplifies the 'kind of cultural and social sadness' expressed above. In some other context, 'feels like a much more private reading experience'[86] might be seen as a positive development (as with reading privacy, discussed in Chapter 5), but in terms of sharing it is a profound loss to that reader, a reason for considering e-books unreal, and a profound lack in the incomplete book. And the link between 'you can't. . .lend it to someone, discuss it with a friend' highlights how, for some, digital makes even book recommendations more difficult.[87]

Sharing Reading with Unsharable E-books

Word-of-mouth recommendations remain highly important, and unless the book is only available in one format, there is nothing to stop a reader acting on a recommendation by obtaining a book in whatever format they prefer. Acting on a recommendation by obtaining an e-book can be considerably faster. As one respondent put it: 'I have had people message me on Facebook, "I've just read this, it's great" and I'm messaging back, "I'm reading it now, yes", and I'll buy before I know I've done it'.[88]

One form of sharing that combines elements of connection with elements of display is the spontaneous public transport book conversation. In one personal story shared in a focus group, a print book, explicitly labelled 'the real thing', is critical to making 'that connection'.

> *'I was on a train reading a book, about three months ago, it was a brilliant book, I was just reaching the end and getting excited, and then this woman suddenly said to me, "It's great, isn't it?" I said, "Yes, it's just so wonderful. I can't believe I didn't read it 30 years ago" and then we had a discussion about*

*it. [comments from other participants: 'great!' 'that's wonderful!'] If I hadn't had been reading **the real thing** [in the form of a print book] I wouldn't have had that connection with her, and it was really nice and special.' (FG 5 respondent 4)*

Qualitative data highlight the degree to which the two sides of the book recommendation equation – serving as the giver and serving as the recipient – are not symmetrical; while both are important, they are driven by very different motivations and satisfy different needs. As discussed in Chapter 2, seeking out or acting on recommendations is most often noted in the context of trust, in finding good books and having the confidence to invest time and/or money in a given title. While this does clearly represent accepting something from the recommender, feelings of connection and strengthening of relationships are not emphasised the way they are when the information is imparted in the other direction. Richards draws a critical distinction between conscious recommendations, valuable because chosen and selectively passed on, and the 'data exhaust pipe of personal information devoid of context or real content' that is Facebook-style 'frictionless sharing'.[89] Offering recommendations is instead noted in the context of sharing or giving, incorporating elements of ownership, and also (as I will discuss in Chapter 5) identity and love.

While 'sharing books' has multiple meanings, taking different forms for print and digital books and incorporating elements of gift, loaning (and hence ownership), discussion, social connection, image, and display, it is not a particularly important motivator for choosing print or digital formats. Only 29.4% of all respondents in my own survey choose print because it is 'easier to share.' (There was no significant difference between print-only and e-book readers, a sharp contrast to values such as enjoyment of print and ease of reading in print.) Choosing print because it is easier to share was stable over the eight years of the survey. There was no significant variation due to age, but men were slightly less likely to agree.[90]

Sharing is correlated with every print value in the survey other than availability, most strongly (and unsurprisingly) with 'better for borrowing or buying secondhand' (78.0% vs 41.7% of others). Those who value sharing were, predictably, more likely to have obtained print books not only from secondhand bookshops and libraries but also independent bookshops, direct from publishers, and via gifts. (It's frivolous but tempting to speculate that friends and family might like to give them books as gifts because they will go on to share the books.)

Impersonal Library? Defining a Digital Collection

Participants in my study placed enormous importance on personal libraries. Almost two-thirds (64.3%) choose print because it is 'better for keeping as part of a personal library', making it the second-most important motivator in the survey (just behind finding a print book 'more enjoyable to handle and use', at 67.9%). While only 15.6% choose digital for the same reason, between the two preferences almost three-quarters of respondents (72.6%) choose format with their personal libraries in mind. While the overlap is very small (just 28.5% of the already small group of those who choose digital as better for keeping as part of a personal library also choose print for the same reason), it's not insignificant: this indication that sometimes cloud storage is better than a shelf, and sometimes a shelf is better than cloud storage, harmonises with Buchanan, McKay, and Levitt's findings on how university users (academics and students) pragmatically select digital or print access depending on when and where they intend to use books[91] and resonates strongly with responses from focus groups and interviews. These data also sharply contradict earlier theoretical conclusions that in an era of widespread digital reading, the concept of a personal library might not remain relevant. But participants diverged sharply in their description of their own personal libraries and what role, if any, digital could play. Some explicitly link 'personal library' or 'home library' to print, for example, 'I also lean towards digital for books I don't require in my home library, such as a guidebook for a specific trip'.[92] (The way that a set of e-books can have the function but lack the feeling of a personal library was highlighted in several groups.) Others, however, will readily apply the term 'library' when describing digital books, as with 'I love the feel of print books, and have thousands, but ebooks allow for an even larger library without having to curate them (moving) or find space'.[93] A number of survey respondents wrote in, as reasons for choosing digital, variations on 'to have a more portable library', 'carry my entire library wherever I go', 'more portable (whole library in my bag)', or 'I can carry a huge library in my handbag'.[94] This sense of a portable personal library can be powerful enough to, by itself, make the entire e-reading experience worthwhile: 'the ability to carry a huge library in a small space makes e-books wonderful'.[95]

E-book readers are less likely than print-only readers to choose print because it is better for keeping as part of a personal library (60.9% vs 73.9% of print-only readers). Agreement rose significantly over time,

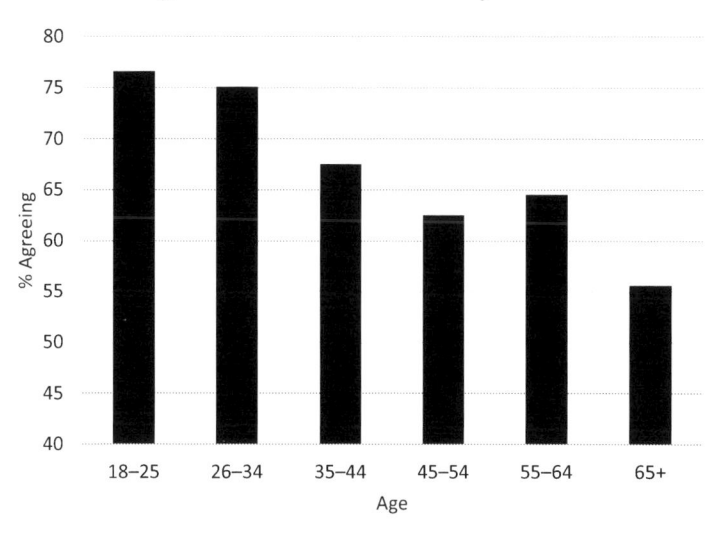

Figure 3.3   Reasons for choosing print: 'better for keeping as part of a personal library', by age.

peaking in 2022 at 73.9%. The one striking demographic factor is age: younger respondents are significantly more likely to agree (Figure 3.3).

This finding initially appears to defy conventional wisdom that youthful digital natives are more comfortable than their elders with cloud storage and digital longevity. But greater confidence with digital may be outweighed by greater attraction to the physical: Price and Pressman[96] demonstrate that bookishness is as seductive to the digitally savvy as the digitally reticent, and as with the revival of vinyl records as an alternative to unsatisfying or untrustworthy digital music,[97] the romance of analogue is most pronounced for younger generations.[98] And an obvious further link between younger readers and print collections is the importance of photographable print editions to Bookstagram, BookTok, and bookish content on other social media, presently more actively pursued by younger users.[99] If the readers most enthusiastic about physical personal libraries are young, this could point to a coming resurgence of interest in print. However, another potential explanation is that the appeal of a print library is most powerful when book collections are small, hypothetical, or stored in someone else's house (as two respondents put it, 'I keep them, even really bad books...I send them all home to my family' and '[at parents' house] I have, like, eight boxes. And I was like, please keep these and don't throw them').[100]

For print-lovers whose collections are of any size, and who have to shelve and dust the volumes themselves, the overwhelming problem is domestic storage space. Responses noting that choosing e-books 'saves physical space in a small flat' or 'I only have so much shelf space'[101] were extremely frequent across all surveys. Storage efficiency was noted not only in positive terms, as an affordance of digital (e.g. 'I love that I can keep reading new titles [digitally] without completely cluttering up my house') but also negative terms, as an example of regret and capitulation (e.g. 'like paper books better, but I have no more room to store them!').[102] When available storage space shrinks, or the book collection continues to expand, the only option is to relinquish books (an exercise many collectors find 'really hard',[103] profoundly unpleasant, or actually traumatic).[104] As one respondent put it, 'having had to cull hundreds of print books for reloca- tions, e-books mean space/weight is no longer an issue...also the trauma of letting books go is lessened because there is less personal attachment to an e-book'[105] – notable in that the 'personal attachment' is described *less*, not absent, when the book is an e-book. The hybrid book collection, part- print and part-digital, spares this individual pain, but at the cost of 'less personal attachment' to their book collection as a whole.

Those who choose print for this reason are print enthusiasts in another way: they are more likely to agree with almost every other print reason in the survey, particularly 'a print book is more enjoyable to handle and use', but also bibliophilia, a desire to support traditional bookshops, and print being better for giving as a gift. This confirms the intuitive connection where 'print personal library' sits alongside bibliophilia, book-gifting, support for traditional bookshops and other values (including, intri- guingly, print privacy, a link I discuss further in Chapter 5) in a constella- tion of bookish values.

Roles of E-books in Personal Libraries

Attitudes towards personal libraries are quite different when it comes to e- books. Only 15.6% of e-book readers agreed that when they choose digital, one of their reasons is 'better for keeping as part of a personal library'. Agreement did not vary according to age or other demographics and, perhaps surprisingly, was highly stable across the survey: pandemic conditions, including the common experience of sheltering away from physical book collections,[106] did not move the needle. Links to the devices readers use to access their digital personal libraries revealed intriguing patterns. Respondents who had read on tablet or smartphone were more likely to choose e-books for this reason – but those who had read on an e-ink reader, laptop, or desktop computer were not. As noted earlier, Amazon advertises its e-books and e-readers with a message of a personal library at one's fingertips, using the term for both one's cloud-stored cluster of purchases and one's device-based history of files, including expired loans (a practice singled out as 'annoying').[107] And as noted, a number of participants have adopted this terminology, describing their e-reading devices as a 'huge library in my handbag', a 'whole library in my bag' and so on.[108] For Kindles to sit alongside laptop and desktop computers, with their well-founded associations with work- and education-based reading (and, for many readers in this study, with e-books as a last resort for books they can't access in print), might by itself suggest that Amazon's messaging is not successful. However, examining correlations with sources of the kinds of e-books commonly read on Kindles offers a different explanation. Choosing e-books because they are better for keeping as part of a personal library is linked to obtaining them from Amazon, both as purchases and as loans via Kindle Unlimited or Prime Reading,[109] as well as direct from publishers. What is not linked, even very weakly, is obtaining e-books from the free-to-user sources of a library or Project Gutenberg. Acceptance of e-book personal libraries as meaningful libraries appears less associated with the device itself than with specific kinds of personal investment: in short, who paid for the book. Sources where the books are paid for by individuals stand apart from sources where books are paid for by institutions, taxpayers, or donors and volunteers. If the link were purely a matter of temporary versus permanent custody of a book – of feeling differently about an e-book that will be out of one's hands in a matter of days or weeks – we would expect to see Project Gutenberg grouped with Amazon purchase and libraries grouped with Kindle Unlimited and Prime Reading. The fact that they are not suggests that a personal financial stake – in a specific title (or in the case of Amazon, in the purchase of a conditional use licence) or monthly membership – changes readers' feelings towards the e-books.

This possible connection between financial transaction and feeling makes the link between obtaining e-books directly from the publisher and a greater likelihood of valuing digital libraries is an especially interesting one. These e-books were not necessarily purchases. A number of respondents wrote in options such as 'Netgalley or publisher', 'publisher provided pre publication [sic] pages', 'review copies from publisher/author' and 'received for review':[110] exchanges more reminiscent of gift, with at least some of the attendant connection between giver and recipient that commemorates a relationship between reader and publisher. It may be that the hand of the publisher changes the way the e-book file is perceived, and how it feels to have it on one's device: that the sense of a direct relationship or personal touch may transform the previously impersonal, generic file into something unique. It is also possible that the files themselves are, unlike e-book files, obtained via other channels: the respondents who read galleys and other pre-release materials are confronted on a page-by-page basis with the fact that theirs is not an ordinary commercial product but something special, reserved for those with connections to and relationships with book creators. This could make them, in a sense, digital collectables, for which enduring digital status is authentic and desirable, and for which digital could be more easily experienced as satisfyingly real.

In terms of relationships to other reasons for choosing digital, 'digital personal library' is positively correlated with most other reasons in the survey, though these correlations are modest compared to those between 'print personal library' and other print reasons.[111] While convenience motivators such as value, selection, and digital being easier to read are prominent, the strongest correlations are with 'I would describe myself as a technophile' and 'a reading device is more enjoyable to handle and use'. Technophilia and digital enjoyability are rare motivators, chosen by only a very small proportion of respondents overall. But they share a clear orientation towards digital reading as genuinely superior: not a thing to be done when print is inconvenient or expensive, but something to choose as the preferred option whenever possible. This group may be small, but it is distinctive and important, suggesting that beside bookish values lies a (much smaller) parallel constellation of e-bookish values, and perhaps corresponding e-bookish behaviours and identities (though unlike bookish values, the constellation is not effectively separate from convenience and cost considerations).

E-books do offer kinds of ownership not possible with physical copies, such as access from a distance or (in some cases) use on multiple personal devices. But these extra affordances were not discussed by focus group participants as an acceptable trade-off. Many described not a sense that e-books are owned differently, but that e-books are not properly owned at all. Participants particularly fear losing digital books: not misplacing them, but watching helplessly as tech giants such as Apple, Google, or Amazon purge books – out of neglect or, after a 'tantrum', with malice.

> *'I always worry that Amazon will go out of business and my eBook purchases from them will dissolve in the digital wind.'* (Survey 2015).

'If something goes wrong with your e-book collection, it's gone forever. I know you've got iCloud and things, so you can store it somewhere but it's just the sense that you might lose it all, for me. So the special books that I'd like to keep referring to, I'd like on my bookshelf as a hard copy.' (FG 3 participant 4)

*'I have a minor concern about [digital books] being under the **control** [emphasis mine] of someone else (amazon, google) who could at any point change their rules of access. But then, I remind myself that I could lose all my physical books in a fire/flood/etc and they're pretty replaceable'* (Survey 2016)

'I don't like the idea that ebooks are only licensed, not owned, and AMZN can take them away in a tantrum if it wants.' (Survey 2020)

'Control' is the key word: the promise of future access appears to mean little when the access is (as terms and conditions invariably emphasise) entirely at the discretion of a distant megacorporation. Thompson observes that trust in the sense of existing commercial relationships was crucial to the tech giants' early footholds in the e-book market: for the many consumers who had already created accounts with Amazon or Apple, storing credit card details and becoming comfortable with delivery systems, buying e-books on top of other goods was simple and low-risk.[112] But the very ubiquity that gives Apple or Amazon or Google an aura of permanence (they're less likely to go out of business than, say, Oyster) also gives a stench of dominance; a sense that the seller dictates the terms to helpless customers.

Shaping a personal library requires multiple kinds of control: the power not only to securely and meaningfully hold but also to bar or remove.[113] 'Keeping as part of a personal library' is far from synonymous with 'keeping', just as 'building a personal library' is far from 'accumulating the greatest possible number of books'. The possibilities of e-books for sampling, trying out, and effortlessly discarding open up new possibilities for finding the ideal level of 'keeping': to read without owning, to access without owning, to license without owning, and ultimately to use many books but own only a special few.

Gatekeeping for One's Collection by Means of 'Digital Audition'

'Digital audition' allows readers to use an e-book to sample a title and, if it proves itself worthy of inclusion in the permanent collection, 'upgrade' to print.[114] Although digital reading makes audition, in many cases, simple and near-effortless (as with 'public domain books I read online first to see if I want a copy'), auditioning books is nothing new: many readers describe sampling books via library or personal loans and upgrading not from digital to print but from borrowed (or shabby, or cheaply produced) print to other print, for example, 'if I borrowed [a novel] from the library and I really liked it I would go out and buy one', 'in the past, if I've really enjoyed a book that I've got from the library I'll buy one', or 'there are books that I've got out of the library and then gone and bought afterwards' (a practice Noorda and Berens found extremely prevalent in the US, where 31% of their 2020 survey respondents had purchased a print book after first discovering it in print form in a library).[115] Reading a print copy borrowed from the library understandably does not offer the same feeling of ownership as reading a personal print copy.[116] But unlike .EPUB files, which might seem to belong to no one, these auditioned print books often do have owners, and readers can feel obligation towards the book owners as well as the books themselves. As one focus group participant put it, a print library copy imposed a special burden of responsibility: 'No [I don't feel a sense of ownership for a physical library book]. If anything it feels like I'm looking after someone's pet and then I'm going to get in trouble if I do something with it [entire group laughs]'.[117] The borrowed book is not just someone else's valuable possession, but something far more unique and treasured, demanding special care but conferring no special value in return for that care.

The emotional dimension of a personal library could suggest that how readers use and conceptualise them is somehow beyond conscious control: that one 'feels it' or one does not. However, respondents in this study sometimes describe conscious reconceptualisation: a decision to think of one's collection differently. This is most prominent when a change of circumstances puts a large physical book collection out of reach. On a daily commute, the collection might be out of reach for the length of a train journey, but sometimes the separation is prolonged or permanent, particularly after moving house or moving to a new country. Some tell, in the space of a few lines, a complete story: one of finding a way, in the face of adverse conditions, to remain a book collector and someone for whom a growing, current personal library is important and meaningful, even when one's books are taken away.

> 'Advantage to digital: easier to transport/move personal library. I'm in a mobile profession, and I have to limit the physical books to take with me to professional references (almost universally unavailable in digital) only – no room for (physical) 'personal' books.' (Survey 2015)

> 'I switched from mostly print to mostly digital some years ago for my personal library because I move frequently and a large collection of print books is

> *physically cumbersome: it takes up a lot of space, is tedious to pack and unpack, is backbreakingly heavy to cart about, and is tiresome to dust. So now I limit the number of print books I keep to less than a hundred.'* (Survey 2017)

> *'I dramatically increased e-book purchases over printed books when I made a transatlantic move. I had to get rid of much of my print library as transporting it was prohibitively expensive, and I wanted to retain access to books I purchase from now on if I move again.'* (Survey 2017)

Un-owning Books: Choosing (and Sometimes Failing) to Let Go

Readers do discard some books: painfully for owned print copies, less so for loans and digital files. In promoting any book to the permanent collection, but especially the personal print library, respondents cite something more than admiration: they describe these 'favourite' books as those they 'really like' or 'love'.

> *'I have been known to buy a book after reading it on my e reader and **loving** it.'* (Survey 2014)

> *'My physical library has started to get too large so I've mainly switched to e-books when I read something new. If I **really like it**, I buy a physical copy.'* (Survey 2016)

> *'I frequently have digital and print copies of the same book…this is especially the case with **favorite books**.'* (Survey 2016)

> *'Occasionally I have bought books in both print and e-book versions because…I read the ebook and **really liked** it'* (Survey 6/2021)

> *'for [digital] books I **really like** I'll probably buy a physical copy as well* (FG 1 participant 2)

> *'I'm sort of a sole e-book reader these days; that's all I read. But if I do come across a book that I absolutely have **read and love**, then I'll go out and buy the hardback…I read [a particular biography] on e-book and I thought, "**I must have** a big, thumping 600 page hardback on my shelf".'* (FG 3 participant 2)

Respect alone is not enough to qualify a book for retention. In a typical conversation from focus group 6, participants unanimously agreed that there were numerous examples of books they thought well of – that they considered *worthy* of keeping – but did not care enough about to include them in their collections. The need to include a book in a personal library can come from a sense of importance and personal meaning inseparable from emotion: the signal that a book must be included is described as not only an intellectual one but also as something that comes from the heart. In one particularly eloquent exchange from focus group 5, participants drew fine distinctions between the kinds of owning possible for a deeply treasured book: the meaning conferred by gifting; the gulf between 'a copy' and the same novel 'in electronic form'. But just as evident are the burdens of print ownership. After the trauma of books lost to a fire, there is the ceremony of replacing books one might 'really feel' are 'needed...in the house'... plus the requirement to supplement that 'needed' print with an e-book edition, without which 'you won't read it!'

> P5: *I had a copy of* [A Prayer for Owen Meany] *I'd had for a long time, and then [a friend] was reading* A Prayer for Owen Meany *on holiday, and I went "aaah! I love that!" He finished the book whilst we were on holiday and he gave me his with as little inscription on it. [sounds of approval from group]. So I have two copies, one I'd read four times anyway and the other was this lovely thing I have. I can't find either of them. I don't know if they were* **lost in the fire** *we had last October...I've bought another copy. I didn't buy it in electronic form, which I might've done and it would've been more logical to, because* **I really feel I needed to have a copy in the house,** *but actually, because it's so big and thick...*
> P6: *You won't read it!*
> P5: *I won't read it.*
> P8: *So, you* **need to get it in electronic form as well so that you can read it** *in bed at night!*
> P2: *Absolutely!*

This liftable, usable second version is one instance of the 'digital reading copy' many participants describe using or, pining after bundling,[118] wishing they could use. While there are many reasons to employ a digital reading copy, such as sparing tired wrists ('carpal tunnel makes it hard to hold books') and reading conveniently backlit versions at night ('Read at night without disturbing my husband'),[119] this usage is also a means of reading the text without sullying the pristine physical object. The more loved the print book, the more important digital can be for preventing wear and tear: 'I love print books, but I love to keep them in good condition, so I will often get the e-book as well', a second purchase that means one can 'read the ebook when travelling and the print copy at home' and also 'read it without bending the spine'.[120] These 'copies [they] don't particularly want to damage'[121] may be signed copies or first editions, and may simultaneously be the kind of long or physically bulky books for which they want e-book affordances such as light weight and searchability: reasons for keeping a digital reading copy can be layered. This is especially relevant for comic book readers, where the community values both deep, detail-oriented repeat readings[122] and the preservation of poly-bagged mint-condition archives for investment purposes. For collectors, digital offers a means of obtaining new titles with no trade-offs regarding the existing collection and of reading without risking the agony of a physical collection cull. And for book-lovers, adding a new zone to the edges of a book collection, a buffer of demi-owned digital files, offers the opportunity to effectively hang a velvet rope around the core collection, creating a VIP area where books can be treated with even greater solicitude. Digital can allow one to have it both ways. But for a reading copy to be meaningful, for it to represent time spent with the original rather than with some impostor, it must be a digital proxy,[123] not a real or *ersatz book* in itself.

Readers feel deep responsibility to their physical book collections[124] but little or none to their virtual, indestructible digital book collections. Fear of personal failure in losing or neglecting a physical collection (including 'someone's pet' in the form of a print library book) is replaced by fear of institutional failure in the sense of a tech giant bungling its cloud storage; loss in either case, but in the latter instance the individual is spared the blame. The smaller and safer the physical collection, the less one needs it for daily use, the more special and separate it can become, and potentially the more sidelined and irrelevant. 'Personal library' and 'book collection' remain distinct. Though each means different things to different people (as exemplified by my groups, where many used the terms interchangeably), the latter does not as directly imply personal use. An eighteenth-century bibliophile's priceless rare volumes, or a contemporary comic book investor's bagged and sealed issues, can confidently be called collections whether or not they are ever read. The use of digital as a means to spare (some) physical books the strains and risks of being read, replacing in many cases earlier use of cheaper, more disposable paper reading copies, could lead to ever-higher standards for preservation, an ever-higher standard for what it means to cherish a deserving book. In the given example, the book-lover who bought her new print copy of *A Prayer for Owen Meany* in a cumbersome edition unsuitable for reading[125] will then need an electronic version if she means to actually access the text. This in turn could lead to a situation where the most ardent print-lover could no longer be as regular a print-user, and for the most beloved personal library to be less a used, lived-in, occupied space than a safe-deposit box – not Price's 'vulgar owning without reading', but reading without touching – or a shrine.

Conclusion

Readers describe meaningful book ownership as complex, but ultimately inseparable from a sense of control. Dominion over one's own books is essential. Suffering anyone else to control one's books (or worse, to be personally controlled through one's books, like a buyer manipulated by 'AMZN') is intolerable. The threat of books being lost, deleted, or taken back is felt deeply and taken seriously: a fear of such actions is enough to drive many readers away from digital, as a blanket policy or as the format for a given book.

The idea, widely shared and deeply felt, that readers have a natural right to own, keep, and give away e-books in the same way they do print books indicates a sense on a profound level that e-books are books, enjoying realness and bookness. However, viewing e-book legitimacy through the lens of ownership reveals the ways that readers not only hold seemingly contradictory senses of e-book realness but also toggle pragmatically between them as the situation demands. A sense of meaningful ownership can be seized and reappropriated, via principled resistance, digital audition, or a conscious decision to accept a digital book collection as a personal library. An idea of e-books as real is of clear benefit to the expat book collector who has transitioned to a digital collection. It is also of value to the proud pirate, the one for whom defiance of Amazon is a matter of self-respect. The sheepish pirate, however, would benefit from seeing e-books as *ersatz books*, as would the disposal-averse book collector who deletes an unwanted e-book: both are treating 'files' in ways they would not wish to treat a 'proper book'. The *Owen Meany* owner needs a digital reading copy to spare both her print copy and her overtaxed wrists; a digital proxy can give her the sense that she is connecting with her personal copy of her treasured novel. This recasts e-books as an integral part of building a personal library: sometimes as components, but sometimes just as tools. This fascinating and nuanced usage, combining conceptions of e-books as real books, *ersatz books*, and digital proxies, further demonstrates how readers are able to move flexibly between visions of what an e-book is – a flexibility we'll continue to explore in the next chapter, on enjoyment and pleasure.

CHAPTER 4

Materiality, Convenience, and Customisation
E-books and the Act of Reading

'Reading on a Kindle I forget I'm reading on a Kindle. It feels like I'm reading. Apart from the fact that it's not as heavy, it feels like I'm reading a real book.'

(FG 1 participant 1)

'Yes, [an e-book is real and] the same book, but not as pleasurable for all the senses.'

(Survey 2022)

The e-book has been chosen. It has been obtained. A screen flickers to life – pixels on a smartphone app, or e-ink flowing into a new configuration of grey and lighter grey – and actual reading begins. The reading may be real, but is the book?

This chapter explores the actual reading event. Contrasting devices and platforms, it considers what kinds of pleasure readers seek from book reading and rereading (in different settings, and at different times), and the ways in which an e-book does or does not deliver such satisfactions. Examining aspects such as tactile dimensions of embodied reading, the role of the material object, convenience and access, optimisation and customisation, and narrative immersion, it contextualises original findings with recent empirical research on screen reading and offers insights into how, where, and when intimacy, sense of achievement, and the feeling of being 'lost in a book' can be found in e-reading.

The Pleasures of Paper

To the degree that scholarship can reach consensus on any point in the interdisciplinary field of reading studies, there is agreement that print remains the medium of choice for most readers. As Baron puts it, 'the majority—sometimes the vast majority—say they prefer reading in print'.[1] This preference is not the result of any overwhelming advantage in terms of comprehension. Pre-1990 studies using first-generation screens did find large differences, but experiments using more modern screens generally do not.[2] In 2015, summarising late twentieth- and early twenty-first-century screen-reading research, Baron found that despite 'nearly all recent investigations are reporting essentially no differences' in terms of comprehension and speed,[3] a broad conclusion more validated than challenged by later studies, including those employing newer technologies for data collection, such as eye tracking and electrodermal activity, that are undergoing constant and rapid advancement. Scrutiny is, rightly, constant. Fervour of debate on the comprehension question – meaningful to any reader, but an immediate and critical issue for teachers and governments making decisions about classroom technologies that affect an entire generation's education – is such that even hints of potential new sources of data can trigger intense media interest.[4] Meta-analyses of reading studies by Delgado, Vargas, Ackerman, and Salmerón (2018) and Clinton (2019) found some small advantages for paper over screen reading when it came to reference and educational texts, but not for narrative texts – the category that accounts for the majority of commercial e-books. Though advantages specific to particular groups (i.e. that older readers may read fractionally more quickly on tablet, or that readers with 'poor vision' may benefit from the high contrast of a backlit screen) are very real, the long-held dictum that most people, at most times, prefer print[5] still stands. (Subtle differences can still be very important, as I will discuss later in the chapter.) This recognises the existence, and importance, of the minority who prefer digital. The question is what widespread and enduring enjoyment of the material print object means for readers' experiences of the bookness and realness of digital book objects.

Enjoyment of the Material Print Object

In my own study, asking survey respondents 'when you choose print, what are your reasons?' elicited a wide range of responses, but among them many odes to the codex. As noted in Chapter 1, though materiality is not synonymous with realness, digital materiality offers powerful support for arguments regarding the realness of a digital object. Responses were varied and often poetic in their expression of enthusiasm for various aspects of the material object and the multisensory experience of interacting with it. (Not every respondent used the free-text boxes to deploy emotive language, but many did.) Common references to touch and the 'tactile thing', and abundant attention to book smell, emphasised what Mangen describes as 'embodied' experience inseparable from the 'physicality of reading' (and invite study via the holistic view that Hillesund, Schilhab, and Mangen embrace as an 'embodied, enacted, and extended approach to the research on digital reading').[6] Many responses foregrounded the specific pleasure of lifting and holding a print book, as with 'I feel more satisfied when holding a print book', 'the feeling and weight of paper in my hands feels good', and 'nothing for me will replace holding and reading a traditional book!', a tether to one conception of realness summed up by 'a real book is nicer to hold'.[7] Respondents frequently used the words 'hands' and 'hand', but with a notable difference depending on medium. They conspicuously link the plural to print reading, as with 'I much prefer to hold a real book in my hands' and 'Sometimes I just want the feeling of a book in my hands',[8] or measuring progress through a book by the weight in the left hand versus the right. They link the singular to digital reading, as with holding an e-reader in one hand on the beach, while distracted by children, or standing on a crowded Underground train.[9]

One aspect of pleasure frequently cited in relation to print, but not in relation to digital in this study, is aesthetic pleasure derived from the material object. Respondents found value in beauty ('collector's editions of print books have more aesthetic value than pixels') and even require-ment for beauty, as in 'certain books are aesthetically necessary to me on paper—children's picture books, art books, etc.'[10] and noted that this appreciation was not just recognised intellectually, but felt. As one put it, 'If the book has an aesthetic reason to be in print – such as format or pictures – I will always go with print. It's more satisfying'.[11] While some respondents noted that certain texts can be more beautiful and more artistically successful on screen, such as born-digital works like Emily Carroll's graphic novel story *Into the Woods*, no one spoke of an e-reading device in terms approaching 'printed books are a thing of beauty' or '[hardcover books] are so pretty!'.[12] Some noted particular pleasure in craftsmanship – 'Print feels more indulgent, a luxury, particularly when reading well-produced hard backs – like sitting in a well crafted chair or wearing well tailored clothes – you feel the difference';[13] the enjoyment was not only from the object itself but also from appreciation of the effort and skill that its creation required, recalling how for some respondents, as discussed in Chapter 3, the effort of authors and editors is what makes e-books real. (While a parallel argument could be made for appreciation of the design of an electronic device, such as an iPhone, no one in this study made it – despite the intense feelings many of us have for our phones.)[14] Some responses framed digital as an enemy of aesthetics, an assault on print, as with 'digital alternatives ruin and take away the art of reading and the beauty of books'.[15] But questions of aesthetics apply to print versus other print as well as to print versus digital, and other respondents noted that a print book can fail as an object: 'small font size/tight layout/smudgy print on poor quality paper puts me off buying some print books' or 'I test out books in store and if the analogue is horrible, I buy an ebook'.[16]

While aspects of print books were sometimes noted as inconvenient, this did not necessarily detract from their desirability. Physical weight was simultaneously a cherished feature of print books and a primary reason to read digital instead. Few participants expressed any negative impressions of the sensory experience of reading print. Even if they considered elements such as beautiful endpapers[17] as items they were willing to forgo as a trade-off with other affordances, participants were overwhelmingly likely to speak of such aspects in positive or at least neutral terms. When 'materiality scepticism' was aired in the focus groups, it often became one of the rare flashpoints of heated disagreement: disliking the smell of a new book, or the feeling of holding a hardcover edition, invited rebuke and scolding. Participants in my study are readers (as noted, nearly all survey respondents and all focus group and interview participants are regular readers of print books) and as readers are heirs to the traditions of print culture, including relationships to print as a material object. While they are not required to share the sentiments of ardent print admirers, they are inevitably in contact with discourse on the subject. (The formation and expression of bookish identity, of which acknowledgement and display of one's appreciation for the material object is a part, is a thread I'll continue to explore in Chapter 5.) One participant spoke for many in explicitly linking this form of pleasure to realness, as something print books have and e-books do not, *can* not: 'when reading for pleasure, I need a real book in my hands, not just printed words on a screen'.[18]

Preference in Practice: Influence of Enjoyment of Print on Reading Choices

Taken on their own, these paeans to print could be dismissed as lip service. But survey results indicate that this appreciation for the physical object of the book is not a distant abstraction but a primary consideration in their reading choices: it is the single most important factor captured in the survey. More than two-thirds (67.9%) choose print because a print book is 'more enjoyable to handle and use'. But younger respondents were even more likely to agree: 81.3% of those aged 18–25 versus 63.9% of those aged 65 or older (Figure 4.1).

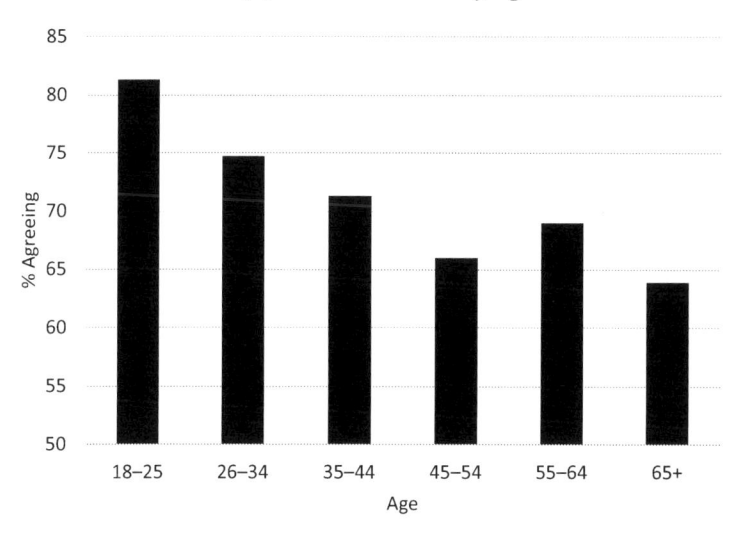

Figure 4.1   Reasons for choosing print: 'a print book is more enjoyable to handle and use', by age.

A link between youth and enjoyment of print books is entirely plausible, particularly in light of younger respondents' greater interest in print as a component of personal libraries (see Chapter 3), the continued dominance of print for children's books,[19] and signs of increased interest within mainstream publishing on the material object of a print book. James Daunt, CEO of Waterstones, speculated that the e-book option has forced publishers to stop 'cutting back on production values' and produce instead 'proper books with decent paper and decent design'.[20] Print-only readers (81.3%) were more likely to agree than those who read e-books (63.3%). But more than six out of ten e-book readers is still a large majority: most e-book readers still enjoy print, and choose print (when they do choose it) for the pleasure. This underscores the fact that avoidance does not necessarily mean dislike, or even indifference, as even the most devoted digital readers can still value the pleasures of print. It also underscores the fact that enjoyment of the material object of a print book is not by itself enough to make someone a print-only – or even a print-ever – reader.

Enjoyment and Book Buying

Enjoyment of print is not an isolated taste. Choosing print because a print book is more enjoyable to handle and use is strongly and positively correlated with obtaining print books from every source in the survey, including Amazon, libraries, and gifts. Of those who choose print for this reason and also read e-books, they were slightly more likely to have obtained them from Project Gutenberg. Links to Amazon, the main source of e-books, are more complex. Between 2014 and 2017, those who chose print for enjoyment were significantly more likely to obtain their e-books from Amazon (76.7% vs 56.3% of others, purchase and loan combined). But in 2020–22, splitting out purchases and loans reveals that those who enjoy print are completely ordinary in their Amazon purchases, but markedly less likely to borrow from Amazon (17.4% vs 30.0% of others). (This is not a blanket aversion to e-book subscription services: they were typical in their use of non-Amazon services such as Scribd.) Differences in device use were minimal: those who chose print for enjoyment of the physical object were slightly more likely to have read e-books on laptop computers (41.6% vs 30.6%), but otherwise typical in this regard.

Much more strikingly linked than reading behaviour are certain reading preferences and values (though not always the preferences and values one would expect). Unsurprisingly, choosing print books for enjoyment of the material object correlates with choosing print books because they are easier to read (58.4% vs 18.5% of others),[21] but it is not the most dramatic correlation: these are a belief that print is better for keeping as part of a personal library (77.5% vs 36.5%)[22] and a desire to support traditional bookshops (56.9% vs 16.5%).[23] Other significant correlations are with choosing print because of identification as a bibliophile (44.8% vs 13.1%), because print books are better for giving as gifts (59.8% vs 29.3%), and because print is better for borrowing or buying secondhand (62.0% vs 32.0%) and, to a lesser degree, because print is better for privacy (14.0% vs 3.1%), print being easier to share (34.4% vs 18.7%), and print having better selection (16.5% vs 6.5%). (The unsurprising relationship between enjoyment of print and bibliophilia is discussed in greater detail in Chapter 5.)

This further emphasises a cluster of linked priorities. Placing a different variable in the centre offers a glimpse of a subtly different web of relationships, and examining print as enjoyable highlights particular closeness to what could be described as 'book experiences', but not all book experiences (e.g. gift-giving to a greater degree than book sharing).

'Materiality' of E-books: The Physical Object Trapped in Scare Quotes

Compared to the codex, the e-reader does not demonstrate the same capacity for inspiration. To participants in my study, the material object of an e-reader was not just an inferior object: in many exchanges, it barely registered its existence as an object. Study participants were not in any way confused about the fact that users only encounter e-books via some physical interface. They are entirely aware that while 'texts displayed on screens' can be described as 'intangible and virtual' and 'are physically separable from their display medium',[24] this means that e-books can be moved between physical display media and stored apart from them, not that e-books could ever be read intangibly; it is self-evident, too obvious for them to mention. But much of the vocabulary of digital reading – virtual, cloud, file, download, and so on – foregrounds the untouchable storage or transfer stage rather than the reading stage; and in my focus groups and interviews e-books are often referred to in terms of their untouchable states as 'just all, like. . .data', 'a big Word file', or a 'Word document', or with characteristics like 'tangibility' linked with a definition of 'book' that excludes digital, as with 'on a screen . . . it feels less tangible, like it's not really there' and 'there is something wonderful about the tangibility of a book. I just don't see myself switching to digital'.[25] While print enjoyed its own rich vocabulary of sensory pleasures, the physical interface with digital was rarely praised, and compared to that of print rarely even mentioned. Very few comments touched in any way on the physical characteristics of the e-readers, and those that did, such as 'I also like my kindle as a tactile object – it produces a certain kind of intimacy'[26] often expanded on how that 'tactile object' is valued for what it does (in this case, foster closeness) rather than what it is. An exception, of course, is 'screen'. This term carries enormous weight in discussions of e-reading, in part because it is almost the only term that has meaning across all devices (in contrast to words such as 'e-ink' or 'app' or 'keyboard' or 'touchscreen' that apply to some but not all common devices.) While there is no reason why an e-reading interface need be touched (e.g. the technology to project text onto a surface viewed but not held, and for actions such as turning pages, 'flipping' back to a previous passage, annotation, or starting or pausing an audiobook to be handled by voice commands is long since in the mainstream), the e-book reading interfaces common to the market and described by study participants are touched, and largely (excepting laptop and desktop computers) handheld.[27] Exchanges in my focus groups and interviews demonstrate how discussion of e-reading and pleasure can flow around issues of e-book materiality, as participants respond to questions about the e-reading object by describing instead what they like, or do not like, about the book-object it is not. E-books are sometimes 'light' but more often 'lighter'; sometimes 'easy' but more often 'easier'.[28] (To describe new reading technologies in relation to an ancient reading technology is logical and unsurprising, and the questions, asking about print and digital separately but side by side, were always likely to elicit direct comparisons, but the asymmetry is still striking. For more on narratives of revolution versus narratives of conservatism and continuity in technology adoption, please see Chapter 5.) Discussion of the materiality in relation to e-books is primitive, constrained by a self-evidently false yet highly persistent conception of e-books and other digital texts as bodiless; to return to Gitelman, signalling 'a certain ambivalence about the bodies that electronic texts have'.[29] But in the years since, discourse on e-book materiality remains thin and barren compared to the vivid complexity and sensory richness of discourse on print book materiality. (The study of textual materiality enjoys its own academic discipline, and as a theme in fiction and belles-lettres it is a genre in itself.) Readers are perfectly aware that e-books, like all electronic texts, have physical form, whether the form is as readable as projection of letter forms on a backlit screen or as unreadable as binary data inscribed on a hard drive.[30] Yet electronic texts remain 'elusive as physical objects' and hence 'digital texts can seem to have no body' even if on an intellectual level the reader knows that this can't be true.[31] For participants in my study, personal accounts abound with descriptions of the tactile dimension of book appreciation, Dibdin's 'pleasures of sensual gratifications' in the look, feel, smell, and sound of pages (though even the most enthusiastic admirers of print in my study drew the line at taste, rolling their eyes at a record collector's belief that vinyl has a 'flavour' and dismissing concerns about used books and germs with 'it's not like you're licking it').[32] At the same time, e-books frequently 'seem to have no body', even among those who enjoy digital reading and reading devices. Placed alongside the print book, the sometimes-disembodied e-book is experienced as less present, less complete because it is not entirely there.

Enjoyment of E-reading Devices

Enjoyment of e-reading devices is a minority taste. Asked about their reasons for choosing digital, 'an e-reading device is more enjoyable to handle and use' was cited by only 12.1% of e-book readers. It presents a near-mirror of the enjoyment of print profile, with enthusiasm rising rather than dropping with age (Figure 4.2). Respondents aged 65 and older were five times as likely as those aged 18–25 to choose digital for this reason.

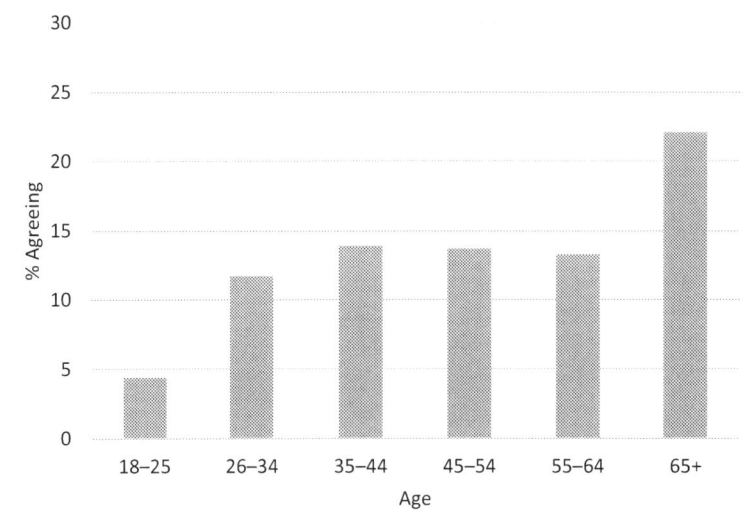

Figure 4.2   Reasons for choosing digital: 'a reading device is more enjoyable to handle and use', by age.

Only continued monitoring will determine whether this is an enduring effect, and if so whether it is a matter of age or instead linked to generation. For now, the youngest respondents' lesser agreement is likely to reflect the importance they place on the tactile dimension of print books, harmonising with their greater enthusiasm for print personal libraries (and correspondingly lesser interest in digital personal libraries). For the oldest respondents, reasons may be more practical. Survey and focus group respondents specifically linked the very commonly cited affordance of adjustable font size to age ('I think digital books are very good for people with poor eyesight such as mature people'), as well as lighter weight and one-handed page turns; 'Kindle works best when mobility is an issue because [of] arthritis'.[33] (As I'll discuss in greater detail later, in relation to convenience as a form of pleasure, older respondents were considerably more likely to choose digital because it is 'easier to read'.)

Examining the values of the small minority that finds e-readers more enjoyable, one correlation stands out dramatically: 66.5% also find digital easier to read, compared with only 14.7% of others.[34] If enjoyment of e-reading devices were strictly a matter of convenience, one might expect to see equally strong correlations with other convenience factors. However, ease and speed of obtaining e-books, like value and availability, have weak or no connections to enjoyment of e-reading devices. (The e-bookish values of finding digital better for keeping as a personal library and finding digital better for selection, in contrast, are more strongly correlated, though still in the shadow of ease of reading.) Other than being slightly more likely to have read an e-novel in the past twelve months, those who found e-readers more enjoyable to handle and use were not distinctive in their e-book genre choices or sources of e-books. Sources of print books were, in fact, more revealing than sources of e-books. Those who enjoy e-reading devices are less likely to have obtained print books from the typically in-person options of chain bookshops, independent bookshops, and secondhand bookshops. This indication that those who enjoy e-reading devices are less frequent consumers of print books, but generally ordinary consumers of digital books, contrasts with print enthusiasts (who are more active consumers of print but ordinary consumers of digital) is potentially quite telling: these enthusiasts may be not reading digital instead of print but reading less overall.

Perhaps surprisingly, there are no meaningful relationships to device choice. This counterintuitive finding challenges current thinking: as the interfaces and affordances of various e-reading devices are so different, it was unexpected to find that the minority of readers who hold this view are relatively normally distributed. This finding suggested that what readers are responding to, what actually gives pleasure as they 'handle and use', was not necessarily something physically bound up in the reading device such as size of screen, location of buttons, or system of navigation, or even e-ink versus backlit screen (a very surprising result given that readers consistently find e-ink less fatiguing).[35] (It is important to keep in mind that these populations of device users are not separate but overlapping: most e-book readers in my survey used more than one reading device over the past twelve months. Hence, their feelings about device usage are informed by experience with more than one interface, and their response to the question may refer to aspects of one interface or multiple interfaces.) This could indicate that readers are responding to some aspect common to different e-reading devices, such as adjustable font size. Another possibility, however, is that the appeal lies in a mode of reading where the physical object is temporarily forgotten. This possibility is one I'll explore in greater detail later in the chapter, as we consider e-reading and immersion.

While there is an extremely small population of respondents who choose print because a print book is more enjoyable to handle and use *and* choose digital because it is more enjoyable to handle and use (1.3%), these are for the most part incompatible preferences.

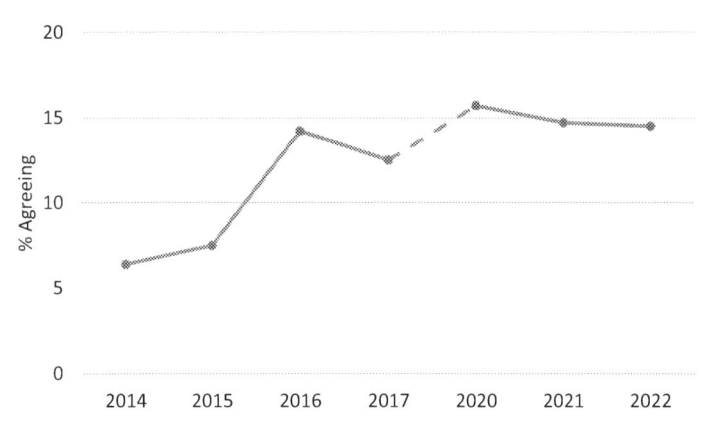

Figure 4.3   Reasons for choosing digital: 'a reading device is more enjoyable to handle and use', by year.

The Rise of Enjoyment of E-reading Devices

Enjoyment of e-reading devices did vary significantly by year: while remaining very low compared to enjoyment of print, enjoyment of e-reading devices doubled over the eight-year span of the surveys, leaping upwards between 2015 and 2016 (Figure 4.3). There was a dramatic increase, but not one obviously linked to increased e-reading during the pandemic.

Given the general lack of relationships to most demographics, sources of e-books, most genres of e-books, and choice of device, it is reasonable to conjecture that this is a genuine increase. Since February 2014, e-reading technologies have developed (though nothing to rival e-ink breakthroughs of the 2000s), and Amazon, the primary source for e-books in my survey, has introduced new functionality for both Kindle devices and Kindle apps. Pew Research Centre estimates that although Americans' laptop/desktop computer ownership was approximately stable (at roughly three-quarters of adults) between 2014 and 2021, tablet (to roughly half by 2021) and particularly smartphone (to more than five out of six in 2021) ownership increased.[36]

For dedicated reading devices, the trajectory has not been ever upward, or ever closer to any one idea of ideal screen reading – or whether that ideal includes emulation of the codex. Pew Internet has not asked about e-ink reader ownership since 2016, but it is interesting to note that the last data, collected in November 2016, found that ownership had rebounded from 17% in spring 2016 to 22% in autumn 2016, calling into question the dominant story of plummeting e-ink reader ownership.[37] Further iterations of the Kindle introduced new features, some of which address (or are meant to address) kinesthetic dimensions of interaction with the text. The PagePress haptics of the 2014 Kindle Voyage offered tactile feedback in the form of a very slight push-back on the reader's fingertips when transferring to a new page.[38] This feedback was very different from the tactile experience of turning a paper page, but is timed to offer some sensory input that coincides with the same action, punctuating the reading experience at a similar pace, and presumably to give readers some of the 'whole process of turning the page'[39] that many in my own study value highly. *Wired* described PagePress to its audience of technology enthusiasts as, alongside the 'grit' of the very slightly textured screen, 'tactile qualities that approach actual paper'.[40] However, other new Kindle features were not designed to emulate paper but to introduce enhancements impossible in a traditional print book. The Kindle Oasis, the model following the haptic-feedback Voyage, abandoned PagePress and added, instead, additional ways to navigate, interrogate, and share the text. These included image-navigation systems, links to Goodreads, features such as Timeline, which promise a new way to keep track of and navigate between key points in a narrative, and X-ray, which promises the chance to 'see all the passages across a book that mention relevant ideas, fictional characters, historical figures, and places or topics of interest'[41] (a perspective familiar in the early 2020s to viewers of Amazon Prime Video, where paused programmes sprout links to the Internet Movie Database [IMDb]). For non-fiction books, the X-ray feature frequently appears alongside a traditional index as well as the more mundane Kindle search function, and might not represent a meaningful augmentation in terms of searchability, but for novels any indexing offered participants in my study a degree of pleasing novelty (the long history of indexing fiction notwithstanding).[42] Some focus group respondents had tried X-ray, and reported that it 'tells you about the characters' in a way that was genuinely new to them; the resource was often primitive and trivial ('quite often it's just a few sentences from when they first appeared'), but sometimes detailed and useful ('in some books, you get a huge amount of information').[43] This opening up of the text to elements from outside, institutional or crowdsourced, are the kinds of 'word-based enhancements' that McCracken considers to be 'centripetal trajectories', forces drawing the reader more deeply into the text[44] but into the text via avenues impossible for print. And in an advance that offered a desirable but profoundly 'unbookish' (or at least unpaperish) shift, the Voyage fulfilled the dream of generations of beach- and bath-readers: it is, at least to a depth of two metres, waterproof. (Though no participants in my study mentioned this Kindle feature, their enthusiasm for beach reading and avoidance of digital near water, for example, 'read in the bath – don't want to drop electronic devices in the water!'[45] confirm that waterproofing would counter one key objection to e-reading. Amazon's later decision to incorporate waterproofing into not only its then flagship model, the Oasis, but its midrange Paperwhites,[46] attests not only to the feature's value to readers but also its value as a luxury add-on: something that, like freedom from advertising, that differentiates the plus model from the basic model.) More recently, the 2022 Kindle Scribe introduced limited forms of written annotation. The stylus allowed for scribbling notes in the margins of PDFs, though not yet in the margins of reflowable .AZW or .EPUB files. Annotations in e-books required creating virtual sticky notes: these handily translate between different devices and the cloud, preserving one's personalised text in a way unimaginable before digital platforms, but are very far from faithfully replicating the experience of jotting down thoughts in a print book.[47]

Amazon's decision to quietly discontinue the haptic-feedback Voyage in 2018 did not represent a wholesale rejection of the bookness strategy. Rather, it indicates continued experimentation with emulation of print, adding and removing features in a search for combinations that tempt – for the lowest possible cost – the greatest number of customers, and advance Amazon's broader agenda of folding users ever more deeply into the Prime membership ecosystem.[48] Designers began the Kindle project "'pushing for the subconscious qualities that made it feel like you were reading a book'" and continue to do so – while still serving Bezos's reported directive to "'proceed as if your goal is to put everyone selling physical books out of a job'".[49]

The Incomplete Book

This rich experience of materiality for print books, and thin, oblique, elusive experience of materiality for e-books, means that when it comes to enjoyment of the physical object, e-books do not function for readers as real: a piece is effectively missing (at least part of the time), leaving a void in its place. This is a form of unrealness very different from the unrealness of a digital proxy or *ersatz book*. The incomplete book is not so easy to present as an inferior replacement; it is only a real book chopped (by no fault of its own) into pieces, more to be pitied than feared. And the metaphor of the incomplete book suggests at least the theoretical possibility of ascension to realness. If it could by some means be reunited with the rest of itself, the incomplete book would become a real book, in a way that an *ersatz book* or proxy never could.

Convenience as Pleasure

Convenience is its own form of pleasure. To participants in this study, it is more than removal of barriers to enjoyment; they 'enjoy the convenience' itself.[50] Noted explicitly by a great many participants as a reason for choosing digital, the term encompasses a wide range of practical concerns and emotional responses, from the brisk 'it saves me having to drive all over town' to the emotive 'love the accessibility and convenience of digital' and 'embrace' of certain conveniences as 'godsend[s]'.[51] Convenience can mean luxury, but also freedom, equal access, intimacy, and power. The beneficiary, however, is not always the reader.

Relative Value of 'Ease': More Important for Obtaining E-books Than Reading E-books

Looking at all survey respondents, just under half (45.6%) choose print because it is easier to read. But even for those who read e-books, optimising for ease is not as simple as a direct swap: only 36.7% of those respondents choose print because it is easier to read, and only 21.0% choose digital because it is easier to read (Figure 4.4). This figure of one in five might on the face of it seem low, but convenience plays a greater role earlier in the process. More than twice as many (44.1%) choose digital because it is easier to obtain, and three times as many (60.4%) because it is faster to obtain: one 2015 survey respondent spoke for many in choosing digital because it is 'faster to buy e-books'.

'Faster to obtain' and 'easier to obtain' were closely correlated,[52] but still separate. Fewer respondents were motivated by ease than speed, perhaps in part because some found e-book purchasing and borrowing to be a finicky process (see Chapter 3).

The appeal of speed is widely shared and largely stable: agreement with 'faster to obtain' did not vary significantly by year (though it peaked at 68.6% in 2020, during the first lockdown) or according to any demographic measure. A number of survey respondents noted that work reading was often particularly time-sensitive (and, in fact, the connection for laptop but not desktop computers may indicate that it is working outside

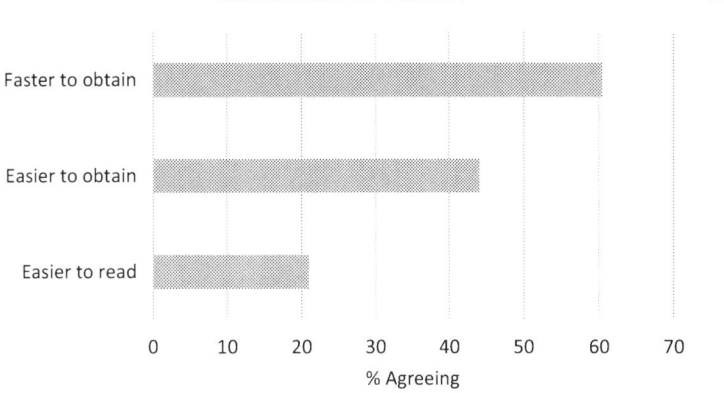

Figure 4.4   Reasons for choosing digital: 'convenience' factors (e-book readers only).

the office, e.g., on business trips, research days, or out-of-hours work, when print copies are not always to hand, that speed is a higher priority). The key word is 'sometimes': they frame it as a strictly emergency measure. 'Sometimes, if I need to start something quickly as research, getting [e-books] is immediate', or 'sometimes, I need a play script for use at an audition. . .when that's the case, I tend to need it quickly (no time to wait for shipping)', or 'sometimes, when I need to read something quickly for learning, I opt for the ebook'.[53] The link to work reading is unsurprising: Buchanan, McKay, and Levitt's 2015 study of academic e-book usage indicated that even where print was preferred, digital was often the choice for speed (and that while academics in the study tended to use laptop computers for quick reference when off campus, students often turned to smartphones for academic purposes 'when the phone is the "to-hand" device').[54] To take advantage of such an affordance is not described as luxury so much as failure: admission of guilt for having been caught short, as with 'I have my paper to write, and there was this one book. . . I needed it quite urgently, because it was a bit late? I was procrastinating a bit. . .that's why I bought it. From Amazon'.[55] But obtaining books quickly and easily offers its own kind of satisfaction. Participants explain that they enjoy the 'instant gratification', and like the 'instant access to many books', especially at the height of the pandemic, when 'the instant accessibility [of e-books], especially during lockdown, was a huge boon'.[56]

'Easier to obtain' did rise during the pandemic, peaking in 2021 at over half (51.7%) of respondents who read e-books. Qualitative data from 2020 to 2022 underscores how many pandemic-specific issues made e-books more obtainable and print books less, from the extremely frequent mentions of library and bookshop closures (such as 'I began reading

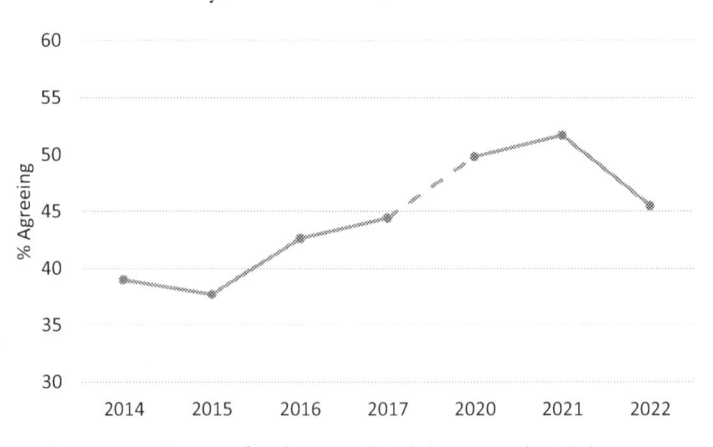

Figure 4.5   Reasons for choosing digital: 'easier to obtain', by year.

ebooks when my library closed down due to covid. Even once they opened back up for borrowing, ebooks are more available than print'), to new and/ or temporary sources (as with the 'Internet archive pandemic library'),[57] to safety concerns not only with bookish settings but also the books themselves ('borrowing an e-book from the public library is safer, no bedbugs or Covid').[58] Agreement in 2022 had already fallen to near-pre-pandemic levels (Figure 4.5).

Non-UK residents valued it somewhat more highly; this group included a number of expats, some of whom used free-text comments to underscore how e-books are the 'only cost-effective'[59] means of obtaining desired English-language titles in some parts of the world. Those who choose digital because digital is easier to obtain were more likely to have obtained e-books from libraries, and somewhat more likely to have obtained them from Project Gutenberg, Amazon, non-Amazon online retailers and, intriguingly, chain bookshops.[60] The library advantage could be due less to some special convenience of library online interfaces than to a comparison (even before the pandemic) to physical libraries, particularly e-books being 'easier to quickly borrow from the library without attending' as well as 'easier to return to the library'.[61]

The Portable Text and the Flexible Reader

The portability of e-books is perhaps the most frequently mentioned affordance in the free-text boxes of my survey. Movement between devices is a predictably common theme, with respondents appreciative of the ability to 'change between [their] devices for e-reading, my kindle, laptop and mobile and read the same book and be bookmarked at the same place' and 'you can read it on multiple devices and it always takes you to where you were in the book'.[62] As one explains, this is not just handy, but wondrous: 'if I have to get up and go for whatever reason I just put the book down and keep listening... *basically, I never have to stop reading*, which is wonderful' [emphasis mine].[63] But even more prominent is the role of e-reading in travel and the reader's movement between spaces. A tremendous number of participants, across all surveys and focus groups, emphasised the value of e-books as a way to be sure of access to chosen reading material when away from one's home or personal print library, either for daily travel such as a work commute, occasional holiday travel, or (as discussed in relation to ownership in Chapter 3), disruptive changes of residence. In addition to the frequent theme of access to a book (and sometimes to the ease of a one-handed grip on a device rather than a two-handed grip on a codex when on a crowded train), there is a powerful sub-theme of access not to *a* book but *many* books. 'One kindle vs a number of books' or 'easy to carry more than 1 book with me' goes beyond a few physical items in a suitcase, where one device can take the place of 'taking multiple books on holiday'.[64] This replaces a single item of commute reading with any book in one's device storage – or, if the WiFi is working (not a given while travelling), almost any book in the world. 'If I'm on the subway and the book I'm reading gets dull', one explains, 'I can switch to a short story, or comic, or completely different book without adding any extra weight to my commute!'[65] It's not only the ability to bring enough reading but also far more than enough: not just choice but surfeit, abundance beyond what could possibly be needed. It is 'not running out of book while travelling' and enjoying the fact that 'tablet with a dozen books = no finishing book on bus and not having another'.[66] The result is a reassuring plenitude, and freedom from the fear of 'running out of book' or being trapped with nothing to read but an inferior book.[67]

> 'Plus you can take [an e-reading device] anywhere, and you always have a new book. So if you go on a train journey with a book you're really excited about and it's crap, you'll probably be able to find another one.' (FG 1 participant 4)

> 'Gone are the days when I felt the need to carry two enormous hardcovers because I was almost done with my book – now I can just slip the kobo in my bag and have a backup that way. **Abibliophobia begone!**' (Survey 2016)

There is a specific kind of safety that comes from carrying, in addition to any books one might be reading, the books one is *not* reading, and are not likely to read. Some respondents very rarely use their device as an e-reader, but value having the reading there in case they ever needed it: 'I bought a smart phone so I always have a book with me but I rarely use it for reading'.[68] This language of 'backups' where 'you always have a new book' speaks to a conception of the e-book as real book. It recalls iron rations and emergency supplies: spartan, never used if there is a more sumptuous alternative, but adequate. A spare tyre is smaller and less durable and only used for short distances, but it is still a tyre, not a part of a tyre or a representation of a tyre or a tyre-shaped substitute. The e-book as spare book may be reserved for emergencies, but it still rolls down the road. (This kind of safety, and closeness, also represents a new kind of intimacy with books; as I discuss in Chapter 5, this offers a new way to be tied to one's books and inseparable from one's reading.)

The safety of e-books is, of course, undercut by the vulnerability of a device to theft, breakage, loss, or simply loss of power. While the need for meaningful ownership of e-books focussed on long-term threats such as changes to terms and conditions, retailers going out of business, and problems with inheritance and with download to generations of personal devices, the need for constant and reliable access to one's reading material leads to concern over short-term threats. Readers place value on the safety net of e-books being there when wanted, 'I always have my smartphone with me (no need to carry the book)'.[69] They noted that '[print] removes dependence on power chargers', that there is 'no electricity required', and asked 'why use expensive electronic technology which requires power to operate, can fail or break?'.[70] However, the nightmare scenario of book-lessness was rarely realised: vanishingly few gave stories of specific instances where an e-book was unavailable, as with an account from 2020 of 'I lost power recently and read a paperback for the first time in years' that stood very nearly alone. Rather, they described hypothetical situations where an electronic device *could* fail them. This speaks less to the experience of unreliable technology than to the fear of it (though that fear is quite authentic, and a genuine motivation for choosing print as a 'more reliable technology').[71]

Some readers, however, find that carrying books one does not intend to read interferes with enjoyment of the book one is reading, preventing 'commitment' to one book.[72] In this sense, e-books can be less intimate than print, or at least less monogamous; a young woman in a focus group was joking when she declared that 'print is the wife and digital is the mistress!',[73] but the comparison does speak to the way in which a primary relationship is affected by the flagrant presence of a backup option. This added burden of a task, the need to select a book and 'commit' to that book, requires self-discipline and, for at least some readers, stands in the way of pleasure. (I will discuss the issue of choosing between books an aspect of digital distraction later in the chapter.) As with concerns over failing batteries and dropped devices, shot through the comfort of abundance is worry over the loss of it; new safety comes packaged with new fears.

The Accommodating Book

But a profound source of intimacy with texts is the way in which digital access allows some readers to integrate reading into settings, physical and social, previously incompatible with reading. The most common story is that of night-time reading. (Reading to manage insomnia is such a common theme that e-books as enablers of bed-based reading is a matter of health and well-being as well as pleasure.) The ability to read in the dark is a frequently cited affordance for participants in this study. Sometimes this is for the convenience of an individual, 'don't have to wake myself up to turn off a light, even a book light' or 'if reading at night I don't have to have light on' (or indeed 'bedtime reading when I might want to switch books without getting up') but often the light-equipped e-ink reader, or backlit tablet or smartphone, enables reading 'without having to keep the light on' so as to not 'disturb my partner', 'disturb others', 'disturb anyone else in the room' – area lighting for a silent activity being evidently disturbing in the extreme.[74] The e-book does not bring books into a previously bookless space – the shared bed, where they have long existed – but merely eliminates the need for the exceedingly familiar technology of the bedside lamp or book light. The person being accommodated is not so much the reader as the reader's partner. In other stories, the person being accommodated is not an equal but a customer, boss, or a beloved dependent. E-books are 'easier to read between customers at work' and 'easier to wrangle while travelling…work travel is becoming quite difficult with print'.[75] Nursing infants are particularly prominent as people whose needs can be more easily reconciled with e-reading than print reading: e-books are 'easier to read during specific situations (when I wouldn't be able to read a print book, e.g. breastfeeding in funny positions!)' and '[e-books make it] easier to multitask, only needs one hand (for example, can breastfeed)'.[76] Baby and toddler care makes the one-handed reading affordance particularly useful: 'I was not expecting this, but with small children, I find [an e-book] easier to pick up and put down and read when I have limited use of hands'.[77] But e-books are also invaluable for reading around childcare when the children are old enough to walk, talk, and take solo train journeys.

> *'I know what I loved when the children were at school was I could be reading a book at home, I could leave it by my bed on the iPad and if they were late out of school I could carry on reading it on my phone, or whilst I was waiting for them to get off a train or something.'* (FG 5 participant 8)

Here, integrating a digital book with a previously bookless setting is not only a matter of taking advantage of a compact or backlit or portable interface. These stories are accounts of personal control reclaimed. Constraints imposed by the wishes or needs of other people – a supervisor, or a child being cared for – can be circumvented by putting the book in a different container, using a platform that is either physically convenient for the 'funny positions' of breastfeeding, physically durable and hence usable around small children, or unobtrusive (and possibly furtive) and able to evade notice. This use of protean reading to evade demands placed on the reader by other obligations and relationships, with its dimensions of gender and class, suggests that digital reading could amplify an existing 'post-Romantic paradigm that makes reading the recourse of the poor, the lonely, the marginalised, the physically or socially powerless'.[78] Those with power shape their environments to suit their needs, while those without power use reading to escape their environments. In contexts where e-books and e-reading devices are costly luxuries (as in 2007, when the first-generation Kindle cost over \$400),[79] this would represent a means of escape only for the 'powerless affluent', those who enjoy some economic advantage but not necessarily autonomy. But as reading-ready devices become less costly and more commonplace (as noted earlier, 85% of American adults, and 96% of American adults younger than age 30, now own smartphones) contexts where e-books become the 'cheap' option, particularly for academics and students at institutions where 'electronic resources have grown as a cost-effective alternative to print resources', offer a more direct parallel to the falling price of print and transformation of reading, in general, from 'a sign of economic power' to 'the province of those whose time lacks market value'.[80] The prominence of caring responsibilities, and possibility of a gendered aspect to this protean reading, also recalls enduring anxieties about women's reading (especially 'absorptive' novel reading)[81] as a strategy for escape from domestic duty. Devotion to reading has been depicted as a signal of insufficient devotion elsewhere, including outright neglect of children.[82] Hence, centuries-old admonitions that women treat reading as an indulgence that should wait until work (including affective labour) was done, or even limit reading as a practice of healthy self-denial.[83]

Digital reading could in this context be seen as even more disempowered: while a reader with relatively more power may adapt their environment to enable the preferred print reading, for the reader with relatively less, the choice may be digital or nothing. As with the backlit screen for reading in bed, the text is accommodating, but the reader is not necessarily the one being accommodated. It can be seen in one light as ingeniously outwitting external control and in another as avoiding confrontation with external control, and potentially prolonging the dynamic. These findings problematise ideas of digital reading as appealing specifically because it pampers a reader with personalisation: the Amazon slogan of 'read books your way'[84] would be better described, for many, as 'read books that get out of other people's way'.

The e-book as accommodating book is in a curious position with regards to realness. Like the backup book, it does its job: the squeezed reading is still reading. But here, the e-book functions more as incomplete book: it is less the non-perishable, freeze-dried version for consumption in a blizzard than a portable slice, the smallest and least troublesome section taken along for some enjoyment even as all that is obtrusive, anything that might inconvenience others, is left behind.

Ease of Reading

The importance of ease of reading was stable: neither print nor digital varied significantly by survey year. This stability, in the face of advances in reading device technology and the increase in usage of tablets and smartphones over the period, suggests that, like enjoyment of an e-reading device, ease of reading digitally is not simply a matter of features on a particular device.

Ease of reading had intriguing relationships with age. Examining all respondents together, print-only and e-book reading, choosing print because it is easier to read dropped sharply with age (Figure 4.6).

However, this trajectory was due to e-book-reading respondents, not readers on the whole. Separating e-book readers from print-only readers, the contrast is sharp. For e-book readers, the decline according to age is not a straight line – there is a sudden dip for readers aged 35–44 – but

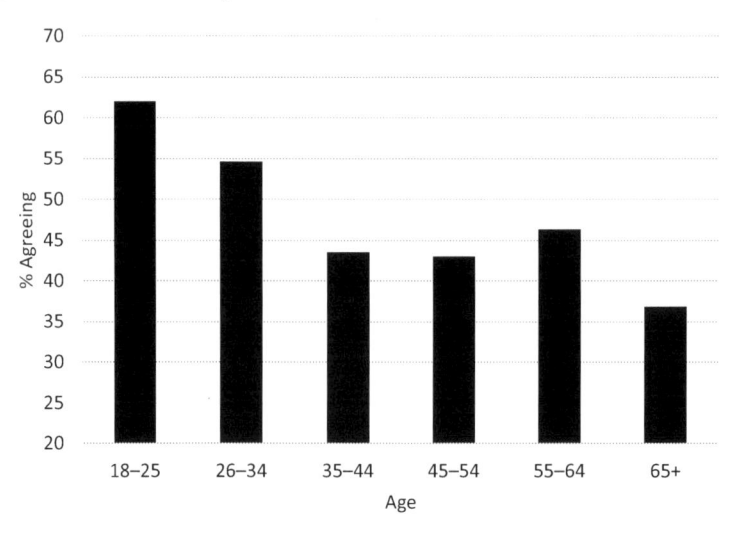

Figure 4.6   Reasons for choosing print: 'easier to read', by age.

it is a significant correlation, and sees the youngest respondents twice as likely as the oldest respondents to agree. For print-only readers, it is not a steady decline but rather a sudden drop among the oldest respondents (Figure 4.7).

Choosing digital because it is easier to read, however, increased with age (Figure 4.8).

It's important not to overstate this effect, as even among the oldest respondents only a minority agree, and conditions such as visual impairment are of course neither limited to nor universal in the oldest group. (For example, in one study cited by Phillips, participants with good vision preferred print for reading, but participants with impaired vision preferred screen reading.)[85] Such affordances could be easy to dismiss as belonging to some lower category of pleasure: the means of overcoming a barrier to enjoyment rather than a source of enjoyment. However, the importance to an individual can be profound. As one respondent put it: 'I have a visual impairment, so the ability to enhance font size etc in Ebooks is a real godsend'.[86] Though the removal of difficulty may seem a small reward, 'pleasure as less pain' inspired emphatic responses. Fewer than one in ten (7.8%) chose digital because they are 'helpful for dealing with a health issue that can interfere with my reading'[87] – but fewer than one in a hundred print readers (0.8%) chose print for that reason.

A case in point would be the experiences of readers who use their chosen technology to overcome barriers presented by dyslexia. Dyslexia

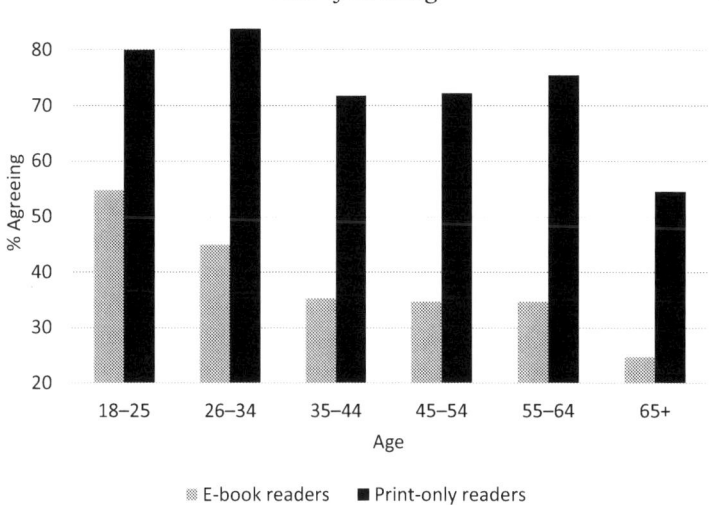

Figure 4.7 Reasons for choosing print: 'easier to read', by age, print-only readers versus e-book readers.

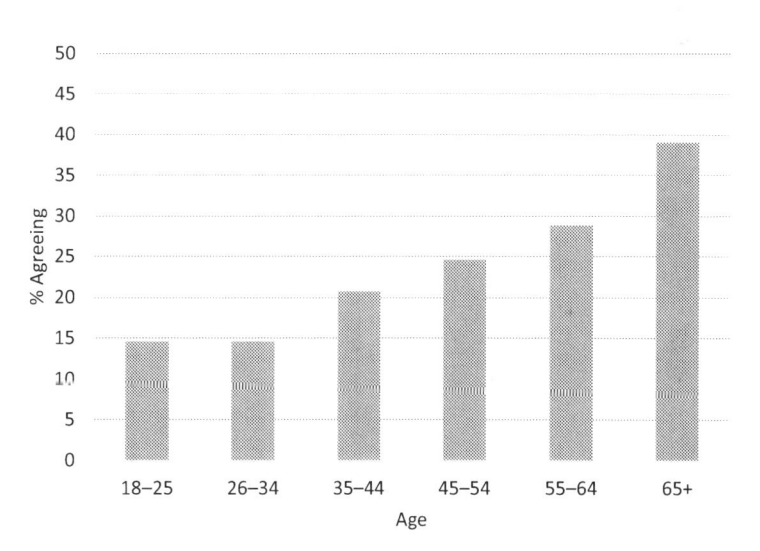

Figure 4.8 Reasons for choosing digital: 'easier to read', by age.

was cited as both a reason to use e-books instead of print ('dyslexia', 'due to having both Dyslexia and ADHD...I have trouble reading hardback book due to the font') and a reason to use print instead of e-books. ('I believe my mild dyslexia also impacts on how much easier I find it to read hard copy text').[88] Studies of dyslexia and screen reading have found that there are aspects that may hinder as well as aspects that may help, indicating that two individuals, even two individuals with the same form of dyslexia, could have drastically different screen reading experiences depending on device and device settings. For example, glare from a backlit screen may exacerbate fatigue and reduce speed and comfort,[89] but adjustable text and shorter line length,[90] and larger characters and more space between characters, have been demonstrated to increase comprehension and comfort.[91] Commercial screen reading products promise benefits, but these promises are not always supported by evidence. Amazon offers 'Open Dyslexia' font as an option for its Kindle app, though some independent studies have found no benefit from either Open Dyslexia[92] or proprietary versions such as Dyslexie.[93] What the respondents in this study have in common is that medium matters for their reading experiences, and choosing print or choosing digital is part of individual dyslexia management strategies.

Ease of reading, in print and digitally, had few links to device choice. When they do read on screen, e-book readers who choose print for ease of reading are more likely to have read an e-book on laptop (48.9% vs 30.8%). It could be that people who read on laptops are frustrated by the interface and hence are more likely to prefer print, or it could be that people who prefer print are less likely to bother with dedicated devices or even dedicated apps, and make do with browser windows. (Those who choose digital for ease of reading are more likely to read on smartphone, at 56.1% vs 44.4%, but have no other meaningful connection to choice of device).

'Read Books Your Way': Convenience as Power and Agency

Amazon sells Kindles (however misleadingly) as a means to 'read books your way'. While e-book retailers (as discussed in Chapter 3) may at times be unacceptably controlling, e-books themselves are accommodating. They change their shape when readers ask it, altering font, text size, page turn animations, colour scheme, lighting, and so on. Many common dissatisfactions with e-books, such as inconsistent pagination and unwanted advertisements and comments, are ways in which an e-book changed when they did not want it to: the pliability of e-books is a benefit when the reader is in control, but a liability when the reader is not. (This, again, recalls the central role of control in relationships with e-books.) Many respondents in my own study noted 'e-book adjustability functions re: serif/non-serif and font size' and the 'search function. . .for long/complex texts' as exceptionally useful (particularly in relation to non-fiction reading), 'attractive' and 'really nice'.[94] Responses in this vein were particularly powerful when linked to disability or age-related impairments: 'convenience' in this sense is nothing less than equal access to books. The customisation affordances of digital are judged in the context of diminishing accommodation by mainstream print publishing. Some participants observed that 'when it comes to magazines and newspapers they are making the print smaller (odd given the aging audience)' and 'as an avid reader with a visual impairment, eBooks have become increasingly valuable to me as print standards decline. Mass-market paperbacks are often badly printed and use a too-small font size'.[95]

Customisation: Comfort at the Cost of Ceremony

E-books offer tremendous opportunities for customisation. Some readers take full advantage of this affordance by personalising in ways reminiscent of commissioned binding:

> *'I tend to specifically organise and convert [e-books] into the right file formats and procure the covers I like. Like fan-made alternative Game of Thrones covers and things because that's much more fun, and the Penguin-style Harry Potter covers[96] are great [note: participant showed samples on her personal iPad]'* (FG 4 participant 4)

But such flexibility is, to others, unsettling: one respondent found that 'changing titles is a bit disrespectful of other people's books, so I'm not quite sure'.[97] Flexibility can be irritating, as when readers are confronted with disliked generic covers, or find that a book has become detached from a cover without their permission:

> *'When I'm looking at my e-reader I really dislike it when I get a book down and they haven't included the front cover [murmurs of agreement]. . .you've just got this Penguin logo or something and they haven't put the front cover on.'* (FG 6 participant 3)

This interference with what is perceived as the normal and expected situation, with 'normal' defined with relation to print (where 'the physical book. . .means that each book has a different cover', unique and appropriate to that book even if elements of design are dictated by publisher or series)[98] speaks further to a conception of e-book as incomplete book. Aspects such as Kindle popular highlights can be switched on and off by the reader, though in practice the means of doing do can be obscure, leaving readers the choice of either investing time in mastering the intricacies of Kindle settings or acquiescing to Amazon's default choice. But customisation does help to combat what some readers describe as an inherent weakness of e-books: an 'impersonalness', 'something that all looks the same', lacking the distinctive annotations and even distinctive damage ('I even like the occasional chocolate, bath water or similar stains on books'), where 'there's nothing different between your copy of [the book] and mine'.[99]

The pleasure of a compliant book is countered by a loss of pleasure where aspects of the print book experience functioned, for an individual, not as chores but as rituals. Some readers celebrate and enjoy the e-book's transformation according to their needs, but others lament the loss of a sense of occasion, even ceremony. Some reminisced about treasured rituals of pre-order (for a few exceptionally awaited books, not everyday purchases) where they 'had the pre-order form… "I want my Harry Potter book"…and then you would go in and queue up and the counter and get your book. In a nice little envelope'.[100] Purchasing an e-book was in comparison, lacking.

> *'It's not as…special? You know when you go into a bookshop and buy a book, and you get it home and you're really excited? ['yes', murmurs of agreement from group]…when you get a book though the post, that's exciting? Whereas downloading a book is just like 'eh'.'* (FG 1 participant 1)

Even the 'the thump of a package on my doorstep'[101] offers some excitement, compared to the 'eh' of online purchase, and this lack – another way in which the e-book is, to these participants, incomplete – further influences book-buying behaviour. As one put it, 'the books I would hope for a sense of ceremony wouldn't be the ones I'd be buying [in digital form] anyway'.[102] Even settling down in a favoured reading spot 'snuggled up with tea and a blanket!' with a print book has the satisfactions of ritual for these readers: 'There's something extremely soothing and wonderfully visceral about settling down with a physical book' one explained, 'that I don't think e-books will ever be able to emulate'.[103]

As Price notes, William Morris designed for non-compliance, creating awkwardly luxurious, luxuriously awkward tomes; 'high-end, high-volume volumes' that 'offered conspicuous inconvenience' to the discerning customer who enjoyed the money to buy them, the space to open and read them, and the time (as McGann argues) to decelerate and give the material object due attention.[104] With e-books, readers do not have to approach literature; the literature comes to them, figuratively and literally. Not only do they no longer have to journey to bookshops, they no longer have to set aside a specific time for reading, or to return home, sit in a suitable chair, set down their coffee, or wait until the baby is asleep. Reading 'when lying on the sofa or in bed', buying or borrowing books while on a moving train to 'get a book whenever I want', and being able to 'switch books without having to get up' is a reading experience unrecognisable to even the most affluent (or lavishly supplied with personal servants) reader from an earlier era.[105] The question is in how this affects their perception and experience of the literature: not only of the book-object (as with Morris's volumes) but also of the text. If the reader no longer has to meet a text on its terms, but may expect it to adapt and meet them on theirs, does the reader's relationship to a text fundamentally change? If an accommodating text grants new power to the reader, that might lead to a diminished power differential between readers and the publisher/authors, even reduction of reverence and deference, or indeed of esteem and respect. However, fan studies consider the effects of hierarchy on properties (textual and otherwise) where readers and other cultural consumers appropriate and remix; this kind of customisation facilitates intimacy and affect[106] but does not necessarily disrupt hierarchy or diminish the distance between creators and fans.[107] Choosing to access a book in print is often linked to esteem: most participants in this study find print better for collecting and better for giving, and some (as I will discuss later in the chapter) find it better suited for sustained concentration, and print books are hence often the 'good books' they honour with special attention and dedicated space.[108] However, the link between print and esteem does not automatically translate into the reverse, a link between digital and disdain. As one survey respondent put it, digital is their format of choice for 'things [they] think of as « lighter » reading (not lesser, mind) such as romance or funny books'[109] specifically because such books are not of the types they usually collect, not because they are in some debased category of 'lesser' reading. It is worth remembering that if much digital reading, especially of novels, is 'light', so is much print reading. In a recent large-scale face-to-face survey of book purchasers in UK high street bookshops, Frost found that most buyers had chosen their print novels to gain 'entertainment, escape, and relaxation', with very few seeking 'an intellectual challenge or for an aesthetic experience'.[110] As one participant put it (to emphatic agreement from her focus group cohort), 'the choice of [print] novels in the supermarket, they're really all beach reads or best sellers'.[111] I asked all focus group and interview participants whether they agreed with the statement that 'digital is for "light" reading,' but serious reading requires print. They were unanimous in considering that as a sweeping statement this was 'rubbish'.[112] They noted that while there were many instances where they and people they knew used digital for 'light' reading (including 'beach read' novels and 'airport novels'),[113] there were also many instances where they chose digital for 'serious' reading, especially when the book to which they needed quick or on-the-go access was not light entertainment to help pass the time on a commute (as much of their digital reading is) but an essential work of such importance that they could not be without it. This could be the 'handapparat' of a scholar who keeps her core texts to hand on a tablet or laptop at all times,[114] but also a great work of literature that they could, or already do, own in print, yet download in digital form because easy access will help them pursue reading they consider important.[115] It can even be the Bible, especially where it is 'easier to take an electronic bible [sic] along to meetings'.[116] Hutchings's work on digital reading of devotional texts confirms that while some scholars express concern that digital access will change the nature of reading scripture, for example, by facilitating the reading of short sections with less emphasis on sequence or context, they are not concerned that digital access equates with disrespect.[117] For Bible publishers (frequently distributing e-book and app versions for free) and readers that have made the Bible so successful on e-reading platforms, all access is good access: lower barriers means more time with scripture. According to Bible app developers YouVersion, 'a striking 77% of users in a recent survey claim to "turn to the bible more" because it's available on their mobile device'.[118] If an individual considered digital formats in any way diminishing, they would probably not have chosen digital for their own sacred text. Accessing a book in digital form is not in itself an expression of contempt for that book. Further, there is not compelling evidence in these data for a link between an accommodating text and reduced reverence, deference, or respect: though one participant described someone else's cover-altering customisation as potentially 'disrespectful', no one characterised their own customisation as in any way disrespectful, or as action that either generated or expressed contempt.

These 'convenience' pleasures are real pleasures, even if they are not universally shared; for some readers, the part of the book that is left is still capable of offering profound enjoyment. A further question is in how the unreal-because-incomplete e-book – flexible and accommodating, instantly available, spoken of as immaterial even when its materiality is beyond question – can or cannot offer a particularly treasured form of pleasure: the feeling of being 'lost in a book'.[119]

'Lost in a Book': Distraction, Immersion, and Narrative Engagement

Deep engagement with a text requires not only overcoming external distractions but also achieving a state of focus, concentration, and connection. For a subset of participants in this study, digital reading presents considerable, even insurmountable, barriers to both.

Viewed through the lens of pleasure, distraction is not necessarily a problem. Though the possibility that the internet era presents critical threats to the concentration required for certain cognitively demanding reading practices,[120] to 'literary reading',[121] or to coherent thought,[122] makes many commentators examine distraction as a danger to literature or literary culture, an individual reader might find distraction perfectly enjoyable. For at least some readers, especially those who enjoy switching between books and between reading and other tasks during travel, movement between media may be part of the fun, and books can be the thing that distracts as easily as the thing distracted from. But for many in my study, distraction was unpleasant, a thing that interfered with their enjoyment of books, and a reason to avoid digital reading.

For some, part of the pleasure of reading was to offer escape from the ubiquity of screens and digital interaction in daily life: an opportunity to 'unplug' and 'get away from electronics' after 'spend[ing] all day staring at computer screens'.[123] This 'break from looking at a screen + does not involve using a potentially distracting electronic device' only became more important during pandemic lockdowns, when participants reported they 'have actively been choosing print books...to counteract all the zoom screen time' and find it 'nice to look at real pages during the pandemic, when we spend so much time on a screen'.[124]

For others, however, it was not the device but the unwanted opportunity to access alternative reading material. 'Bringing ONE physical book to the coffee shop to read with [their] latte' is sometimes essential as it 'prevents literary multitasking: skipping from e-book to e-book on my Kindle':[125] a form of distraction where the competition is between e-books, a dark mirror of the pleasure of choice discussed earlier. 'With e-books', one focus group participant explained, 'you can switch between them really, really quickly. Whereas if you're out and about on a train, with a print book, you're stuck with a print book, so you might get over the hill with the text'.[126] Agreeing, another added that they feel they 'have more of a commitment to a print book than an e-book'.[127] Or, it could be a broader form of multitasking, with competition from non-book reading or non-textual digital entertainment. When on screen means online (as is the case for most reading devices) the 'communication network' can serve as an active antagonist to concentration:

> 'When I read I am doing an activity that is specifically not screen time. In our Black Mirror society our entertainment is consumed in tandem with a communication network that doesn't want you to ever get off of it. My nontech hobbies allow me to disconnect.' (Survey 2020)

The only recourse, for some, is to stop reading on screen.

> 'I can't read on my computer…I've tried, and I have the attention span of a newt… [general chuckles, agreement] Even if I like it, I struggle? To concentrate? [agreement] There's just too much else to do, there's too many tabs open, flashing at you. [agreement, 'yeah, that's true']' (FG 1 participant 3)

Devising an e-reading interface to combat such distraction could, in theory, be as simple as altering device settings. As the 'slow reading' movement manifesto would have it, turning off the WiFi is enough to meaningfully change the e-reading experience (though using a dedicated e-ink reader whenever possible also helps).[128] But other research investigates the possibility that the screen itself presents serious barriers to concentration and engagement. This explores distraction in the sense of the reader/viewer/listener's 'mind wandering', the competing demands on attention not as alternative information or entertainment options on a multi-use or network-connected device, but as 'thinking about other things', with distraction defined as 'the presence of thoughts that are unrelated to the narrative'.[129] Empirical studies of the experience of reading immersion are, like reading research in general, carried out in a wide range of fields. Some current enquiries into potential differences between print and digital reading (of which e-book reading is a subset) build on studies of reading speed and comprehension, and consider immersion largely from a perspective of minimising barriers such as physical demands imposed by an interface (e.g. eye strain from backlit screens or delays in transfer between pages) or cognitive demands imposed by an interface (e.g. keeping track of one's place in a text presented on a scrolling page, or managing non-intuitive navigation) or by the text itself (e.g. hyperlinks, enhanced text features such as sound or embedded video, Amazon features options such as popular highlights or X-ray, etc.). These often examine e-book reading in terms of general internet use, with its preponderance of factual and short-form information and material framed as 'journalism' rather than 'books'. Others draw on studies of narrative engagement, considering e-books in terms of stories told via film, television, text, and, more recently, interactive media. This perspective groups many forms of non-fiction with novels and short fiction, approaching story as 'a mental representation...not tied to any particular medium and...independent of the distinction between fiction and non-fiction'.[130] This grouping excludes many examples of e-books, including non-narrative poetry, many forms of reference, and some books under a general 'non-fiction' umbrella (though the role of narrative in books such as academic monographs is a matter of debate).

Hou, drawing on her own past work on gaming and on Wittmer and Singer's work on virtual environments,[131] defines immersion as 'a sense of engagement or a sense of losing oneself in an environment'.[132] Busselle and Bilandzic also evoke the sense of being lost in an environment, but theirs is 'transportation into a story world', building not on human–computer interaction theory but media, film, and literary studies and 'the literature on narrative experiences' (following theorists such as Green and Brock) and connecting explicitly with Csikszentmihalyi's conception of flow as 'a complete focus on an activity accompanied by a loss of conscious awareness of oneself and one's surroundings'.[133] For all, achieving the desired state requires not gain but loss: a situation where the reader may 'lose track of time, fail to observe events going on around them',[134] to be temporarily free of self-awareness and rid of unrelated thoughts. Scholars also order the terms differently, with some, like Hou, describing engagement as a component of immersion, and others, like Busselle, Bilandzic, and Green, describing immersion as a component of engagement. Pleasure is described as an 'outcome' of engagement,[135] and not necessarily an important outcome.

Unlike empirical studies of reading comprehension and speed in print versus on screen, which are numerous and broadly in agreement,[136] empirical studies of print versus screen reading in terms of immersion or engagement are recent and comparatively few.[137] (It is also important to note that while any study finding no difference between screen and print reading in terms of immersion would be very valuable, negative results are not always published or reported widely.) The studies that do exist can offer contradictory conclusions regarding the meaning of their results.

There are competing models to explain effects like the dislocation felt by some readers when reading a reflowable e-book, as where they report that they 'don't like not having a physical eye-view of where [they are] in the book', want to 'know where [they are] in a book' when they 'can't get a feel' for progress when reading on screen and miss turning pages when 'turning pages tells you where you are in the story – part of the reading experience – knowing that the climax is coming etc'.[138] Mangen and Kuiken propose a medium materiality model in which the haptics of turning the page, feeling the weight of completed pages in the left hand, and so on are indispensable to grasping one's place in the text, which in turn is indispensable to remembering and understanding a text.[139] Many respondents in this study find print more 'engaging' (mentioned in free-text responses in 2014, 2015, 2016, 2020, and 2022 surveys). A few go further to explain that print also offers them a more significant connection to the author and/or the text itself, as with 'when you're reading on a Kindle, or whatever [the reading device]…you're not as attached to the author or something?' and 'some of the ones I've read on Kindle only so far, I really enjoyed them, I liked them a lot…but I feel like I don't know them fully'.[140] Many respondents in my study specifically note retention and memory. Though, as noted, most studies of reading comprehension find little overall difference between print and screen, some have found advantages to print for intensive reading of highly complex texts such as academic documents,[141] suggesting that some forms of learning may be more sensitive to platform than others. Following Noyes and Garland (2003), Mangen, Walgermo, and Bronnick use Tulving's Remember–Know paradigm (1985) to distinguish between information recollected and information applied, and conclude from their experiments that paper reading is more conducive to the deeper and more lasting applied knowledge.[142] In discussing their experiences of e-reading as less memorable, some of the respondents in my study noted that the different materiality of the e-book lacks elements that make print superior for recall. To say that they 'retain print information better', 'absorb/remember what is in a printed book better' is a common experience, meaning that 'When [they] need to read something carefully and to remember it well, [they] go for printed matter'.[143] Several specifically note the 'physicality' of a print book as crucial, as where print is described as 'better for remembering/more of a physical memory aspect'.[144] (It is telling that its plastic and non-distinctive materiality is frequently framed as the opposite of 'physical' books, a form of words used at least once in free-text responses in five of the seven yearly surveys.)[145] This potentially supports Mangen and Kuiken's medium materiality model. However, others draw attention to the fact that the 'non-physicality of e-books' only makes them 'easier to forget about if the content is not all that engaging'.[146] This suggests that even in a medium materiality model, there is 'content' sufficiently engrossing, sufficiently powerful, that it can overcome the shortcomings of a digital medium. That power may be narrative power, and the crucial distinction may be, in defiance of Green, who stipulates that story is story regardless of genre, fiction versus non-fiction[147] (meta-analysis having concluded that print's slight advantage on performance, according to certain metrics, applies only to non-fiction).[148] Other experiments found the situation for fiction more complex. Mangen and Kuiken, in a 2 × 2 study that gave participants the same text as a 'booklet' of 'letter-sized pages stapled in the upper left corner' and on iPad, and introduced as fiction or non-fiction, found a statistically significant reduction of narrative engagement when the material was presented as non-fiction, but not when presented as fiction; in fact, for the fiction condition, measures such as 'perceived narrative coherence' actually increased, though not at levels that reach statistical significance.[149] Mangen and Kuiken found it 'difficult to explain' why fiction was not affected, and hypothesised that the unfamiliar and uncongenial 'rough assemblage of stapled pages' that made up the sample booklet affected fiction and non-fiction conditions differently.[150] Their conclusion is that screen reading interferes with readers' engagement, and that this is because without 'physical, tactile, and spatiotemporally fixed cues' as to progress through the text (as with turning pages and feeling a weight of completed pages in one's left hand) specific to paper, 'overview of the text's organization and structure...may be diminished'.[151] In a follow-up study that used Kindle devices instead of the Kindle app on iPad, examining engagement alongside other measures of reading comprehension, Mangen, Olivier, and Velay found that while 'on most tests subjects performed identically whatever the reading medium...on measures related to chronology and temporality, those who had read in the print pocket book, performed better than those who had read on a Kindle'.[152] If this is the case, then no existing e-reader can offer an experience equal to print. Hou, Rashid, and Lee, however, challenge this conclusion, finding instead, by comparing readers' engagement with a Marvel Comics graphic novel when read in print form, fixed-layout PDF form on iPad, and in a dynamic panel-by-panel presentation on iPad, that print and PDF were entirely equal, with reduced engagement for the dynamic presentation only.[153] Their conclusion is that barriers to engagement in screen reading are real, but due to page reflow and the resulting difficulty in forming a cognitive map of the text, making remedy as simple as reading e-books in PDF rather than reflowable .EPUB form.[154]

Participants in these studies by Mangen, Kuiken, Hou, Rashid, and Lee, like my own participants, tend to describe digital as at best equal to print in terms of immersion. Many are confident that digital is 'as good', explaining that for them the platform is irrelevant and the reading experience is the same: 'I have no particular favourite medium', 'I don't really have a preference', or 'I really don't care if it's print or electronic most of the time' (keeping open the option of caring some of the time).[155] They 'read in all formats: hard copy, paperback/hardback, audiobook, e-audiobook, ebook, mp3, manuscript, advanced readers, flipster...the format is unimportant'.[156] Separating work and leisure reading was a common theme, but there was no consistent connection between work and print or leisure and print: this depended on the individual. Some report that 'most of reading for leisure I do in print. Professional reading almost entirely digital if possible' while others say that 'I use e-books when reading for pleasure, when I study I use printed books'.[157]

The instant when awareness of the physical interface falls away, when they 'forget [they're] reading on a Kindle',[158] is both the moment of immersion and the moment when the e-reading device becomes as good as (but generally not better than) print. There is no barrier between the reader and the narrative, realising the device's potential as 'this whole world of stories that you can dive into'.[159] This finding, that transportation is impeded or impossible for some e-book readers, but perfectly achievable for others (either minimally impeded, not impeded, or conceivably assisted), harmonises with Hayler's theories of experiences of e-readers as devices that intrude versus technology that recedes into the background.[160] Further, it has echoes in even the earliest empirical research on Kindle reading. Clark, Goodwin, Samuelson, and Coker's 2008 qualitative study of thirty-six university employees, examining their experiences of using first-generation Kindles for one year immediately after the device's 2007 release, revealed that for about half of their respondents the Kindle remained a 'noticeable, obtrusive device' with which 'they were not fully engaged with the text as they would be if reading a traditional book'.[161] However,

> '...the other half said they did become accustomed to the Kindle as a reading device, and that it did eventually fade into the background. "At some point it felt like I was reading a book and not a Kindle anymore." For some this happened quickly, while for others it required a longer adjustment period. "If you stay reading on it long enough you forget it's a Kindle." One participant remarked that the transition was almost immediate, taking only "five seconds".'[162]

Notably, transition was partially dependent on genre: 'many agreed that immersion was less difficult when reading fiction'.[163]

This idea of an unobtrusive ideal interface echoes Beatrice Warde's analogy (specific to typography, but applicable to any other design choice in a printed book) of a 'crystal goblet', 'invisible' and the only suitable choice for the 'connoisseur'.[164] But it also speaks to an idea of the 'insides' of a book – framed as story, text, ideas, 'content', or otherwise – as being both separate from and elevated above the 'outsides' of a book – a conception I'll return to in Chapter 5.

Transported by Part of a Book

One participant's description of a Kindle as a 'world of stories'[165] both supports and challenges the idea of digital as an obstacle to overcome. The moment of transportation is not described by these participants as different from print, or the immersion in the narrative any less (or any more) satisfying, even if the journey to that moment was less satisfying in terms of the tactile experience. The question is whether the convenience, customisation, and 'intimacy'[166] of e-books, confirmed advantages for some participants, can hasten that moment. An argument could be made that an uninviting, functional interface could hasten transportation, as there is no reason to linger; this would present the beauty of and pleasure in handling a material book as a distraction in itself. However, no participants made that particular argument. Rather, those who described easy transportation with an e-reading device (when they achieved it at all) framed it as being as good for the purpose as print, not better. In 2008, very early Kindle users were (in Clark's focus groups) 'united in their opinion that. . .the print book functions as an inconspicuous container once the participant began reading'[167] and Amazon's publicly stated goal for Kindle design was to match, not exceed, print's capacity to 'disappear', and for the Kindle to 'get out of the way, just like a physical book, so readers could become engrossed in the words'.[168] (If there is a wave of young readers growing up without skills for print, they have not yet arrived, and if my data on the greater enjoyment of and ease of reading in print among young adults is any indication, they are not arriving anytime soon.) Hayler argues that 'all technologies must begin as devices, novel solutions to particular problems. . .that might trend towards being technologies over time', with the 'fully technologised' codex enjoying a millennia-long head start; the trend, however, is neither inevitable nor one-way, and e-reading interfaces feel most present, and most frustrating, when they 'move back from the technological to the "devicive".[169] If so – or indeed if transportation via digital reading can be understood more simply as a skill acquired via practice – this could help explain the doubling of enjoyment of reading devices between 2014 and 2016, and points to potential further increases as experience with e-reading (and exposure to a greater range of e-reading platforms, each with their own advantages) takes more readers towards the 'inconspicuous container' stage. As one survey respondent put it, in 2017:

> 'Digital reading is very much something people need to get used to, need to learn and familiarise themselves with, just as print reading is. Often people expect the experience to be the same as print and hence they reject digital reading. We need to remember that it took us years as kids how to learn to read print. We need to expect to also have to learn how to read digitally.'
> (Survey 2017)

Utility as Realness: It Is What It 'Does'

The power of an e-book to transport a reader, to foster that state of immersion (even some of the time), forms a core argument for e-book realness. The way readers 'can get just as absorbed' and e-books 'convey ideas, tell stories, enhance perspectives and bring new worlds to life just as powerfully as physical books' were frequently cited reasons why an e-book is a real book: 'whether reading on a page or a screen, a book is a book. Its pages transport you'. The e-book's ability to effectively serve as a gateway to a 'world of stories' was the decisive factor: 'reading from an e-book or listening to audio book gives you the same immersion into the story itself'. Respondents expressed bafflement as to how this could even be in question, 'not understanding,' one explained, 'how the medium in which [they're] enjoying a story is supposed to diminish its "storyness"—thus, 'to me, the electronic medium has no bearing on whether the book-...remains, in fact, a book.' If 'a book is a vehicle for the story' then a book is 'real whether in analog or in digital'; if 'books are about the story', and 'ebooks still share a story'; if 'you experience the same story through reading', then e-books are, ipso facto, real books. This framing foregrounds utility, both in Drucker's sense of 'what something *is* has to be understood in terms of what it *does*' [emphasis his],[170] and in the less complimentary sense of something like a utility belt or World War II–era utility clothing: valuable because useful, despite aesthetic shortcomings; perhaps 'not as pretty to look at', but that gets the job done. In the context of pleasure, that means a book that's real, not only because it's 'another way of transferring text' and 'anything you can read that communicates the information counts' but real also because it delivers the experience of transportation and immersion in a narrative world.

'Experience', however, is a word that cuts both ways: readers invoke it to grant realness or withhold it. If 'a book is about the words and the experience they give you' and 'a book is the experience you have while reading it', e-books can be classed as real because they offer 'still the same basic experience'; as one respondent put it, 'if I can get the same book, the same words, the same broad experience from both, why would I consider one "unreal"?' However, they can also be 'not the same experience but definitely still a real book': real because 'different experiences – but the same story'. But even respondents who answered 'yes' to the question of whether they consider e-books real books can use the word 'experience' to qualify, and specify how those e-books are real yet missing valued aspects. 'I used a Nook for several months', as one put it, 'and I don't feel like I really experienced those books I read as fully as I normally do.' Others explained that 'intellectually, yes: I know they're books in a different medium. But I do find the E-book reading experience qualitatively different. An E-book is less likely to lodge in my mind' and 'as far as content yes [an e-book is a real book]. But you can't browse the shelf and check the blurb in a kindle which removes much of the anticipatory pleasure.' Still useful, but not as useful; still readable, but with a 'loss of palpable pleasure'; 'they do light up your brain in a different way but they are still part of the reading experience.' Free-text answers return again and again to *removed, not as, loss, less*. The books are not defective, but not completely satisfying because they are not complete.

Sense of Achievement as Pleasure

Some respondents noted having a greater feeling of accomplishment from reading in print, like the previously quoted respondent who enjoyed the 'tactile feedback' of print for its value in 'taking note of [their] progress through the book'.[171] For some, print makes it 'easier to feel like you are making progress through weighty books', and, fascinatingly, 'printed books urge you to complete them', another instance of print experienced as demanding in positive as well as negative ways.[172] A common form for this feedback to take is the sensation of completed pages amassed on the left side of the book, 'first from turning pages, from dog-earing the corner to mark my place, and taking note of my progress through the book', a tangible and satisfying alternative to a situation they might actively 'hate': reading material that 'weighs the same, the whole time in both hands...

[they] like having "I've read this much, I've read this much...".[173] (Unfortunately for device designers, the wedge shape, pioneered in the NuvoMedia Rocket eBook and mimicked by the first-generation Kindle, and described by Jeff Bezos as 'a tapering...that emulates the bulge towards the book's binding', was static and hence useless in terms of pleasurable feelings of accomplishment.[174] However much Amazon intended to 'project an aura of *bookishness*' by stashing batteries to one side [emphasis his],[175] Bezos's storytelling does not explain why the wedge disappeared in Gen 2.)

As noted, print was for some participants easier to recall, either in terms of details of the text or simply in terms of having read a particular book: 'with e-books, I often have trouble retaining a memory of what I've read'.[176] And this gap appeared in explanations for why e-books were not real books, including 'it's harder to flip back to find earlier passages when you want to remind yourself about something which happened or was described earlier', and 'no somatic memory for pages/incidents/quotations' (again recalling findings on the importance of sensorimotor cues).[177] Much of this struggle to recall was linked, as with a feeling of accomplishment, to being able to see a particular title on the shelf (though this of course depends on owning and keeping the finished book, which so many respondents due to loans, house moves, collection culls, or being stranded away from book collections during COVID-19 lockdowns[178] could not do). Some respondents report that 'with e-books, I sometimes not only don't know the cover art, I can't even recall title' or that 'I would remember it more if I'd seen the physical copy'.[179] For others, however, digital was a better way to remember: '[e-reading] helps me keep track of what I've read/bought' or 'I track my reading (title and format) and in 2015, I read 55 books, of which 32 were e-books'.[180] But a number noted that they were completing books more quickly on screen: this was either a subjective feeling ('I seem to get through books more quickly when reading digitally')[181] or, thanks to active tracking, a quantifiable difference. Faster reading could be for some an achievement in itself. But reading more books was expressed as both a goal ('I can read more often digitally') and a confirmed attainment ('I must admit that since getting a Kindle as an unasked for birthday present, I've increased the number of books I complete per year by at *least* five times').[182] This impression of abundant reading is supported by general surveys over the past decade: people who read e-books also read more overall.[183] This could, as the earlier respondents suggest, be because they are reading faster on screen, or it could be as much or more a function of the 'wonderful' state where they 'never have to stop reading',[184] where digital reading (e-book and audio-book) has brought books into previously bookless spaces.

A dimension of immersion not specifically cited by respondents – tellingly so – is empathy. While some (but not all) describe a lack of connection to a text, or to an author, none mentioned a lack of connection to characters, or difficulty in empathising with the people or situations depicted. This kind of immersion, studied by researchers like Mangen and van der Weel, relies heavily on definitions of 'literary reading' as a unique activity with a unique utility in developing an individual's capacity for understanding of and sympathy with other points of view.[185] Quantification of potential benefits has proven challenging: enthusiasm for the widely cited 2013 Kidd and Castano study where experimental psychologists tested participants on their ability to identify emotional states based on expression in a series of photographs of faces, and found a statistically significant improvement after participants had read a sample of 'literary' fiction, and no such improvement after reading a sample of 'commercial' fiction, was sharply checked when their results could not be reproduced, despite attempts from multiple teams.[186] However, Dodell-Feder and Tamir's 2018 meta-analysis of studies does identify a significant, though small, positive correlation between fiction reading and perform-ance on certain social cognition tests (keeping in mind that they drew on data with either 'no reading' or 'non-fiction' as the comparison group, excluding data seeking to compare 'literary' and 'popular' fiction condi-tions).[187] This idea of engagement, where the reader is measurably elevated and improved by the experience, touches on both conceptions of reading as a means of self-improvement, an 'intellectually stimulating' pursuit,[188] and fiction as a means to this end, with 'literary' fiction providing a cognitive service that makes it measurably different from less serviceable 'non literary' fiction

Conclusion

These layered, varied, and often contradictory experiences of pleasure cast e-books as predominantly unreal things that nonetheless give real pleasure. The experience of pleasure is, as it must be, subjective. Individuals are under no obligation to feel pleasure consistently, or 'logically', and owe no explanations as they make their own trade-offs between forms of pleasure, or between pleasure and other outcomes. Aesthetic pleasure in the material object is, for these participants, something effectively exclusive to print, and tactile and sensory pleasure in handling the material object nearly so. That lack alone denies e-books realness in this dimension.

However, other forms of pleasure are preserved or even heightened with digital reading. The 'backup book' relieves 'abibliophobia' and eases fears of being caught bookless precisely because, in this light, the e-book is a book: potentially an austere and impoverished book, the literary equivalent of freeze-dried emergency rations, but still a nourishing and capable of sustaining (reading) life. While ceremonies of approaching literature on its terms (going to libraries and traditional bookstores, setting aside times and places for reading in print, etc.) are often lost, interacting with literature on one's own terms, choosing the available, adaptable, accommodating book (overcoming limitations imposed by disability or health concerns, summoning reading to oneself instantly and without travel, reshaping reading technologies to avoid conflict with work and caring commitments) fosters a new kind of intimacy, and carves new spaces for reading in participants' lives – for those who enjoy high status and ample resources and those who do not. The alignment of pleasure in the material object with 'experience' values in the case of print and a more complex mix of 'convenience' and 'experience' values in the case of digital underscores the fact that print and digital pleasure are not mirror images, and the degree to which 'convenience' is not a trivial consideration but a pleasure in its own right, embracing satisfactions that include those of agency and self-determination. Ultimately, pleasures such as immersion and sense of achievement appear to be impeded by digital for some readers but not for others, and for some even facilitated. There is some evidence that enjoyment from novels and other forms of fiction is less likely to be impeded than with other types of e-book. This frames the unrealness of e-books as most often incompleteness, casting the e-book as part of a book, but specifically the most important part: as the text or content or story. For some participants, this part is something that cannot thrive on its own, and the text/content/story is less satisfying or effectively inaccessible when separated from the physical print object. For others, it is something that can stand alone, meaning that the incomplete book can deliver important, perhaps the most important, reading pleasures just as well as print. This vision of the e-book as an incomplete book sits alongside other visions (of the e-book as *ersatz book*, and the e-book as digital proxy) as readers consider what digital books mean to them as bookish people: a topic for Chapter 5, on reading lives and reading identities.

CHAPTER 5

Reading Lives and Reading Identities
Genre, Audience, and Being a Reader of E-books

'Books mark important moments in life. Just looking at the spines brings back memories. That's why I keep books.'

(Survey 7)

'[E-books aren't real books] Because I feel a "real book"...can be passed on and shared, looked at and admired.'

(Survey 2022)

The laptop is shut; the app closed; the e-ink screen blurs and resolves into its latest placeholder image (perhaps a fountain pen or stack of battered leather tomes, or, if one has a lower cost 'With Ads' Kindle, a pitch for a toaster). What comes next? What role do e-books play in the formation and expression of readers' self-image and public image? And how can a reader's self-image and public image shape their use of and attitudes towards e-books? Previous chapters have examined the ways in which e-books are real or unreal, and useful or not useful, in terms of ownership, trust, and pleasure; these intermingling roles of e-books as real books, *ersatz books*, digital proxies for books, and incomplete books come together as we consider how readers reconcile book-love and bookish identity with use (or rejection) of artefacts when they function as near-books, stand-ins for books, or dismembered parts of books. This chapter brings the reader's journey full circle, investigating how finished e-books are shared or not shared, displayed or not displayed, and made a cherished part of the reader's personal history or barred from such status. It examines aspects of display, cultural capital, and sharing (both conscious and 'frictionless')[1] in forms specific to digital and forms specific to print. It investigates how stereotypes (of some readers as unqualified and some reading practices and communities as inferior) and assumptions (regarding the reading behaviour of low-status audiences and e-book readers as a whole) can interact with and further entrench existing narratives, including narratives of literary decline, technology as a threat to culture, and women as incompetent readers in need of professional and/or masculine guidance. It further examines how the bookish groups taking part in this study policed or did not police orthodoxy on bookish positions (such as pleasure in the material object of the print book) and considers how changing attitudes towards print privacy signal the emergence of concern for intellectual privacy as a bookish value in its own right. Finally, it examines e-book realness through the lens of love. It investigates readers' experiences of powerful emotion and digital reading, including how previously discussed dimensions of control, trust, pleasure, and identity intersect for those novels that attain special status and with which a given reader establishes a meaningful and lasting relationship. It explores love for reading devices as well as love for print, how love for books and book-related activity does and does not equate with identity as a bibliophile (or as a technophile), and what it means to feel real emotions for an e-book that is only sometimes real.

Reconciling Bookish Identity with Reading of Low-Status Books

As discussed in Chapter 2, from a consumer perspective, e-books do not enjoy equal status with print. While there is no certainty that this will remain the case, for now the reputation issues of digital-only and self-publishing – categories that only include some e-books, but the stigma of which affects all e-books – casts them as lower investment products that may or may not have been approved by traditional gatekeepers. The large proportion of book readers who read digitally are hence aligned, at least some of the time, with lower status books.[2] They must incorporate readership of lower status or ambiguous-status books into their public and private reading personas and contend with entrenched narratives of 'print vs digital' as they negotiate their readerly identity. The lower status of digital, however, is also due to its association with lower status audiences.

Influence of (Perceived) Audience on Book Status

Books, like other artistic works, are defined not only by the intentions (or background) of their creators but also by their audiences.[3] Bourdieu finds that 'there are few fields (other than the field of power itself) in which the antagonism between the occupants of the polar positions is more total' than for literature, amplifying the impact of association with an 'intellectual', 'bourgeois', or 'mass' audience.[4] The 'negative relationship...established between symbolic and economic profit, whereby *discredit* increases as the audience grows and its specific competence declines, together with the value of the recognition implied in the act of consumption'[5] [emphasis his] devalues any work appreciated by a mass audience. Damage caused by their appreciation can be, to a degree, counterbalanced by critical approval and simultaneous attention from high-status 'intellectual' audiences, but not cancelled out. Within this exceptionally polarised literary field, the novel ranges across a wider territory than drama or poetry, offering a great number of possible locations along axes of size of audience and degree of consecration.[6] With many consumers, but also many producers (not limited as, say, late twentieth-century French drama was limited by the number of Parisian theatres) and low unit price (compared with, say, paintings), and much profit and critical attention to distribute between works, the outcomes for any particular novel are volatile; identification with a particular audience has the power to move that work nearly to the poles of either axis (and hence to any corner of a legitimacy grid). Digital-era measures of esteem can make the relationship between wider audience and lower prestige even more visible, and to the general public as well as literary insiders: for example, Kovács and Sharkey's analysis of Goodreads star ratings of novels before and after major awards found that winners tended to experience, in addition to the expected spike in sales, a drop in average star rating, while shortlisted books saw a more modest increase in sales and no obvious drop in star rating.[7]

Bourdieu presents this as an essentially irreducible problem: the novelist needs a mass readership if there is to be any possibility of making a living wage,[8] but growth of an audience lacking in 'competence' leads to increase of discredit. Later theorists have noted how problematic a binary opposition between prestige and wide readership can be for interpreting contemporary literary fields, proposing a more nuanced approach that recognises the role of audience while respecting the significance of other factors. Squires notes that 'the value-laden nature of this principle too quickly suggests a delineation of the field into markets for mass and elite audiences, as Q. R. Leavis's does', and goes on to demonstrate in *Marketing Literature* how factors including literary awards make it impossible to so directly couple status with audience size in twenty-first-century Britain.[9] English performs similar work on the American literary field in *The Economy of Prestige*, emphasising the role of 'journalistic capital' as a third force interacting with economic and cultural capital and challenging the idea of a direct trade-off between the economic and cultural.[10] But any increase in discredit due to changing readership depends on the visibility of the 'competent' portion of the audience in proportion to the 'incompetent' portion: if the incompetent, low-status readers were somehow concealed, their 'loving a book in public'[11] made less public, the author could in theory accumulate economic profit without risking discredit. (Raising the possibility that authors such as Jonathan Franzen, eager for an Oprah's Book Club sales boost but frightened that association with female readers and feminised reading institutions would drive away male readers,[12] can now enjoy income from female readers without being seen with those readers in public.)

This concealment of audience is in fact under way. The generic exterior of the e-book is not so much a veil of discretion as a blank canvas, a space onto which observers can project their ideas of what 'that kind of person'[13] would be reading. In the absence of data, stereotypes can rush in to any gap, and lower status readers contend with automatic assumptions that they are reading lower status books.

E-book Privacy: Reading a Book Without Showing Its Cover

With highbrow material a source of cultural capital, and low- or middlebrow material a source of discredit, readers are justifiably concerned about what image their reading choices might project. The question is whether this feeling affects reading choices, and if so what role digital reading might play.

The perception that individuals choose e-books for furtive reading is widespread and longstanding; an 'opinion piece cliché'.[14] Data on furtive reading, however, is almost absent. A Royal National Institute of Blind People (RNIB) survey from 2013 (based on responses from general readers, not only readers with sight loss) found that 64% 'admitted feeling embarrassed about reading certain types of books'.[15] It represents a very rare instance of an actual survey on 'embarrassing' screen reading (even if a brief one, disseminated via press release) and even there the key question is framed as a hypothetical. The RNIB survey reported that 'less than one quarter of e-book readers (23%) said that they were more likely to read an "embarrassing" book electronically as no one would know about it'.[16] My survey, asking about actual rather than hypothetical reading choices, found an even smaller proportion in agreement. 'Better for privacy – no one can see what I'm reading' is a real but rare motivator, a factor for only 6.5% e-book readers. Agreement did not vary significantly by year (though it sagged slightly during pandemic lockdowns, to 4.4% in 2020 and 4.2% in 2021, possibly because of the frequently mentioned loss of commute reading, and fewer opportunities to read in public settings in general). Women were most likely to agree.[17] However, more important than

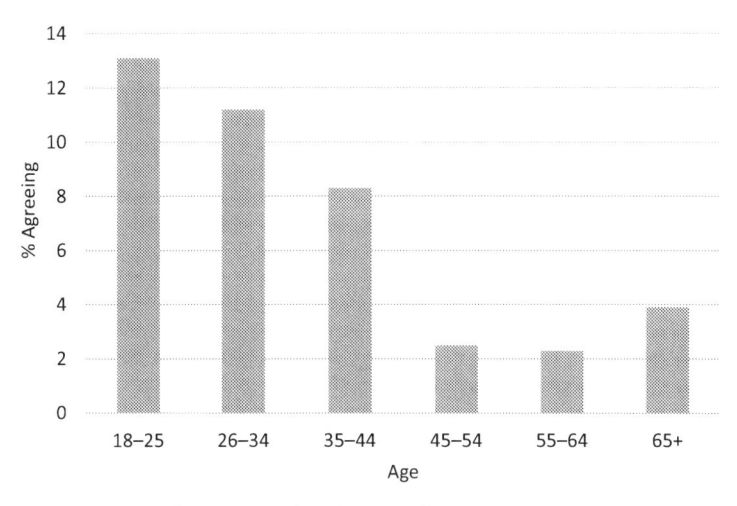

Figure 5.1   Reasons for choosing digital: 'better for privacy – no one can see what I'm reading', by age.

gender is age.[18] Respondents younger than 35 were more than twice as likely to agree (12.0%) as respondents 35 and older (4.7%), with the highest level of concern among those 18–25 (13.1%) (Figure 5.1).

A desire for this form of privacy emerges as a rare concern, and one disproportionately shared by young women. (Only one survey respondent – young and female – used the free-text boxes to describe secretive reading, and that individual did not mention genre: 'plus I don't want people to see what I am reading').[19] These digital privacy-valuing readers appear otherwise largely ordinary in their reading behaviour. They are typical in their sources of print books, no more likely to read novels or any other genre of e book, and there were no meaningful links with reading device (including the Kindle, confidently cited by journalists as the device of choice for furtive reading).[20] They are slightly more likely to obtain e-books from the unusual source of chain bookshops. But when it comes to e-books from Amazon, a potential pattern emerges. Between 2014 and 2017, when Amazon purchases and loans are grouped together, there is no connection. But between 2020 and 2022, when I asked separately about e-book loans, those who value e-book privacy are no more likely to buy from Amazon, but slightly more likely to borrow from Kindle Unlimited/Prime Reading (42.3% vs 21.1% of others) (though no more likely to borrow from a non-Amazon service such as Scribd). The connections to other digital motivators of 'cheaper/better value' (63.9% vs 42.8%), 'better selection' (18.1% vs 3.8%), and 'the books I want aren't always available in print' (49.4% vs 22.5%) (though this limitation that would not apply to mainstream romance or even mainstream erotica of the *Fifty Shades of Grey* moiety, these genres being widely stocked in bookshops, supermarkets, and public libraries) further suggest that Kindle Unlimited might be particularly appealing to this group both for digital-only offerings, exemplified by the prototypical Kindle Direct Publishing (KDP) self-published novel, and for the all-you-can-read monthly price. This raises the possibility that the readers most concerned about reading without public scrutiny – or judgement – are more active consumers of the genres most closely associated with Kindle Unlimited, including self- or Amazon-published[21] romance.[22] (Though intriguingly, not to a degree that would lead to unusually active use of Kindles, or Kindle apps on tablet or smartphone.) However, the lack of connection to choosing digital because it is faster or easier to obtain does not support any special link with chain reading. Obtaining books for chain reading, where after finishing one book in a series one immediately starts the next, was noted by several participants as a reason to read digital, and one theory as to the success of romance fiction in digital form has been that romance novels lend themselves to this kind of one-after-another 'binge reading'.[23]

In gathering empirical data on a widely shared but previously untested belief, this study emphatically challenges conventional wisdom on the topic and calls into question theories based on an assumption of widespread furtive reading (and assumptions as to who those furtive readers might be). The question is whether this small population of readers is drawn to digital for freedom from scrutiny, or driven to it. The reasons why young women might be especially sensitive to scrutiny of their reading have roots in the long history of anxiety over private reading and focus of that anxiety on women's reading.

Enduring Stigmas: Women as 'Incompetent' Readers

The strong connection between e-reading and novel reading would by itself link e-books to women readers. The novel has been associated with women readers since its inception: not only as a genre shaped to accommodate the requirements (or what were assumed to be the requirements) of female customers but also one that developed in tandem with mass female readership and conceptions of female readership, and even tasked, to a greater degree than other literary forms, with defining what a modern woman could and should be.[24] 'By the middle of the 19th century...the novel was already known as a female form of writing', and 'throughout the [Victorian and Edwardian] period novels were at the centre of discussions concerning women and reading'.[25] But e-books, associated with lower status texts, are also associated with female readership because of the persistently lower status of women readers, 'women's genres', and women's reading practices.

Most readers are women, and women, on average, read more books than men,[26] but women do not enjoy equal status as readers or occupy most positions of power and influence in the literary world. The 'woman reader' is a figure identified as both different (an essential point in separating out women's reading as both atypical and in need of anxious examination) and inferior for millennia.[27] 'Men have historically been associated with elite culture, while women have been linked with more commercial forms'[28] and women's mass participation, with reading and with the novel in particular, has led not to full participation in the elite but rather a sectioning-off of literary culture, where women (and the books they read, the books they write, the literary institutions they patronise, etc.) are corralled into lower status zones. Though the majority of publishing professionals are now women, the majority of senior positions are still held by men,[29] and the majority, sometimes the overwhelming majority, of both book reviewers and authors reviewed in elite literary magazines and journals are male.[30] In library and records management, the UK workforce is approximately gender-balanced (in contrast to the global workforce, where four out of five librarians are women), but men have higher average pay and are nearly twice as likely to hold senior management positions.[31] At present, 'the literary field that fosters modernist fiction gendered male has its related mother-field, the field of mass-market books, in which middlebrow women readers exert power'.[32] Driscoll defines the literary middlebrow as 'a broad phenomenon...allowing for different registers and formations' that nonetheless can be tracked by a 'family resemblance' where all middlebrow institutions share most of a set of eight features: middle class, reverential, entrepreneurial, mediated, emotional, recreational, earnest, and, crucially for digital reading, feminised.[33] Humble explains that 'texts move in and out of bounds [of the middlebrow] depending on who is perceived to be reading them', and popular success demotes a book down the highbrow-middlebrow-lowbrow axis, the more dramatic the success and the more populist the venue, the more severe the damage; 'selection as a "Book of the Month" by a newspaper would inevitably push a book into the middlebrow category, as, often, would "bestseller" status...indeed, there is much evidence to suggest that…a predominantly female readership very often automatically consigned a text to the category of middlebrow'.[34]

E-books are also associated with women because of the prominence of women as creators in modern self-publishing. Though there are few reliable statistics for self-publishing, several studies indicate that the majority of self-published authors, both for Amazon's KDP and similar models and for free sources such as Wattpad, are likely female.[35] Just as the texts they produce are held at arm's length, only sporadically granted the designation of 'book', the writers are frequently fenced off from the designation of 'author'.[36]

'Guilty Pleasures'

A major factor in perceptions of women's digital reading as furtive consumption of 'guilty pleasures'[37] is the status of romance fiction, particularly stereotypes of voracious and exclusive readers of popular fiction caricatured as 'undiscriminating, without judgement, a passive consumer gulping down rubbish by the gallon'[38] while ignoring more nutritious fare.[39] Romance is a major category in both print and digital formats[40] and a genre with a unique publication history.[41] Its complexities make it a zone of disagreement and debate among literary scholars,[42] but three points of agreement are its importance to the publishing industry, its association with female readers, and its low status. While the idea that this one genre is somehow uniquely lacking in worth, inherently less valuable than any other form of popular fiction, is ludicrous, this is a charge levelled at romance and an image with which readers must contend. While it is reasonable to investigate whether privacy (rather than, say, lower price, speed of access, or availability of digital-original titles) is a primary reason for the genre's success on screen, it is not reasonable to skip the investigation and assume that correlation is causation, leading to 'train commuters reading spicy novels on iPhone but crime stories in paperback'.[43] This assumption was visible in focus groups. Privacy of this kind was rarely mentioned, but when it was the furtive reading was instantly associated with 'women's genres' of erotica and romance. One participant, a student pursuing her master's degree in publishing (who did not read romance herself or choose digital for reasons of privacy), knew about digital romance sales figures and leapt to the conclusion that the cause was romance readers' desire for privacy.

> 'The success of Mills and Boon in digital form, certainly [comes from the choice to access 'light reading' digitally] particularly if people are embarrassed to read it. People no longer have to buy book covers, which was a thing that they would

> *use that was actually sold because you can just hide whatever dodgy novel you're reading by reading on a Kindle.'* (FG 4 participant 4)

Only one (female) individual in any focus group or interview described privacy of this kind as important to her personally; she was one of only two respondents who spoke about reading romance novels. She was teased by a (male) fellow participant.

> P1: *'And then there are some books I might not necessarily want people to see that I'm reading. For example, some romance books. There's an author I quite like called Shelley Lawrence; she writes kind of like the romance thing and the covers are always quite sort of, of, like, I don't know...'*
> P2: *'[laughing] Do they have shirtless men?'*
> P1: *'[sounding nettled] No, not necessarily. [laughter from other participants] Well, it depends, because they have different versions, now, of [covers]. It's just, you can more easily hide what you're reading on a Kindle.'* (All FG 2)

Later, when the same respondent (P1) was discussing the experience of strangers striking up a conversation with her regarding the print copy of an Orwell classic she was reading in public, the other participant (P2) continued to tease her: 'secretly, you had the romance tucked under it!', making it clear that her earlier statement had been noted as a meaningful admission (or confession) and was neither forgotten nor forgiven.

This display of teasing (in this instance, it was between coursemates and appeared to be done, and accepted, in a generally good-natured spirit) also demonstrates the next step of the folk wisdom that women habitually conceal taboo reading: that whenever a woman's reading can't be seen or verified, it is assumed that the reading is taboo. This assumption is prominent in the discussion even in the face of immediate reminders (including, in this case, shortly beforehand in the same conversation, 'I read a lot of classics on the Kindle, 'cause you can get them for free' that female as well as male e-book readers frequently choose classics, in part because so many are available for 'free of charge' on Amazon and via Project Gutenberg).[44] There is explicit recognition that because anonymous e-book reading means sacrificing cultural capital attached to public reading of prestigious titles, readers are discouraged from accessing such titles on screen.

> *'...a lot of it is genre and romance that people don't necessarily want to be seen reading on the Tube [exasperated, sarcastic 'yeah' in background, from Participant 1, the previously teased romance-reading participant], I also think*

there's a kind of corollary to that, which is that if it's literary fiction or a classic, everyone almost does deliberately want to be seen reading it.' (FG 2 respondent 2)

Romance was unique in these focus groups as the only genre singled out for ridicule and derision. The respondent teased earlier for her romance reading had elsewhere in the conversation noted that she reads (in addition to high-status classics and literary fiction) fan fiction, young adult (YA), science fiction, and fantasy. None of this reading attracted jeers. (In focus group 1, one reader, participant 4, was tentative and apologetic in discussing Harry Potter fan fiction that she had read, but no one in the group picked up on this as embarrassing or even noteworthy.)[45] In focus group 6, participant 4, the only other participant who openly discussed reading romance, did not wait for it to be criticised by the group but instead criticised it herself: 'don't [read romance, as she does]. You shouldn't, it's all garbage [General laughter]'.

Fifty Shades: The Only E-book Published in the Twenty-first Century

More than a decade after its release, *Fifty Shades of Grey* remains embedded at the centre of debates on digital reading privacy. In studying commentary on the topic, I have encountered virtually no journalism published since 2012 on the trope of Kindles used for furtive reading that did not mention this series: journalism on any aspect of digital reading is, in fact, highly likely to mention it. There are reasons for its prominence in these debates. It was unquestionably a publishing phenomenon: even the least prominent books in the series were bestsellers[46] and the series as a whole was a fixture (not to say fixation) of early twenty-first-century cultural conversation, invoked in discussions that range far beyond books and publishing. Its colourful origin story (e.g. a work of fan fiction that stunned industry insiders and made its author fabulously wealthy) is exciting and widely known, and easily invoked by commentators to support a wide variety of arguments, from women's empowerment to women's triviality to a new cultural frankness to imminent cultural collapse. And the theory that its success is bound up with secretive digital reading was raised early by a woman with an insider's knowledge and perspective: James's agent, Valerie Hoskins, told *The New York Times* in 2012 that 'one of the things about this is that in the 21st century, women have the ability to read this kind of material without anybody knowing what they're reading, because they can read them on their iPads and Kindles'.[47] Nicolas Carr goes further, concluding that benevolent supervision had, pre-Kindle, protected the publishing industry and the culture from the likes of *Fifty Shades of Grey*: 'We may even be a little embarrassed to be seen reading them, which makes anonymous digital versions all the more appealing. The "Fifty Shades of Grey" phenomenon probably wouldn't have happened if e-books didn't exist.'[48] His hypothesis curiously overlooks *Fifty Shades'* parallel success in print; as Colbjørnsen observes,[49] the mega-selling paperbacks sold in a plethora of formats, sporting a wide array of cover designs, all of them visible to the naked eye. The series' overwhelming presence dominates and skews discussion of digital reading, but most particularly women's digital reading, and similarly skews perceptions of what is 'typical' screen reading and what the motivations of a typical e-novel reader (at least a female e-novel reader) might be.

Fifty Shades of Grey bears almost every possible stigma in terms of literary legitimacy. It is genre fiction, and a hybrid of two of the most derided forms, erotica and romance. It began as a piece of fan fiction. It was originally self-published, and in digital-original form. It was written by a woman for a female audience. It is not generally regarded as well-written.[50] (In its defence, Archer and Jockers marshal machine learning data to argue that while the line-by-line prose may be awkward, the first novel in the series is, in fact, expertly paced.)[51] And, as noted earlier, it is a bestseller of historic proportions, which according to Bourdieu would by itself accrue historic levels of discredit.

No one in the interviews or the free-text boxes of the survey mentioned *Fifty Shades of Grey*, but it was mentioned (not raised by the facilitator, but by participants) in half of the focus groups. Focus group participants were aware of the *Fifty Shades of Grey* assumptions as something widely shared in the media, but notably did not express agreement: it was couched as something 'they' said and thought (a hallmark of reputation as meta-belief).[52]

> 'That's one of the things **they said** Fifty Shades *benefitted from, wasn't it? That people could read it without anyone knowing they were reading it. (Laughs)'.* (FG 3 participant 3)

> 'It's one of the reasons **they thought** so many copies of Fifty Shades of Grey *was sold, because people could read it anonymously and no one would know.'* (FG 5 participant 5)

It is interesting that both participants quoted earlier (one male and one female) said 'people' rather than 'women', whereas James's agent spoke specifically of women. While the success of the series is attributed to (and resulting damage to literature blamed on) women, it is acknowledged that men do sometimes read it; to avoid censure, they must ensure that their interest is perceived as critical or academic, not personal. (Charles McGrath, author, past *New Yorker* fiction editor and *New York Times* book review editor, and confirmed member of the literary establishment, laughed at himself for hiding his childhood copy of *Little Women* behind a homemade brown paper wrapper, but still takes pains to make clear that his and his friends' Kindle reading of *Fifty Shades of Grey* was for professional reasons.)[53] If they are suspected of enjoying such books, sharing such tastes (feminine, juvenile, or both), mockery can be harsh and enduring, as with a participant deriding her father: 'he's got the taste of a teenage girl. He actually, like, legitimately likes *Twilight*, and I'm still judging him for it many years later'.[54]

While journalism on 'Kindle smut' frequently features headlines about guilt and shame (e.g. 'A cover-up! Guilty secret we hide in our Kindles' or 'Ebook readers' guilty pleasures revealed'), interviewees the articles quote often tell more complex stories about public mockery and the variety of possible responses to it.[55] Sarah Wendell, author and co-creator of the romance website *Smart Bitches, Trashy Books* (www.smartbitchestrashybooks .com) agrees that concealment is a major factor for digital sales of romance and erotica because 'women get enough commentary when they check out at a bookstore with romance novels. The commentary when you go to buy an erotic novel is even worse, so if you have the safety of doing it anonymously online, you take it', but she herself 'no longer cares what people think of her reading habits' and while fellow commuters still regularly bother her, they do so at their own risk.[56] An anonymous reader recounted a story of moving to digital reading after being teased on a plane: 'but I was like, gosh, never again can I be out in public with these books with questionable titles and creepy people on the front all draped over each other'.[57] These are not stories of 'guilty secrets' or 'guilty pleasures' so much as stories of anticipation of and pragmatic response to pestering. In general, what readers are describing as their own experience of furtive reading is embarrassment, with shame reserved for much more specific book-related transgressions.

Embarrassment versus Shame

Any specific mention of shame by participants is noteworthy, all the more so as shame is a cultural preoccupation and recent fixture of the bestseller lists,[58] whether filed in the Self-Help section with John Bradshaw or Humour with Jon Ronson. While older participants in my study came of age in a time when, in the US and the UK, shame was discussed as a valuable means of managing behaviour,[59] current debates are shaped more by Gilligan's hugely influential theories of shame as unproductive and profoundly damaging to the individual and society.[60] Philosophers, psychologists, anthropologists, sociologists, historians of emotion, and researchers and clinicians from other disciplines distinguish between embarrassment, guilt, and shame in different ways (some describe embarrassment as a lesser version of shame, some as a distinct but related emotion), but there are areas of intersection. One is that they are not equally painful: embarrassment is less intense, an emotion suited to a relatively minor transgression, or simply to being caught doing in public something normally done in private (it is not for nothing that the reader of popular fiction is 'imagined as. . .virtually masturbatory').[61] Another is that they have different relationships to outside judgement: while shame may be either public or private, embarrassment typically requires an audience. Shame researcher Brené Brown (whose bestselling popular books and famous TED talk, at 61 million views one of the most-watched in the organisation's history, have made her an extraordinarily prominent academic)[62] has popularised a definition of shame as 'an intensely painful feeling or experience of believing we are flawed and therefore unworthy of acceptance or belonging', quite distinct from guilt, 'a feeling that results from behaving in a flawed or bad way rather than flawed or bad self'.[63]

Participants in my study rarely use the words shame, guilt, or embarrassment. Quantifying the mentions reveals how infrequently they appear in these readers' conversations about e-reading, in sharp contrast to the frequency with which they appear in journalists' coverage of e-reading. The few instances where they use the word 'shame' suggest that they do, in fact, subscribe to the above-mentioned concepts of shame hierarchy (where shame is more serious than embarrassment) and the importance of observation. In this set of qualitative data, personal shame is mentioned only twice: one participant described 'shamefully' buying high-quality books but giving them as gifts instead of reading them herself, and another reported that she 'dropped Salman Rushdie in the bath and I've never been so ashamed in my life' (this experience of shame, interestingly, came from the same participant who described romance novels as merely 'embarrassing').[64] There were three mentions of guilt: avoiding it by buying books one wanted to annotate electronically, as one can mark up an e-book 'without guilt' (this relates, like one shame example, to remorse over mistreating a print book), proudly rejecting it for the non-crime of excessive book buying ('I buy far more books than I read and I have no guilt'), and of other people's lowbrow reading as 'guilty pleasures'.[65] Embarrassment is mentioned twice: once, as mentioned earlier, in describing romance novels as embarrassing books, and second, in describing Amazon's dynamic estimated reading time, where glancing away from the page means being branded a slow reader, an 'embarrassing' identity imposed (unfairly) by a 'judgmental' Amazon[66] (this instance of resented surveillance, and the problem of Amazon, is one I'll discuss further in the context of intellectual privacy). These six are the only examples, but they do together suggest meaningful distinctions. Shame was experienced, and came from ruining a print book and from failing to read a book one has bought, but was not attributed to others. Guilt was experienced, from marking up a print book (or rather, avoided by not marking up a print book), and was attributed to others for 'guilty pleasure' reading. Embarrassment was experienced, from being labelled a slow reader by Amazon, and attributed to others for being seen to read a romance novel in public (not, notably, for reading romance, but for being seen with it; readers do not have to agree that their reading is shameful to know that they are likely to be attacked for it). Shame was reserved for damaging or neglecting books. Embarrassment was specific to being caught looking unbookish in public.

E-books and e-novels in this way function as parts of books: the text without publicly visible paratext. E-novels are in that sense precisely what the book-shamed reader quoted earlier wanted: the romance novels she liked to read without the lurid, 'creepy' covers she neither liked nor wanted to be seen with, and indeed the reading experience without the public shaming experience. This represents, in one sense, freedom: the ability to read in public without being harangued by strangers. In theory, this might also, should the reading be low-status, evade discredit. However, stereotypes and tropes of Kindle reading as a tool for furtive readers may invite observers to assume that all her anonymous reading is low-status: that she only reads digitally because her reading is 'embarrassing' (activating eighteenth- and nineteenth-century ideas of private reading as dangerous, with female readers in particular restrained only by fear of censure, and reaching for the trash and smut the moment their benevolent supervisors' backs are turned). If so, her choice of reading digitally does not evade discredit, it invites it; the price of digital reading is not only opportunity cost, cultural capital lost when her high-status reading (as with free classics) is concealed but also a default assumption that any e-book – if it is read by a woman – is *Fifty Shades of Grey* or something like it.

Narrative of Literature in Opposition to Technology

Statements about the virtues or dangers of screen reading are 'position-takings', statements that may express liking or dislike but also declare alliance (with a philosophy, group of actors, etc.) in the struggle to define a cultural field.[67] Position-taking on the issue of digital reading began long before mass e-reading, and, in the form of suspicion regarding technology, before the emergence of the e-book.

Narratives of technology as the enemy of literature, or of reading, predate digital reading and take a variety of forms. (Flint notes that Victorians also considered themselves time-poor and bedevilled by technology, distracted from reading by 'loosely defined "tendencies of the age"'.)[68] Bob Brown's *The Readies*, expanding on ideas first explored in a modernist literary magazine in 1930,[69] described print reading as 'old-fashioned, frumpish, beskirted', and promised that his new machine would free writing 'bottled up in books' and allow literature to advance into the twentieth century.[70] In 1913, Thomas Edison pronounced that books would 'soon be' obsolete; in 1966, Marshall McLuhan pronounced them obsolete already.[71] Sven Birkert's *The Gutenberg Elegies* has proven an extremely influential text in the late twentieth-/early twenty-first-century debates on screen reading, widely reviewed on its release and cited by hundreds of scholars and commentators from almost the moment of its publication[72] to the present day, admiringly[73] and less so.[74] First published in 1994, it refers to digital reading, when it does refer to it, in the sense of hypertext fiction that must be 'booted up' on a 'terminal' in the writing room of a friend who is 'a convert to the sorcery of the microchip'.[75] Rooted in twentieth-century debates on competition between media, it situates reading in opposition to an 'electronic culture'[76] where the anti-literary distractions come from 'music, TV, and videos' emerging from radios, Sony Walkmans, and television sets, not the not-yet-mainstream internet or digital culture as fostered by the Web (which had been invented only five years before). It presents technology in any form more modern than moveable type as antagonistic to 'slowing down enough to concentrate on prose of any density' or literary production; even composing on an IBM Selectric electric typewriter instead of a personal computer is seen as a (deeply contradictory) statement of alliance to heritage forms.[77]

Technology companies' statements about how their products and services would disrupt information exchange landed on fertile ground. The territory was primed by exhaustive debate in literary circles. 'In the early stages of thinking about bookishness,' Pressman 'considered writing a history of "the death of the book" genre, focussing on rhetorical practices and assumptions', so vast was the material for analysis – and so revealing as to the values of the combatants.[78] 'Discourse of resistance surrounding e-reading,' as Hayler observes, 'reflects a rhetorical attitude that is repeatedly played out in the history of the introduction of new technologies'.[79] Colourful insults reducing print books to squid remnants defacing tree and cow remnants[80] may have been intended as playful or provocative (the tendency to whimsical overstatement certainly suggests that the goal was attention, not sober discussion), but such insults were quoted and requoted and requoted again, helping to shape an idea of debates on e-reading as a battle between 'gloomy bibliophiles and triumphant technophiles'.[81] As historian of technology Mar Hicks reminds us, 'narratives focussed on progress or "revolution"', while not necessarily accurate or offering much explanatory value, are ubiquitous in computing.[82] Any romantic attachment on the part of the gloomy bibliophiles to heritage, to preservation-heroes and narratives of decline and loss, has a counterpart in romantic attachment on the part of triumphant technophiles to innovation, to disruption-heroes and 'sociotechnical progress narratives',[83] and all of these narratives rely on conflict, villains, and the drawing of sides. Jeff Bezos did in 2007 assure shareholders of Amazon's essential bookishness,[84] citing as evidence those aspects of Kindle design that emulated print reading.[85] But by the time of the Kindle launch, the idea of opposing teams, like the frequently 'hyperbolic' tone of the discussion,[86] was already well established. In my own focus groups, there are instances where readers are, in establishing their own credentials as readers and bookish people, acknowledging the existence of sides, before beginning the slow and difficult process of determining which side they are on. Participants were often exasperated by what they described as excessive attention to the idea of sides, and by narratives of print in opposition to digital, and emphasised the importance of moving on (not ignoring the fact that in studying digital reading I am myself frequently drawing attention to differences between print and digital reading, and helping reinforce the idea of them as opposing forces; part of their exasperation is very justly with me).

> 'I wish there were fewer value judgements about the whole thing. I mean, fewer people saying... "I don't ever want to use e-books, I hope they plateau and die." Or people **on the other side** saying things like "oh, within ten years it's all going to go, all the print is going to go."' (FG 2 participant 2)

> 'We've **got to get away from this idea** that one [print or digital reading] is better than another...I think the important thing is to encourage the reading, and that's an end to it.' (Interview 2).

The question facing this group of committed readers is where a bookish person should sit: what attitudes towards digital reading are appropriate? It is fair to say that all would, if they were given the choice, be on the side of books; but they are not given that choice, the sides are not defined in that way. Instead, they are left to work out, on a conversation-by-conversation, purchase-by-purchase level, what opinions are approved (winning them inclusion in circles of other bookish people) and what choices are positive (supporting rather than harming books, reading, and literature). 'In our book-centered societies, the craft of reading signals our entrance into the ways of the tribe, with its particular codes and demands'[87] and weary as they might be with the idea of sides, awareness that there are sides is in itself a sign of sensitivity to the logic of the field and hence inclusion in the bookish group.

Choosing Sides

On many dimensions of reading we are prepared to disagree without rancour. On aspects such as genre choice, evaluation of specific titles (such as Becky Chambers's *A Long Way to a Small and Angry Planet*,[88] which some members of one focus group loved and others despised), importance of ownership, or attitudes towards book piracy, it proved possible for focus groups to air conflicting opinions without heated debate. An exception was appreciation of the material qualities of a print book. Groups could comfortably accommodate observations that hardcover books were in some cases too expensive for purchase, too bulky for storage, or too heavy for comfortable reading, as in this exchange in focus group 6:

P5: *'Oh, I dislike hardbacks.'*
P1: *'I never buy hardback.'*
P3: *'I love them.'*
P5: *'I actively dislike hardback. I wish things came out in paperback first, I would buy them.'*
P1: *'Me too.'*
P3: *'I like the hardbacks, for the good ones. You know they last longer.'*
P1: *'They're too big.'*
P5: *'They're unwieldy.'*
P3: *'I've destroyed...'*
P1: *'Big and heavy, compared to many paperbacks.'*
P5: *'They're like heavy and uncomfortable to hold.'*
P4: *'It really depends.'*
P4: *'That's why I like my Kindle.'*

This exchange is typical in the sense that reading is held up as the ultimate good, and materiality scepticism (and even expressing a liking for Kindles) is acceptable when avoidance of hardcovers is presented as a trade-off in pursuit of an even more important bookish goal. The hardcover enthusiasts may even come in for some gentle teasing over the lengths to which they will go to read heavy hardcover books in bed, propping themselves and their reading matter on carefully constructed edifices of pillows (FG 6 participant 5), or rolling over after each page to keep resting a book on its side (FG 6 participant 3).[89] Groups were less tolerant of any suggestion that hardcover books were not beautiful, or did not sit at a pinnacle of desirability such that any other choice of format must be guided by practical considerations. In this exchange from focus group 4, when one member of the group (participant 4) says that she dislikes hardcover books, she is challenged (her account of her experience dismissed as unreasonable) and corrected (told that if her personal reading habits make hardcover books inconvenient, that is her 'own fault').

> P4: *'Also, I don't buy hardbacks ever.'*
> P2: *'Really?'*
> P3: *'Really? . . .why?'*
> P4: *'I hate hardbacks! Because you drop them on your face and it hurts.'*
>   *(laughter)*
> . . .
> P2: *'No, I don't.'*
> P3: *' I have never done that.'*
> P4: *'I have dropped them on my face and that is painful.'*
> P3: *'Well, that's your own fault more than the book's.'*
> . . .
> P2: *'Then don't read like that.'*
> P4: *'They are bulkier and they just don't feel as nice to me.'*
> P2: *'They're so pretty!'*
> P4: *'I hate dust covers. Dust covers are the worst thing.'*
> P3: *'I take the dust cover off. . .'*

The recommended solution is to change how she reads, by holding books differently and removing dust covers rather than not buying books with dust covers in the first place. It is the very definition of the accommodating reader and the demanding book – along with a demanding, uncompromising bookish community.

Opinions about the smell of books were policed as fiercely. Extravagant declarations of love for book aromas, of the fresh-from-the-press ('new book smell never gets old') or years-on-the-shelf ('the smell of old paper is magic') variety, are a familiar means of expressing personal bookishness.[90] When, in focus group 1, one reader (participant 3) admitted to disliking the smell of new books ('they keep talking about smelling books and things, and I have never done that in my life'), the group reacted with incredulous disbelief, shouting 'what?!' and 'you haven't done that?' When the errant participant persisted, she was firmly corrected: told that her facts are wrong (that books do not have a 'strong, unpleasant smell of glue' as she believes) and commanded to educate herself: 'you should go into a bookshop!' This last is an extreme and telling rebuke, insisting that deviation from group norms can only be a sign of ignorance of, and inexperience with, books; in a stroke undercutting the dissenter's bookish credentials and entire bookish identity. Later, a different participant is taken to task for not agreeing that old books smell nice and are pleasant to hold. When she explains that she doesn't enjoy old books because 'you have no idea whose germs are on it!' she is laughed at, and instructed to stop being so silly.[91]

Again, the reader is instructed to adapt to accommodate the physical book: in this case not just to hold it differently, but to change her own habits, tastes, and beliefs. If a heavy hardcover is incompatible with reading in bed, she should stop reading in bed. If she dislikes an approved smell, she should train herself to love it instead. If she avoids 'germs' in every other instance, she should nonetheless make herself indifferent to germs when they appear on books. The rigidity on display here helps explain why for many readers time spent with an e-book that is expected to change itself to suit her, not vice versa, is so appealing (for more on enjoyment of the accommodating book, please see Chapter 4). When readers choose digital to escape such strictures – or judgement for non-compliance – they are treating e-books as part of books, specifically the parts of books that don't come with responsibilities and burdens.

Elusive Display

As noted, reading on screen means sacrificing the cultural capital that comes from public display of high-status literature. If reading on a dedicated device like a Kindle means that observers are likely to make assumptions about what one is reading (including the common assumption that a woman with a Kindle must be reading erotica or romance), when reading on a non-dedicated device like a smartphone, the sacrifice is not only display of a given book but display of reading at all: 'I'd have books on my phone and I'd read them while my wife was in the changing room at the mall or whatever. People think I'm texting but I'm just reading'.[92]

One of the advantages conferred by personal print libraries, and not matched by digital personal libraries, is of course display of one's collection. Reading is, to participants in my study and to the bookish circles they inhabit, both the foundation of and the window unto character: 'hence the persistence of the old saw "show me your book case, and I will tell you who you are"'.[93] (Such quotes are, for people who linger in bookshops and book sites, beyond truisms and into the realm of furnishings, metaphorical and literal: Heidegger's version, like Ruskin's precursor and Mauriac's development, adorns countless posters, wall stickers, screen backgrounds, mugs, scatter cushions, etc.) As US lawmakers put it in a Senate Report stressing the importance of reading and viewing privacy (a report inspired, pragmatically, by a burst of press interest in the video store rental records of politicians), 'the selection of books that we choose to read' is 'at the core of any definition of personhood. They reveal our likes and dislikes, our interests and our whims. They say a great deal about our dreams and ambitions, our fears and our hopes. They reflect our individuality, and they describe us as people'.[94] But 'reflect' and 'describe' are some distance from 'define'. That readers enjoy looking at each other's bookshelves, and wish there were an equivalent activity for e-books, is almost as omnipresent as the observation that readers enjoy the smell of books. To readers in my study, display of books is taken for granted, simply part of life, but as a representation of one's reading invariably suspect: when curated, too calculated to be truly revealing, when not curated too raw to judge.[95] Physical shelves can prompt 'discussion',[96] inspiring a social connection not about a single book, as in serendipitous public transport book conversations, but about one's entire collection (and, potentially, one's more rounded and complete book identity). As one put it, 'you have people over and they like, look at your bookshelf and they ask you about stuff. Whereas. . .I guess unless they're like looking at your Kindle or whatever that really can't come out'.[97]

The people I spoke to for this study overwhelmingly value books and reading, and display of books in any form tends to please them. As one put it, 'I like books. I'm suspicious of places without books in them'.[98] But participants in this study actually spoke much more often of a personal than a public view: how bookshelves (physical or virtual) looked to themselves as the owners, rather than how they might impress visitors. Many descriptions of books that 'look nice on the shelf' and 'make shelves look good' don't specify who is looking, the owner or a suitably impressed guest.[99]

The physical bookshelf, with print books that are 'easier to organise as you can put them on shelf and see very clearly', was specifically noted as a better way to access one's personal reading history, describing the visual review as effective in a way that a digital search was not. As one respondent put it, 'books mark important moments in life', and 'just looking at the spines brings back memories'.[100]

> *'Browsing a bookshelf is very different to browsing a screen. Owning a book [in print] allows you to browse your personal bookshelf easily letting the mood you are in select the book you wish to read.'* (Survey 2015)

> *'I have a large library of print books already, including many favorites, even though I find it easier to read on a Kindle. Sometimes I even buy the printed version of some thing I have read on the Kindle so that I can look at it on my shelf.'* (Survey 2022)

> *'It's random, but I find it harder to remember what books I have in e-book form. Like with my physical books, not only do I know all the books that I own, but I know them almost because of where they are. . .Like if I want to read Lord of the Rings again I know it's on that shelf over there somewhere.'* (FG 6 participant 4)

Digital displays were singled out by several as poorly designed and ineffective for finding the book one wanted, sometimes requiring shifts between different e-reading apps and devices.

> *'I also really don't like the way the library is organised on my e-reader, because I feel like I have to flip through multiple pages in order to find the book I'm looking for. And I'm like, "Is it even in this category? Maybe I didn't file it in this one. I don't know."'* (FG 6 participant 1)

> *'I have all the e-reader apps on my phone, because I find it much easier to search on the phone, "Oh, yes, I have got that one. It's that one." And then I can get the e-reader out and find it on that, because the e-reader is a little more fiddly to use and type on.'* (FG 6 participant 3)

Such displays can be equally inadequate for giving an overview of one's full collection and/or recent reading. For some readers, digital 'helps. . .keep track of what [they've] read/bought':[101] file lists aid in quantifying their reading. But others found that the screen display made it more difficult to recall what they had read recently. Despite options for sorting and searching e-book collections, what they 'do find difficult sometimes is to keep track of what [they've] actually got'.[102] Displays with excessively tiny cover images, or cover images detached from the e-book file, were a particular issue: 'I think the cover thing with that as well, in that I recognise the visual, what a book looks like, because of its cover, and I don't, I just have the title. It's harder to browse'.[103] Books can be effectively lost because without the identifying covers they are neither findable nor memorable.

> P2: *'In a physical copy because you see [the cover] every time you pick it up.'*
> P4: *'Yes, absolutely, whereas I couldn't tell you on the Kindle.'*
> P3: *'Quite often with an e-book, with the Kindle, I don't even know, can you see the cover?'* (FG 5)

Functionally invisible books lead to what was recognised as a common and vexing e-book problem: repurchasing. Interfaces were seen as working so poorly for recollection and display that many respondents recalled buying, or having clicked through to a sale page to buy, an e-book they already had. Without reminders from Amazon about past purchases, readers don't always realise they have it already: 'I'll sometimes be on Amazon looking at something that'll be recommended and I'll be like, "I think I've read that"' or 'I often get it when you get reviews, and say Amazon is giving this special offer and I'll be, "Oh, that looks like an interesting book, but, oh, it says I purchased this six months ago"'.[104]

> P7: *'Yes, or you can go back and add it. You know when you buy the same book and it says. . .'*
> P8: *'"You've already bought this."' [general laughter, recognition of a common situation]* (FG 5)

The endurance of e-books, where purchased and even borrowed e-books leave lasting traces of an Amazon profile, makes the ubiquity of repurchasing all the more startling. For these readers, the e-books are there but not there, in theory constantly accessible but in practice inaccessible, because they have entered the file structure of a digital collection but not the mental map of a book collection.

But visual access to a personal reading history is not only a matter of organisational practicality. Digital shelves, while they have their uses, do not necessarily offer the same utility in terms of commemorating and celebrating one's reading history and reading self. Several participants in my study noted physical shelves as important for the sense of achievement they enjoy in recalling their reading, citing experiences of 'looking at the shelf and saying [ticks finger against imaginary bookshelf] 'I've read that one, I've read that one. . .' and 'having it all on your shelf. . .and you can say, 'I read that!'.[105]

> *'I think it is partly to see. Because the ones that you have on your Kindle, it's sort of like they exist in imaginary space [murmurs of agreement]. If you bother to*

scroll through the whole contents list you'll see it again, but you normally don't. Whereas if you have it, then it's on a shelf, and you read it, even if you don't read it you'll see the spine occasionally and sort of remember.' (FG 1 participant 3)

The personal digital shelf is not the only setting where display matters intensely even when the display is to oneself. Amazon recommendations are, to some, worse than a nuisance: disliked for their uselessness, but loathed for their inaccuracy, for the false image they project of one's reading self. One participant found Amazon's mistaken impression of him as a drug dealer amusing (he had purchased a highly sensitive digital scale to weigh small amounts of artificial sweetener for sugar-free baking, and then found that Amazon was recommending paraphernalia such as 100-packs of tiny resealable plastic bags). But others found unsuitable book recommendations insulting, or actively offensive. Some found Amazon's 'bombard[ment]' an irritant: excessive and not always relevant, as in this exchange in focus group 5:

> P7: *'I go onto the Goodreads site. Again, Amazon do bombard you with...'*
> P5: *[exaggerated sing-song voice:] "If you've read this you might also like to read this", but that's not always the case.'* (FG 5)

Some participants liked Amazon recommendations or avoided them because 'they're too tempting', an indication that they are well-targeted at least some of the time.[106] For others, however, irrelevant recommendations provoked 'hate',[107] largely because they were seen as a symptom of a much larger problem: that Amazon thinks it knows its customers, but doesn't. Amazon was seen as using 'obvious' and 'corrupt[ed]' metrics, such as recent browsing or the time one takes to turn a page, to make broad assumptions about its users: one's taste, one's reading speed, what 'kind of person' one is.[108] This offered constant reminders of how they were perceived by an unaccountable, uncorrectable corporation that observes a fraction of their book-buying and book-reading behaviour and draws the wrong conclusions from what it sees.

> P1: *'I hate [Amazon recommendations].'*
> P2: *'I hate them because they're so wrong most of the time.'*
> P6: *'Really?'*
> P2: *'Oh, yes. They're terrible. They're so obvious. Because sometimes – to do something, some research, and it's nothing to do with anything I'll read* Industrial Tractor Farming *or something, some character I needed to know.'*
> P5: *'Yes; "You looked at* Industrial Tractor Farming, *now we have these for you"'.*

P2: *'And then, "Amazon recommends great tractors"'.*

. . .

P5: *'Yes. They should look at the majority of what you're browsing rather than a one-off which **corrupts** every recommendation they're after.'*

P1: *'And sometimes it's so insulting, isn't it? You turn it off. It's like, "**Really? You think I'm that kind of person?** That's it, go on".'* (FG 3)

To be subjected to constant scrutiny and evaluated by such crude means could be 'embarrassing' (FG 5 participant 5) because 'they're judging you' (FG 5 participant 1):[109]

P5: *'The other thing I notice is that quite often I read in bed so I might read and fall asleep, the thing's still on so it thinks you've taken an hour to read that page [laughter, agreement] and then it says you've got 17 hours left of the book. It turns out there is only 20 minutes. . .' [lively laughter]*

P8: *'But it's got you down as a slow reader!'*

P1: *'They're judgmental aren't they, they're judging you.'*

P8: *'It is.'*

P1: *'It's very judgmental.'*

P5: *'It's embarrassing then.'* (FG 5)

It is notable how often participants refer to the Amazon recommendation algorithm as if it were a person: a 'they' or 'you' that can judge or insult, and inflict pain as though it were another human dismissing or disrespecting them. The practical problems that stem from the existence, on some distant server, of false images of ourselves, false images that can be used against us (and not only in terms of reading recommendations), is a concern confronted in attitudes towards print reading privacy.

Print Book Privacy: Reading Without Page-by-Page Tracking

Like digital privacy, print privacy is at present a concern for only a small minority of readers. That, however, is where the similarity between the two motivations ends. When asked their reasons for choosing print, only 10.5% of all readers agreed with 'better for privacy – no one is tracking what I buy or when I read'. Choosing print books for privacy reasons did not vary significantly by year, country of residence, age, or gender (the latter a sharp contrast with choosing e-books for privacy reasons). The lack of connection to age again defies ideas of digital natives as complacent about (or conversely, highly sensitised to) data sharing and online profiling compared to their digital immigrant elders.

What does correlate with desire for this kind of privacy is print-only reading. Over one in six (18.3%) of print-only readers choose print for this reason, compared with only 7.8% of e-book readers. The issue, however, may be much more to do with e-book use than with book purchasing. Those who choose print for reasons of privacy were no less likely to buy print books from Amazon, and are actually more likely to obtain print books from other online retailers (37.5% vs 23.5%) which can track purchases as well, though perhaps not comprehensively cross-referenced with non-book purchases to the same degree as Amazon. They are more likely than average to take advantage of the typically untracked options of independent and secondhand bookshops. In terms of e-book usage, they are more likely to have read on a laptop computer (another potential suggestion of last-resort reading) and to have obtained e-books from Project Gutenberg (which requires no sign-in to download books or read online, though Project Gutenberg does, of course, have the usual ability to track by IP address). But attitudes towards Amazon appear to be hardening. Pre-pandemic, they were less likely in absolute terms to have obtained an e-book from Amazon (which not only tracks page-level reading but as a major general retailer and tech company has the ability to link reading data to a broad purchasing/reading/viewing/Alexa-using profiles), but the effect was too small to be meaningful (61.0% vs 70.1%[110]). But after the start of the pandemic, the effect is both significant and meaningful (58.5% vs 74.8%[111]). These are not large effects, and it is important to keep in mind that a solid majority of privacy-minded e-book readers still use Amazon. But given the ordinary levels of enthusiasm for other sources that can track purchases and could track some usage, such as non-Amazon online retailers and (at least in theory, though they may not take advantage of the opportunity) libraries, this again isolates Amazon as a source of concern.

The fact that these print privacy-valuers still buy print from Amazon, and in great numbers, but are much more likely to be print-only readers and eschew digital reading altogether, suggests that the freedom from monitoring 'what I buy' is less important than freedom from monitoring 'when I read': that distaste for Amazon's and other e-book retailers' individualised reader metrics is the real issue.

Valuing print privacy is correlated with other print motivators in the survey, with the sole exception of 'the books I want aren't always available electronically'. This pattern aligns a desire for this kind of privacy with core 'book experience' values, including support for traditional bookshops, valuing a physical personal library, giving gifts, and bibliophilia. (The correlations to bookish values are not simply due to the high proportion of print-only readers in the print privacy-valuing group: looking only at e-book readers, every connection other than availability still appears.) As is the case elsewhere, this bookishness does not equate to anti-e-book sentiment: e-book readers who prize print privacy are typical in their attitudes towards e-books.

These factors – the singling-out of Amazon, the aversion to Kindle reading but not Amazon print buying, and the correlation between concern for print privacy and other motivations – suggest that concern for intellectual privacy[112] may be emerging as a bookish trait in its own right. Though rooted in practical protections for individual records of viewing, borrowing, browsing, and web searching, and employed by law scholars such as Julie Cohen, Pauline Kim, and William Geveran in arguments for expanding and updating a wide range of privacy laws to address the disclosure risks presented by new technologies, Neil Richards notes that the concept has 'special applicability to reading in general and social reading in particular'[113] because the freedom to read is inseparable from freedom of thought. Richards argues that intellectual privacy 'protects our ability to think for ourselves, without worrying that other people might judge us based on what we read' and 'rests on the idea that new ideas often develop best away from the intense scrutiny of public exposure'.[114] Richards enshrines books and reading as essential to democracy, and 'free minds [as] the foundation of a free society' and issues a stirring call to action in asking anyone who agrees on books' importance to fight for reading privacy, because 'surveillance of the activities of belief formation and idea generation can affect those activities profoundly and for the worse' (noting, as he should, that librarians have defended this position for generations).[115]

While Richards's argument for urgent changes in privacy law is not directed solely at bookish people, his arguments are predicated on the importance of books to society and hence are calculated to appeal to bookish listeners. My data support Richards's arguments as to the special applicability of intellectual privacy theories to reading, but in identifying line-by-line tracking as an issue of greater concern to readers, my findings complicate his theories of private purchasing as always-better purchasing. Turow, Hennessy, Draper, Akanbi, and Virgilio have demonstrated that 'party affiliation and political ideology impact how Americans feel about [everyday institutional surveillance] far more than do income, age, gender, and race/ethnicity';[116] and in my own study, demographics are also less significant than sentiments: beliefs and values around books, bookshops, and personal libraries are excellent predictors of a desire for print privacy, while age and gender have no predictive power at all. Tracking not only the level of interest in reading privacy, but the association between interest in reading privacy and in bookish motivations, will be an essential area for continued research.

Book-Love

The long history of book-love includes a long history of complicated emotional relationships with book technologies: reverence for a material object vying with a 'language of insides and outsides' that 'makes any consciousness of the book's material qualities signify moral shallowness', and persistent anxiety about the 'proper' relationship with the 'outsides' of books.[117] Twenty-first-century readers are as active and innovative as their predecessors, and use the rapidly evolving menu of interlocking digital and print reading options for more than just access. New book technologies that 'augment. . .and offer alternatives'[118] provide new ways to read, and also new ways to form, deepen, and express relationships to the text. As discussed in Chapter 4, for some (but not all) readers, digital interfaces present barriers to immersion and a sense of connection. But my study finds readers seeking ways to keep and memorialise books as 'peculiarly interiorized objects that stray outside the metonymic logic of the souvenir'[119] and harness the menu of options to construct their own desired relationships with a given book. This section examines emerging reader strategies, such as layering the affordances of print with those of an array of e-reading interfaces, and how readers strive to perform an 'act of reading' that 'establishes an intimate, physical relationship in which all the senses have a part'.[120] The key word, however, is 'desired'. Not every book demands a close relationship: distant, impersonal and transitory may perfectly describe what a reader wants from a given book (particularly if that book is a novel).

As noted in Chapter 3, conceptualising digital ownership as demi-ownership allows book collectors to control their level of obligation to a given text, keeping some accessible for reading but without requiring storage or special treatment. Novels are frequently given as an example of the kind of 'throwaway'[121] reading that does not merit a place in permanent book collections. But novels are also very frequently given as examples of the kind of deeply beloved, personally meaningful texts that form the heart of a book collection, and that readers seek to access in multiple editions and formats. These 'reread novels' are sometimes canonical (as with *Don Quixote*) or more recently acclaimed (as with *The Luminaries*) texts, but sometimes childhood favourites, a 'comfort thing' where with a given novel 'you just feel like dipping back into the old friend'.[122] One respondent compared such reading to 'comfort food, like macaroni cheese books', inspiring raucous laughter and nods of recognition from the book lovers sitting beside her in the group.[123]

Love and Screens: Readers' Accounts of Emotions Related to Digital Reading

E-books can and do inspire powerful emotions. While a few respondents described e-books as 'sterile' or 'impersonal', implying that e-books are incapable of moving us deeply, participants' accounts are in fact rich with emotional language, positive and negative.[124] E-books are, as retailed and accessed in the 2020s, walled off from a number of specific elements of what could be termed 'the whole book experience' (FG 4 participant 3) that respondents in my study explicitly link to love, hate, 'LIKE' (Survey 2014), and so on.[125] Examples include love for handling a codex (particularly a hardcover book with sumptuous endpapers and intense booksmell), seeing print books on a bookshelf, collecting signed editions, and browsing in and buying from physical bookshops: actions beloved by many and set by some as minimum requirements for realness. But 'lov [ing] the object for itself' can include the physical artefact of an e-reading device, even if such expressions of feeling are rare compared to those for paper and spines.[126] This group deployed ardent, not dispassionate, language, as with 'I love my Kindle', 'LOVE my kobo glo!', 'I love my Kindle Oasis' or 'my husband has become a convert and loves his e-reader'.[127] It was more common for respondents to express love for their own, individual devices – love for 'mine' or 'his' – but some were willing to extend their feelings to embrace the entire category, saying 'I just love Kindles' the way that other respondents will say 'I love printed media' or 'I love print'.[128]

When it appears, love for 'e' is wholly compatible with – and in fact, more often than not appears alongside – love the printed book, as with 'I love both ebook and print books' and 'I love both e and non e'.[129] And a number of participants found this love heightened or actually inaugurated by reading during COVID-19. When asked whether their thoughts, feelings, or opinions about e-books changed during the pandemic,[130] several explained that they 'love them now! Was sceptical about the reading experience before but turns out it's great' or 'love them even more' (alongside, it must be said, less enthusiastic praise such as 'I'm more accepting of them' and 'I'm a little bit more okay with them than I used to be').[131] And in light of perceptions of e-books as (as noted previously) sterile or impersonal, this love can come as something of a shock. As one respondent put it:

> *'I have* **come to love** *reading e-novels. I really enjoy the physical experience of it - the fact that I can read in the dark and it is so accessible and easy. I now find a print book almost cumbersome.* **I've been surprised at how much I love e books**. (2021)

The reverse, expressing blanket loathing for an entire format, was unusual. The great majority of statements were positive, either in favour of (more often) print or (less often) digital, or neutral, insisting that 'format is unimportant' or that they are 'entirely print/digital agnostic'.[132] But when it did appear, hatred was exclusively for digital: 'I think E-Books are horrible', 'e-books suck' or 'I hate ebooks :)' [emoticon theirs].[133] (That said, respondents are perfectly capable of making themselves use the hated objects in a pinch: as one put it, 'I hate ebooks! But they are a necessary evil if you need a book really quickly'.)[134] Others expressed hatred for aspects of the e-reading experience, if not for the e-books themselves, as with 'hate reading lengthy text' on screens, 'hate looking at a screen', 'hate reading ebooks before going to sleep!' and 'just hate reading from an e-book after spending most of my working week in front of a screen!' – hatred for reading on screen is not generally expressed as hatred *of* the screen, which would, in a sense, be a form of feeling for part of the device itself.[135] No participants in my study reported that they hate Kindles (though some hate Amazon or Jeff Bezos, feelings I'll discuss further later in this chapter). Even when professing strong dislike for certain aspects of print books, such as 'strong, unpleasant smell of glue' or weight so excessive it caused pain for the reader,[136] no one expressed a view that print books suck.

Bibliophilia

There is nothing unexpected, or even particularly modern, about the fact that not every person who loves books is ready to call themself a bibliophile. Since its origins in the eighteenth century and rise to prominence in the first decades of the nineteenth, the label has bound together the best and the worst of relationships to the book.[137] Modern definitions contrast the two: 'a lover of books; a book-fancier' or 'having a great or excessive love of books'.[138] For every refined, cultivated, sensitive, cerebral individual with a great love, there sits beside a mirror image, the snobbish, ignorant, sentimental, or mindlessly acquisitive individual made ridiculous by an excessive love: a 'bibliomaniac' or 'book fool'.[139] While the term was originally applied to a small population of dedicated collectors, at a time of pre-industrial book production when high costs made all books, not just rare ones, luxury items,[140] its connotations changed and diversified as the price of books fell and more book lovers (including more women) could define themselves as collectors without necessarily being part of a closely acquainted community of gentleman enthusiasts.

Many readers in this study held bookish values without wishing to share the bibliophile label. In addition to questions on bookish motivations (both intuitively obvious ones like enjoyment of print book-objects and less obvious ones like print privacy), my survey asked specifically about bibliophilia. Just over one-third (34.6%) of respondents gave, as a reason for choosing print, 'I would describe myself as a bibliophile'. Compared to other named factors, bookish and not, agreement with bibliophilia is low: out of eleven options given, it ranks seventh (between 'I prefer to support traditional bookshops' and 'the books I want aren't always available electronically').

Focus group and interview contributions highlighted both the level of uncertainty regarding the meaning of the term and the resulting level of anxiety about alliance with it. Some simply embraced the term, wholeheartedly, without hesitation or qualification, saying 'oh, yeah' or (following a unanimous round of 'yes') 'I'd be interested to find a book group where they didn't [call themselves bibliophiles]. It would be a bit weird, wouldn't it?'[141] Others, however, were more cautious, responding with 'probably', or protesting 'I don't even know if I know what [bibliophile] means' and requiring definitions before committing themselves.[142]

> *'Well, I don't know. [I hesitated] just because everyone hesitated. (Laughter) I was like, "Does 'bibliophile' mean something that I don't know?" (Laughter) Is it something creepy?'* (FG 4 participant 3)

One participant, in the face of such uncertainty, backtracked from a confident 'yes, definitely' to a more timid 'I mean, I would say I was, but like, express slight misgivings about, like… [trails off]'.[143] Some initial impressions were distinctly negative, for example, 'It's so creepy, isn't it? It's a weird word' or 'I think it describes me, but I think it sounds a bit pretentious'.[144] But most were generally positive, aligning the term with bookish priorities participants could understand even when they did not share those priorities.

Initial definitions varied widely. Some emphasised enjoyment of the physical object, while others emphasised owning and collecting books in any category 'regardless of content'.[145] One participant narrowed this to collecting books 'beyond novels': an intriguing distinction, as it implies that novels are a special kind of book that even non-bookish people collect.[146] But most considered any kind of book-collecting bibliophilic, as long as it involved suitably enormous quantities of books: 'There's a big "to be read" pile that qualifies me, I think.'[147] Exactly how big the TBR (to be read) pile needs to be to 'qualify' is up for debate. But one easy definition is 'too many', a quantity of books, whatever the number for a given person, that represents a burden and a problem: 'if you define a bibliophile as buried very deep under books that you've bought and then you're struggling to keep up with all the books that you've bought that you need to finish reading, yes'.[148] Such a quantity is explicitly framed as a hoard, a spectacle of extravagance, even waste: 'you've built a pile and you sit on top of them like a dragon!' (this last followed by nods and appreciative laughter from the group).[149] This places an understanding of bibliophilia on the same cusp as the dictionary definitions: one foot in great and one in excessive love, balanced not between feeling and indifference but between feeling and even more feeling. Burden is the point.

Only one participant cited public image as a component, explaining that 'I'm pretty sure I have somewhere a couple of reserve Twitter handles and things for Bitchy Bibliophile, so yes [I am a bibliophile]'.[150] But most defined it in terms of behaviour or beliefs, not outward-facing statements. Only one participant equated bibliophilia with antipathy for digital reading, stating that 'I guess the very fact that I can't bear to read e-books instead of actual books means yes'.[151] However, in this context 'can't bear' actually meant 'can and do bear, but prefer print': she clarified later in the session that she did read e-books and while also identifying as a bibliophile.

Each group in turn effectively embarked on a negotiation of the meaning of 'bibliophile'. The result was generally an expansion of the definition: narrower individual contributions (e.g. that bibliophilia was about collecting art books rather than novels or about smelling books) combining to extend the term until it could cover some aspect of relationships with books that resonated with everyone in the group.[152] By the end of a given session, even groups where one or more individuals disagreed (e.g. 'No, I wouldn't use the term "bibliophile"') could come to a point of consensus ('I think we all just went, "Yes"').[153]

Many focus group respondents took pains to make clear (which, in person, they could, qualifying and adding nuance in a way the survey respondents could not) that they were not the kind of bibliophiles 'rather seduced by the exterior than interior'.[154] Some placed the interior and exterior on the same level, as with 'I love the stories and the objects'.[155] But others firmly assigned higher priority to the interior, as with '...it's love of stories, for me, more than the books themselves' and 'I also love the stories more than the objects, but...different levels of love. You still love the object. I'm a bibliophile, but I'm more a – whatever the equivalent for stories is.'[156] In a separate focus group, one participant coined the term 'readingophile', as a subcategory of bibliophile, to describe herself.[157] The term was instantly picked up by others in the group, who proudly declared themselves readingophiles as well.

Such definitions split decisively from any narrow definition of a bibliophile as someone who collects rather than reads, and realigns the term with someone who loves the experience of reading a book as much or more than the experience of holding or admiring a book. Such a definition, privileging the 'readingophile' over the bibliophile, is not only sympathetic to e-book reading but it also opens the door to use e-book reading to distance oneself from some of the least attractive connotations of the bibliophilic image.

E-books as 'Insides' of Books

The signal quality of the 'book-fool', the book-fancier who loves books in the wrong way, has long been exemplified by someone who fixates on the 'outsides of books' when 'due attention to the inside of books, and due contempt for the outside, is the proper relation between a man of sense and his books'.[158] The trope of a book lover as insensible when faced with a ravishing binding is not only a standing joke, a subject for 'bantering' and friendly teasing, but also a grave accusation of improper relations. The (lightly) fictionalised characters in Thomas Frognall Dibdin's expanded 1811 version of *Bibliomania* are swift to defend themselves.

> "'I will frankly confess,'' rejoined Lysander, ''that I am an arrant BIBLIOMANIAC —that I love books dearly — that the very sight, touch, and, more, the perusal—''
>
> "Hold, my friend,'' again exclaimed Philemon, ''you have renounced your profession — you talk of reading books — do BIBLIOMANIACS ever read books?''

> ... *"Forgive,"* rejoined Philemon, *"my bantering strain. You know that, with yourself, I heartily love books; more from their content than their appearance."*[159] (Dibdin, 1811, pp. 3–4)

Price finds evidence of near-consensus in the Victorian era that 'not content to ignore the outsides of books, a good reader actively scorns them'.[160] Ferris, however, qualifies that, noting the number of passionate readers who maintained that while the 'inside' was of course more important, only a philistine would deny the beauty of a good binding and the emotional connection of a reader to his personal, physical copy of a book that moved him: for 'a real man of letters, the most fanciful bindings are often the emblems of his taste and feelings' (though this was in the days of commissioned binding, when such 'emblems' were not just choices between different editions but often bespoke tailoring for one's books.)[161] Bibliophiles have always in a sense walked a tightrope, wanting to care for 'outsides', but not too much; to show oneself to be not only a 'man of sense' (and it is by default a man, as discussed later) but also of taste and of feeling. Digital reading offers an opportunity to align oneself with the 'proper' sort of book-love. If a reader chooses to think of an e-book as part of a book, specifically the all-important 'inside', reading even one makes a statement, as with 'it's the words, like the content, the information that's in the book, rather than the book itself, I think'.[162] Just as the presence of some (but not too many) lowbrow books alongside the highbrow in an eclectic book collection allows them to demonstrate that they are a cultural omnivore, not a snob,[163] enjoyment of some (but not too many) digital books allows them to prove that they have the knowledge and taste to appreciate a print book's material qualities without being dependent on those qualities: they can appreciate the gem of a fine 'inside', whatever the setting.

A conception of the e-book as the inside of a book – and specifically an elevation of the inside of a book as the part that truly *counts* – is the single most prominent theme in responses on realness in my study. Of 197 free-text responses, over half (103) rooted realness (sometimes alongside other aspects, in the case of a longer response) in arguments such as 'books aren't defined by their physicality or lack thereof. To me, a book is the contents, not the cover/jacket/etc.' – almost a quarter (45) did so using 'content' or 'contents' as nouns (and seven more use the verb 'contain'). 'Content', however, is a fiendishly difficult word to define. It is inescapable in discussion of books, serving as a means of gathering under one umbrella the expanding range of textual and non-textual matter produced by publishers: as Bhaskar puts it, 'content was once a grubby, near disrespectful word in the corridors of publishing. Not any more'.[164] But 'surprisingly, for a buzzword, the concept of "content" remains relatively unexamined', where publishers and readers use the term relentlessly but do not 'state [any definition] explicitly, then it uses [a working definition] nonetheless'.[165] Eichhorn observes that 'as the term grew more ubiquitous in the first two decades of the twenty-first century, critical dialogues about content – what it means in a digital era and its adoption and circulation across industries and disciplines – have remained surprisingly rare'.[166] Eichhorn's study of the concept of content includes charting its shift from twentieth-century usage (when, as Tenen observes, the Open eBook Authoring Group could gather 'to give content providers. . .minimal and common guidelines which ensure fidelity, accuracy, accessibility, and presentation of electronic content over various electronic book platforms' with comparative confidence),[167] to complex and frequently contradictory usages following the web-based explosion of content. 'Content', Eichhorn explains, 'isn't necessarily data, even if the two terms are frequently used simultaneously', but some older definitions corralling content as non-data because it is contextualised information, and/or conveys a message, break down when 'some content – for example, the Instagram egg – seems to exist simply for the sake of circulation alone and not to convey a message'.[168] When 'content' can be stretched to include almost anything shared, even when not created by humans or requiring humans to receive it for its value or meaning, 'content' is a commonplace, mutually understandable, yet supremely fluid way of designating the inside of a book – one that leaves a reader with a great deal of room to manoeuvre.

The many variations on 'same content', 'same number of words and content', or 'the content is what makes a book, regardless of how it's consumed' converge on an idea that 'it's the contents that matter' – or more specifically, it's the contents that matter *most*. Responses that echo the sentiment 'the content is more important than the format/method of delivery' recognise personal preference, noting that even if e-books are 'just another format, that people may like or dislike', 'some people find them more convenient' though they 'might not suit everybody'.

> *'The book is the text, the story, the narrative, the content, whatever you want to call it. The container is secondary. Print and digital (and audiobooks for that matter) have different affordances and are not the same experiences, but are all "real" books.'*

'Whatever you want to call it', however, puts a spotlight on the importance of subtle differences for responses in this category. For one strand, in addition to 'text', 'story' and 'narrative' (all of which appear in multiple responses), the inside of a book is described as 'words' and 'verbiage' (or 'the words and the pictures' or 'words and illustrations'). For another, as 'writing' or 'intent of the author' or 'the work that someone has created', foregrounding the role of the creator and recalling the ownership argument for realness (e.g. 'the content that the writer came up with is still contained in the work', and interestingly separating books as things that spring from *authors*, *writers*, or just *someone*), For a third, as 'ideas' and 'information' and 'knowledge' (and for one respondent, 'structure'). In any of these strands, the book can be defined as that which can 'convey' or 'impart' or 'deliver' or 'communicate' or 'port' or 'share' that 'whatever you want to call it'. But alternatively, and frequently, the book is said to simply 'contain' – leaving unstated who or what is the active agent.

Similarly, words used in relation to the 'outside' revealed varying conceptions of what the inside is, what can hold it, and where it ends. The frequently used 'container' (as with 'narratives in containers, even if the container is my phone/ipad') is highly generic, broadly defining the outside as the thing, any thing, that contains; as one puts it, 'I don't confuse container and content'. Some focus not only on the tangible aspects of a codex with 'paper' or 'pages' but also on the 'cover', 'jacket', or 'ink', in opposition to 'bits' and 'bytes'. 'A book is not a lump of paper and ink – a book is the written word' is crushingly diminishing: the 'lump' not only recalling jibes about bits of tree covered in bits of squid but also firmly defining the book as *not* the material – the words being (as others put it) 'independent' of an outside that's 'almost irrelevant' or 'has no bearing'. But respondents also use 'form', 'format', and 'edition', as well as 'medium' and 'media' and 'method of delivery', concepts that are anything but interchangeable: as one puts it, 'media, format and content are entirely separate things.' A *format* that *delivers information*, for example, is hardly synonymous with a *medium* that *ports knowledge*, or an *edition* that *shares* the *intent of the author*. The number of ways one can splice conceptions of inside, outside, and means by which inside reaches the reader is vast.

> *'This might be the technophile (or perhaps the pedant) in me talking, but the format doesn't matter too much. A book is a book, whether it's printed on paper, read aloud, or displayed on a screen. Sure, you could argue that a "book" is a physical thing, and everything else is specific – but that's just semantics. A copy of some novel is still that novel whether it's bound in paper, or bound in bytes.'*

But a minority of respondents argued exactly that. Free-text responses following 'no' answers included 'for me the definition of a book is printed material with a cover. I'm happy with a separate definition of e-book for online material', 'a book is not just the contents, but also the physical object', and 'a book consists of the content but also the paper, weight, design etc.' All rely for their power on *with* and *also*, accepting the logic of an inside and an outside, but maintaining that shorn of its outside, the inside no longer qualifies. 'A book should have a cover and actual pages' makes covers and pages, like 'content', necessary but not sufficient conditions for bookness. For these readers, e-books 'are the content of story collections/novels/recipe books whatever, but not a book'. The earlier self-declared technophile/pedant dismisses these distinctions as 'just semantics', but those semantics, and their context, leave ample grey area.

> 'The real answer is "yes and no." If someone asks if I've read a book and I read the e-book, I say yes. In that instance, book = story. But when I hear the phrase "real book," I think of something tangible—a particular physical object. Same for audiobooks.'

Adopting a language of insides and outsides does not require accepting that the outside is irrelevant – or irrelevant all of the time.

Compatibility of Bibliophilia with E-reading

The usefulness of this conception of e-book as incomplete book – all inside, no outside – helps explain the compatibility of bibliophilia with e-reading. E-book readers are in fact fractionally more likely to identify with the term than print-only readers (34.9% vs 33.9%), though the gap is so tiny this amounts to a statistical tie. This is doubly striking as a number of bookish values, including enjoyment of the physical object and preference for print as better for keeping as part of a personal library, have strong positive correlations with print-only reading (please see Chapters 3 and 4 for more on these forms of ownership and enjoyment).

This raises the question of whether e-reading attracts those who already identify as bibliophiles, or whether e-reading may potentially amplify, or even activate, such identification. Evidence suggests that the answer is both. Digital readers are, above all else, readers: numerous surveys have confirmed that the great majority of e-book readers are also print readers, and those who read in both formats read more books overall.[169] Even if digital is not their preferred format, format flexibility can allow a keen reader to fit more books into their day, and 'never have to stop reading':[170] filling those last, frustratingly bookless minutes of a life with reading. However, as discussed previously, 'death of the book' debates have for

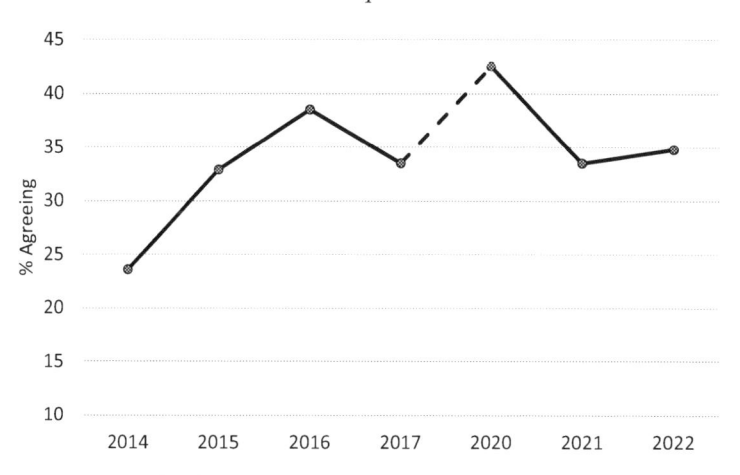

Figure 5.2   Reasons for choosing print: 'I would describe myself as a bibliophile', by year.

generations framed digital reading as the enemy of print reading,[171] and called for e-book readers to explain themselves and their supposed disloyalty towards print culture. Such calls may drive otherwise indifferent e-book readers towards a label that proclaims their loyalty to book culture. These findings demonstrate how unrepresentative opinions like those of the focus group participant who equated bibliophilia with being unable to bear e-books[172] actually are and provides a sharp riposte to arguments that e-reading and bibliophilia are incompatible.

Identification as a bibliophile increased over the eight years of the survey, rising from 23.6% in 2014 to mid-30s in most years. The peak of 42.5% in 2020 suggests that the tremendous importance of reading for solace, comfort, connection, and well-being during the pandemic[173] had at least some – though perhaps temporary – effect on identification as a bibliophile (Figure 5.2).

Men were less likely to describe themselves as bibliophiles.[174] Gender differences on bibliophilic identity are highly intriguing. As Lisa Otty has explained, the positive and negative sides of bibliophilia have been presented, particularly in the early twentieth century, as gendered: 'bibliomania' as feminine or effeminate, and true connoisseurship as masculine.[175] This separation of the masculine 'book-lover' and the feminine 'book-fool' makes the under-representation of men amongst avowed bibliophiles all the more interesting. It could be a point of honour for some female respondents to reclaim the term. Alternatively, it could be that the word 'bibliophile', and all the risk it brings, has been less frightening for non-male readers in the early years of mass e-reading: as discussed earlier in

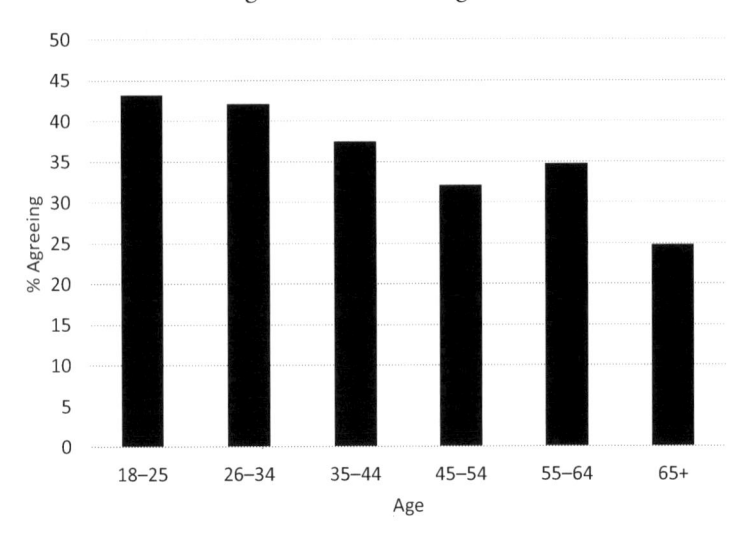

Figure 5.3   Reasons for choosing print: 'I would describe myself as a bibliophile', by age.

this chapter, women are accustomed, and perhaps resigned, to ridicule, condescension, and scolding. But another possible reason for a gender-based gap in identification with the word 'bibliophile' is that its meaning in the digital reading era has been debated in highly gendered reading spaces, such as the book groups, online forums like Goodreads, and festival audiences that are typically dominated by women.[176]

Identification as a bibliophile varied significantly by age, falling steadily for older respondents, a pattern that echoes those choosing print for ease of reading (Figure 5.3).

Identification as a bibliophile correlated positively with every source of print books in the survey, including gifts (underscoring the fact that bibliophilia is not just a matter of personal identity but also public identity: friends know, and buy accordingly). All connections are meaningful, but the weakest[177] was with libraries. While this is a slightly counterintuitive result, it could simply be the result of the higher level of book consumption from every other print source, including gifts. These avowed bibliophiles, who also highly value print for keeping as part of a personal library (see later), may be such active book collectors that book borrowing is less important, and even less feasible, if they commit so much time to their larger collections of owned books that they have little time left for borrowed ones. Even so, avowed bibliophiles' levels of library use are average, not low (or only low compared to their heroic levels of bookshop, online bookshop, and gift use) (Figure 5.4).

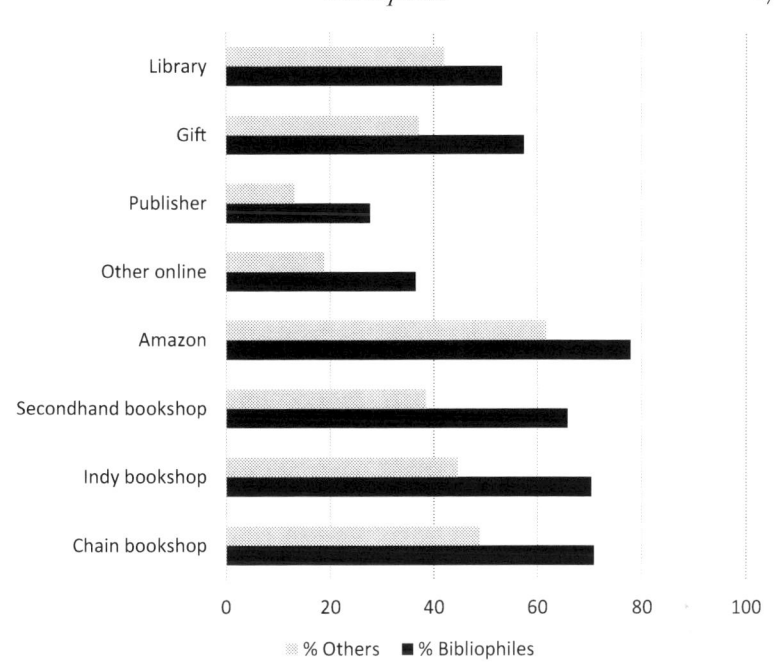

Figure 5.4   Reasons for choosing print: 'I would describe myself as a bibliophile', by source of print books.

Avowed bibliophiles are generally ordinary in terms of their e-book use, with few significant relationships to sources or genres of e-books, or device usage. While they are also ordinary in most attitudes towards e-books, they stand out on a few key e-bookish values. E-book reading avowed bibliophiles were slightly less likely to choose digital because e-books are easier to read (14.8% vs 24.3% of others), or more enjoyable (5.4% vs 15.7%). They were slightly more likely, however, to choose digital for reasons of availability, or 'the books I want aren't always available in print' (31.1% vs 20.6%); a hallmark of being driven to digital rather than drawn to digital.

In contrast, bibliophiles' attitudes towards print books are anything but ordinary. Identifying as a bibliophile correlates positively with every other print value. It is the strength of the relationship that demonstrates what other values are the most bibliophilic. While links to choosing print because print books are more enjoyable to handle and use (87.8% vs 57.3%[178]) and because print is better for keeping as part of a personal library (87.0% vs 52.3%[179]) are notable, the most 'bibliophilic' value is choosing print to support traditional bookshops (68.8% vs 30.7%[180]).

'Love' and 'LIKE' were words many participants used in conjunction with bookshops, and particularly for the 'thrill of browsing in a second-hand bookshop' ('I love to browse!', 'I love to browse in bookshops', 'I love browsing bookstores', etc.) alongside the satisfaction of supporting a traditional physical shop ('I love to support independent booksellers where possible', 'I LIKE to support bookshops', and grief for its reverse, 'While I embrace e-books as convenient and an inevitable advance, I lament the demise of print books and of bookstores').[181] This form of love was only heightened during pandemic lockdowns, where mourning for access to beloved bookshops and libraries was a fixture of free-text responses.

Among avowed bibliophiles, e-book readers and print-only readers are not far apart in their views. E-book readers are, predictably, more likely to choose print because the books they want aren't always available electronically. Print-only bibliophiles, however, exceed e-book reading bibliophiles in their enthusiasm for print being easier to read, the leading bookish value of print being better for keeping as part of a personal library, and the emerging bookish value of privacy – but not on print being more enjoyable or other signal bookish values such as wishing to support traditional bookshops.

The single focus group participant who defined bibliophilia in terms of antipathy for digital reading did not speak for the majority. The special relationship avowed bibliophiles have with print (they are more likely to obtain print books from every source, they have drastically amplified bookish values, etc.) is paired with a very unspecial relationship with digital: ordinary in their usage, mild in their opinions. Declaring love for print books, outsides and insides, is compatible with e-book reading. However, declaring love for the insides of books carries its own kind of risk, especially for female readers, given the negative image of affective reading.

Emotional Reading and 'Untrained' Readers

Novels that inspire empathy and emotional connection may, as there is evidence to suggest, enjoy greater commercial success,[182] 'have a unique role to play in promoting and nurturing pro-social abilities',[183] and further the agendas of policy makers who hope that literary empathy will foster real-world altruism, yet 'disdain for the preferences of feeling readers pervades literary criticism'.[184] As Murray has noted, a flight from affect is part of the history of the formation of English literature as an academic discipline.[185] Despite the work of generations of scholars of reading, including Radway's analysis of romance readership, in questioning such a simple dichotomy, it remains easy to find examples where empathetic reading is casually set up as the antagonistic opposite of analytical reading, as in Jonathan Franzen's account of rewriting *The Corrections* for the 'open-minded but essentially untrained fiction reader'.[186] In the absence of a critical apparatus, and unable to cope with 'difficulty', Franzen's untrained reader supposedly relies on lesser measures of a work's quality, most especially emotional connection: feeling for the story and the story-world, and 'empathy, sympathy, identification, and the reader's "care" for fictional characters'.[187] This confidence that emotional response is a separate and distinctly lower form of response to literature, and that the unskilled reader does not without help ascend past this lower rung, is also gendered. As Studer and Takayoshi point out, the conflict between trained and untrained reading is dramatised in *The Corrections* in a showdown between a male literature professor, Chip Lambert, and a female student, Melissa; Franzen's pivot to the mainstream was in essence a decision to 'turn his back on readers like Chip Lambert and court readers like Melissa'.[188] Longstanding stereotypes of women as emotional, and by definition irrational, beings incapable of analysis (of literature or anything else) live on in feminised middlebrow literary culture where modes of 'sentimentality, empathy and therapy' characterise and stigmatise both emotional reading and the female readers associated with it.[189] Jonathan Franzen's feud with Oprah's Book Club is so often mentioned as an example of literary elitism, and sexism in the 'high-art literary tradition' Franzen defined as his natural home, that it is possible to overlook the role that book-love played in making the Oprah audience, out of all possible mainstream audiences, so threatening to him. It wasn't just the gender of her studio audience, it was the genderedness of the studio discussion: its earnestness, its affect, its extension of the 'sentimentality, empathy and therapy' modes of daytime television to the discussion of books. The 'readingophile' who described her own bibliophilia in terms of 'love of stories [even] more than the books themselves' is using the language of affect to define her relationship to the inside of a book, and this makes it easier for a critic (at least one who accepts a binary division) to consign her to the lower rung of amateurish, non-analytical readers. For women readers, taking hold of the label of 'bibliophile' requires a measure of defiance in reclaiming it from its history of sexist use. It may also offer a counterweight: balancing the outside against the inside of a book, the caricature of the book-fool against the caricature of the 'open-minded but essentially untrained reader'. These excessively, incorrectly emotional readers invite further ridicule when they broadcast unseemly feelings for a novel or novelist. Public dislike need not damage an author's standing: as discussed earlier in this chapter, the right enemies can be as important as the right friends, and the disapprobation of outsiders with low levels of cultural capital can elevate a work's prestige, underscoring how its virtues are beyond the capacities of the uninitiated. But public affection presents risk, and online reading forums, using the 'affective language that is common online'[190] pose a threat.

Bibliophilia and Amazon

Feeling for a text in digital form is further complicated by feeling for the device on which it is displayed, which can be intense.[191] This does not, however, map neatly to a strength of feeling based on device choice or, indeed, to device choice based on strength of feeling, or an easy equation by which novels on beloved iPhones are more treasured than novels on work laptops. This is in part because texts are not fixed to one device. As previously noted, most respondents in my survey used two or more reading devices in the past twelve months, and many regularly switch between devices (e.g. reading on a smartphone while standing for a train commute but switching to tablet or print on the sofa at home). But it is also due in part to the fact that some devices are linked to retailers, and these retailers may be distinctly unloved.

While, as discussed, a number of readers love their Kindles, not a single respondent described love, or even mild liking, for 'the dreaded Amazon'.[192] Rather, the reverse was true. While respondents use Amazon extensively and its lead over other sources of e-books remains overwhelming, their feelings about Amazon as a company range from indifference to mild distaste to active loathing. Some express reservations about its 'business practices' and effect on writers and the literary market-place, even rooting for its demise ('I hoped Amazon would lose money... I am a writer and if Amazon keeps growing I will not be able to make a living').[193] A number actively despise both it ('Hate Amazon and avoid them religiously for all book purchases, print and electronic') and its founder ('[during lockdown] I grew to hate Jeff Bezos so I started reading exclusively on my iphone').[194] The depth of feeling only increased during the pandemic, where some respondents avoided Amazon for print book orders, not only because of their desire to support bricks and mortar bookshops but also from concern for Amazon warehouse workers and deliverypersons. The result is reluctant Amazon purchases ('I might have to buy it from Amazon which I would not necessarily like to do') or no Amazon purchases ('I am now boycotting Amazon', 'I'm actively boycotting Amazon', 'I will not buy from Amazon').[195] This stands in stark contrast to the love many respondents expressed for physical book-shops: while the occasional participant expressed dislike for aspects of traditional bookshops, such as 'bookstore staff are useless',[196] none hated bookshops as a category the way some hate Amazon as a company.

Even more striking is the way some express strongly negative feelings about themselves when they buy from Amazon. They describe themselves as 'a sucker when Amazon recommends something', or 'Amazon's dream customer because I read a review...on Amazon and, "okay, I'll have that."... So yes, [I'm] gullible, stupid...', or explain that they 'don't like buying things from Amazon... But [they] just get suckered in anyway, because... "Oh, look, £0.99".'[197] Among respondents who dislike and disapprove of Amazon, buying on its terms can leave them feeling like a 'sucker', a 'gullible' chump. Aversion to Amazon does not lead readers as a whole to avoid Amazon: it is too ubiquitous, typically the most convenient and often (especially in the case of digital-only books from KDP or an Amazon imprint) the only way of obtaining a given book. But respondents sometimes described themselves as something akin to accomplices in an assault on print culture: weak, unprincipled, cheaply bought. This intri-guingly recalls accusations of disloyalty levelled at all e-book readers during the 'e-book wars': while no one in this study described their own e-book *reading* as contrary to the best interests of print or print culture, in this one specific way a few participants describe their own e-book *purchasing* as contrary to such interests.

Not only are Kindles linked to a widely disliked retailer, they also do not appear to qualify as 'technology', if technology is defined as something alluring to the group Duguid termed 'triumphant technophiles'.[198]

Technophilia

Technophilia is a factor for fewer than one in fifteen (6.6%) survey respondents, and did not vary by age. Men were more likely to identify as technophiles.[199] Agreement was stable from 2014 to 2017, but dropped to an average of 3.5% between 2020 and 2022 (largely due to a plunge to 0.7% in 2021). This general trend could be due to screen exhaustion during the pandemic, but also to the evolving image of Kindle and other e-ink readers as everyday tools rather than desirable gadgets of interest to technophiles (who are more likely to read e-books on tablet or smart-phone, but not other devices). As noted in Chapter 4, since 2010 Amazon has split its Kindle range, selling feature-laden premium models such as the

Scribe and Oasis alongside basic versions where advertising-free interfaces and even chargers are optional extras. But marginal advances such as improved waterproofing and Bluetooth connectivity for headphones are not breakthroughs on the level of e-ink: *Wired*, the technology magazine that enthusiastically reviewed prior models described the 2017. Oasis as 'just not different enough to justify the £229 starting price'.[200] (Technophiles were no more or less likely to obtain e-books from Amazon, however: the only link to sources of e-books were to higher likelihood of direct purchase from publishers).

Building Relationships

Aside from instances where an avowed bibliophile chooses to think of an e-book as part of a book, in terms of legitimacy, a loved e-book is functioning for these respondents as real. The emotions inspired are real emotions. That said, the powerful dislike a few respondents feel for e-books, or for e-book retailers, may prevent them ever encountering enough of them to fall in love with one (if they are boycotting Amazon, they are unlikely ever to fall in love with a novel presented as an .AZW file). The problems some respondents report in becoming immersed in an e-book may also stand in the way of a close relationship. But when participants report that 'one of my favourite books I actually got for free on Amazon' or that they are 'as likely to read or reread a favourite "amateur" story/novel length work as a published pro work these days' it is clearly possible for not only an e-book but also a digital-only book to ascend to the status of a favourite 'reread' book.[201]

Some of the actions readers identify as special, reserved for books that warrant close attention and ongoing connection, are difficult or impossible for digital-only books. To own, give, or handle and use in codex form a given book, a reader may use digital audition to layer on the affordances of print, if there is a print edition to be had. (This can entail paying twice for the same book, but paying twice has its own benefits, as I'll discuss later in considering e-book patronage.) And availability in print is not limited to commercial availability. The practice of fan binding, where readers turn chosen born-digital fan-made texts into physical fan-made codices (what one fan binder calls 'undigitising'),[202] offers readers the opportunity to create bespoke editions to satisfy needs not fulfilled by online originals. Such editions can be as simple as a comb-bound stack of A4 (evoking twentieth-century traditions of photocopying zines), or a Print-On-Demand hardcover from Lulu or Barnes & Noble (though such providers can officially refuse to print transformative works,[203] as they do for any text where copyright permissions are murky). But the most celebrated examples are sumptuously produced book art, one-off book-objects created by fans largely self-taught in desktop publishing software and traditional bookbinding techniques. While preservation is one reason for fan binding, loss being a chronic concern with fan works,[204] two studies of the Renegade Bindery community by Shira Buchsbaum and Kimberly Kennedy indicate that individuals pursue this expensive and demanding practice for a range of reasons, from reading offline to conferring status on the works to bequeathing volumes to heirs and archives to furthering ideals of non-commercial creativity by gifting copies to fic authors – reasons that connect with many desires for realness in obtaining, enjoying, and keeping books as discussed in previous chapters.[205] But both studies find that fan binders are fundamentally motivated by love. Binders 'began binding fic because they love fan fiction' and choose to work on, out of the vast number of available fics, those they love the most.[206] As one fan binder put it, 'the effort of binding an entire book has to be the strongest demonstration of "I loved your story this much!" there is'.[207] These bespoke objects don't supersede the digital, as the losses in converting online fic to print include aspects of 'accessibility, interactivity, and malleability...losing hyperlinks and comments strips the fic of its community context'; as Kennedy puts it, 'at its core, fandom is a conversation' and 'without the source material and the fandom interactions that led to the fic's creation, readers cannot understand the full breadth of meaning held within the story'.[208] The bindings are treasured but not necessarily preferred. To retain their full meaning, the fics remain interlocked with the digital, symbiotic rather than superior.

Without the option of print, however, there is still the valued option of personalisation. One such form of personalisation is through annotation. For my participants, the idea of writing in books was contentious, as in these two exchanges from focus group 4.

> P4: *Yes. Let me show you the book that I have with me today. This was one that I used at university and I've got over half the pages turned down at the corners. The highlighting wasn't me but the pencil notes were me. The highlighting doesn't bother me.*
>
> . . .
>
> P2: *'Oh, goodness. No.'*
> P4: *'Look!' [directing another participant's attention to the annotated page]*
> P2: *'No. Oh my God. I only did that to books I **hated**.' (Laughter)*
> P4: *'No, I **love** this one. I'd do it because even if you pass it onto someone else it's nice to see what they've enjoyed.'*

P3: *'Yes. I lend books to my mum and she finds it interesting because I write little notes sometimes. Not in all of my books but in some of them and she's like, "Oh, that's interesting. I wouldn't have thought of that."'*

. . .

Moderator: *'If you put notes down in a book like that, is it a sign that the book was especially good? It moved you to say something?' (From FG 4)*

P4: *'Or* **especially bad**.*'*

P3: *'Yes, hopefully it's not the other.'*

P4: *'I distinctly remember underlining something and just writing "no" in the margin.'*

For some, writing in print books is 'definitely' a powerful sign of esteem,[209] something they do to books they love and something they welcome from past readers. For others, it is taboo, and something they personally only do to books they loathe. But in both cases, it is a sign of strong feeling, even when the annotation involved 'typ[ing] notes [on a first generation keyboard Kindle] painstakingly!'[210] rather than taking a pencil or pen to paper. In some cases, it is a bridge to other readers, 'the notes in the margins written by my great great grandfather or complete strangers' or Kindle Popular Highlights 'where you can see other notes of people who wrote in it?...I loved that!'.[211] But annotation can as easily serve as a bridge to themselves in another time.[212]

'I write by hand on them, take notes of passages to re-read, they are memories attached to the object called book "where I bought it in which mood, at what moment of my life, they are a personal image of my evaluating centre of interest"' (Survey 2014)

'a physical book can become an old friend. You see the places you've dogeared in the past, pages you marked as meaningful, your maiden name in the front cover because you've had it that long. . .' (Survey 2017)

Marking up is an important action for readers to take for books that matter to them. But readers are split on whether annotation is facilitated by print. In just one year group, Survey 2017, multiple write-in responses gave ease of annotation as a reason to choose print (e.g. 'easier to highlight and take notes' and 'easier to take notes on them') and as a reason to choose digital (e.g. 'annotations and copy paste, especially for scholarly works easier to go digital', 'I like being able to search, add notes' and 'useful to search and highlight', the *especially for scholarly works* serving to emphasise the particular importance of search functionality for non-fiction reading). No one expressed hesitation about writing in digital books – after all, one cannot, when notes and comments are held in a separate file from the text, truly deface an e-book even if one wanted to. But forms of annotation like Amazon Kindle highlights cross a line between writing in books and writing about books.

Amazon has pushed its 'highlights' feature aggressively, emphasising its use as a connection between readers: 'popular highlights' making everyone's copies more alike, not allowing one reader to make their copy distinctive and personal to them. But if the purpose of this type of marginalia is in fact to broadcast one's opinions, broadcasting one's opinions is another key strategy for getting closer to a book. Talking about a book, in person or on social media, is ostensibly a format-neutral strategy: unless one is in a book group where audiobooks are taboo, it is no one's business whether the book is encountered on paper, on screen, or via headphones. That said, the attachment and recollection gap noted in Chapter 4, where some (but not all) readers reported that they did not feel they 'know…fully' or completely 'absorb/remember' e-books, may make it that much more difficult for a digital-only book to move them the way they need to be moved before they write a book review (another sign of strong feeling, good or bad, according to my respondents), blog post, Goodreads comment, or tweet. But once over that obstacle, one can write oneself closer to a novel whatever its format.[213]

Patronage

But if e-book readers can own themselves closer, customise themselves closer, and write themselves closer to a given book, there is one way of deepening a relationship that can be quite different for a book on screen: spending oneself closer, but not in the manner of a typical product purchase. What readers receive in exchange for financial investment in book relationships is less of the privileges and satisfactions of a customer and more of the privileges and satisfactions of a patron.

Buying an e-book is not pleasant. It may be quick and easy, but it is unsatisfying.

> '*It's not as…special? You know when you go into a bookshop and buy a book, and you get it home and you're really excited (agreement)… [and] when you get a book through the post, that's really exciting? Whereas downloading a book is just like…mmmmmugh.*' (FG 1 respondent 1)

Buying is often unnecessary, if one does not mind piracy. (And, as discussed in Chapter 3, many respondents in my study do not.) And buying is, in many ways, futile. Conditional use licenses do not confer either the same rights or the same feeling as print ownership (see Chapter 3). The feeling of being taken advantage of as a customer makes readers describe themselves as 'sucker[s]', 'gullible'[214] and outsmarted – 'book-fools' of a very different kind.

Readers can instead reframe their e-book payments as effectively 'donation', and 'patronage', with reciprocal offerings for an artist's gift, and the transaction as a gift exchange rather than a commercial arrangement.[215] Freely given support for art and for artists establishes a profound but very different relationship between creator and reader.[216] (Thinking of book transactions in this way brings to book buying some of the feeling of book giving, and the connection it forges between two readers; for more on this connection, please see Chapter 3.) This idea of spending one's way closer to a text also helps explain digital audition: not so much buying twice as contributing twice.

Savvy authors and publishers are very explicitly tapping into this sentiment, and not just via non-book-specific creator sponsorship platforms such as Kickstarter (which allows members of the public to commit to prefunding individual projects such as games, music, or films, which are only made, and the patrons only charged, if a funding goal is met) or Patreon (which uses a similar online platform but takes pledges to an individual creator rather than a creative project).[217] Unbound's business model allows reader/patrons to take part, via prepublication commitments of support, from the point of commissioning, and offers levels of involvement. Early commitment allows select patrons to literally write themselves into the book, listed in the first edition like eighteenth-century subscribers.[218] The range of pledge options typically includes print editions (as well as premium packages that bundle hardcover print copies with collectables and experiences such as signed bookplates, sets of bookmarks, enamel pins, or lunch with the author) but also e-books, with one's name included in only the digital edition. Sellers like Humble Bundle (noted by several survey respondents as a source of their e-books), a company that began sharing indie games but expanded into e-books and digital comics, invite users to 'pay what you want', share the proceeds with charity, and post constantly updated leader boards of top contributors.[219] But other authors are finding ingenious ways to bend existing commercial frameworks to address readers as potential patrons rather than potential customers. Hugh Howey, a self-publishing breakout star whose *Wool* series went on to be adapted for television by Apple TV+, used the product description of a Kindle Singles e-book to directly address the reader/buyer and explain his creative aims, apologise for Amazon's commercial ones, and to say 'thank you' (not *readers*, but *you*) 'for all your support'.[220] Despite its length, the passage is worth reproducing in full: what makes it notable is not just its content but also its context. The direct appeal is not before or after the product description, it *is* the product description, in its entirety: the connection between reader and author is what the supporter (not customer) gets for their money. Even within the 'everything store', authors and readers can choose to replace the language of commercial exchange with the language of gift exchange.

> *'This is a short story about a man seeking closure. It can be read in ten minutes. Please don't purchase this expecting a novel for your dollar.*
>
> *This story was written in a small cafe on the corner of Bleeker and Grove in New York City on Tuesday, May 27th. The idea came to me yesterday while walking across the Brooklyn Bridge. I saw the locks on several of the small cables on the bridge. I remembered my time in both London and Paris, taking pictures of all the love locks on bridges there. And I thought about all the couples those locks represent. I wondered how many are still together.*
>
> *Maybe this story isn't worth your dollar. If I could price a work on Amazon for less, I would. It is what it is. I hope this will be the first of many short pieces that I write and publish in a single day while recording what I'm thinking and where I am when I write them. For those who take the plunge, I hope you get your money's worth. Thank you for all of your support.'*[221]

This form of direct bid for connection demonstrates not only how retail venues can be effectively hijacked by authors to further a patronage rather than a commercial relationship but also how such patronage does not require a physical print object to build a reader–author relationship of this type. Support for a self-published, digital-only work, and indeed for a self-published, digital-first author, can employ the same economic and emotive apparatus. When readers choose to become patrons of an e-story or any e-book on the same terms as they would a print book, to accept that they are getting their 'money's worth' in terms of relationships and emotional reward, the e-book is functioning as real.

Conclusion

In terms of image, public and self, the e-book functions primarily as an incomplete book. It cannot contribute to readerly identity as fully as can a print book because its own identity is in part obscured: not only to the subway 'spy'[222] but also to the reader themselves, as their reading history may be less visible and accessible to them, and their reading choices more difficult to meaningfully and intentionally share. At the same time, the granular experience of reading, from annotations to reading speed, is unprecedentedly visible to retailers. Readers who object to e-reading surveillance demonstrate particular concern about Amazon, singling it out as both especially crude and overt in its profiling (which some respondents find not only inconvenient but also insulting, as if the company were a person being personally disrespectful). In a sense, in objecting to being defined as people by a subset of their purchases, they object to being reduced to parts of readers: treated as incomplete people, judged according to their use of incomplete books. This makes Amazon for them a retailer to be avoided for digital (but not print) books. The desire for print privacy has no link to age or gender, but correlates strongly with other bookish values such as a desire to support traditional bookshops; the latter constellation of links underscores the degree to which a desire for this kind of privacy is itself a bookish value. The appeal to bookish readers to resist tracking for the sake of the intellectual privacy of future generations may, if the proportion of readers concerned with this form of privacy continues to rise and continues to correlate with bookish values, add an additional reason to hew to print.

The freedom offered by obscured paratext, allowing readers to access their books of choice in public without fear of teasing or embarrassment, comes at a high price, as anonymous reading denies readers the cultural capital their reading might accrue if it were in print and, for women in particular, invites observers to impose their own ideas of what their chosen reading is likely to be. The lower status of digital books can cost readers cultural capital simply for being seen with a dedicated device, and a non-dedicated device may hide book reading altogether. Despite the image of e-reading devices as vital tools for furtive reading, perfect for guilty pleasures and naughty books, the actual importance of furtive reading as a motivator for choosing digital appears extremely low. The exaggerated image of the furtive reader, however, threatens to further perpetuate gendered stereotypes and distort not only understanding of digital reading but also understanding of the audiences for specific books and of women's reading in general.

The empty space where some elements of the book's paratext would be in a print edition can be filled, and not by the reader. It can serve as one kind of screen facing outwards, where observers can project their ideas of what any particular 'kind of person' would read, and another kind facing inwards, projecting a stream of data towards retailers, who will continue to stockpile such data to profile and target individual readers, and will, unless restrained by refinements to the law, retain it indefinitely for future uses not yet imagined. How to tolerate that empty space is what bookish people must negotiate in order to use e-books while maintaining an identity as a bookish person.

Viewed through the lens of love, e-books can function not only as parts of books but also as real books. Print inspires deep feelings and passionate loyalty for many readers. Digital formats inspire these for fewer, but their love is no less real for being somewhat unusual. While aspects of print books and print book culture, such as the smell of a book or the staff of bookshops, may be disliked, no respondents in this study expressed hate for print books or print culture. Some respondents do hate e-books, as well as e-book retailers such as Amazon. That said, loathing of e-books is rare (much more so than love of e-books and e-reading devices) and the most common stance towards e-books among book lovers is bland appreciation. Notably, e-reading is wholly compatible with book-love: e-readers are in fact fractionally more likely to identify as bibliophiles than those who read books only in print (though this difference is small and below the level of statistical significance). Love for books and book culture is widespread, but embrace of the label bibliophile is not: only a third of participants in this study choose print because they identify as bibliophiles, in contrast with large majorities who choose print because they enjoy the material object, find print better for keeping as part of a personal library, and/or wish to support traditional bookshops. What it means to be a bibliophile in the modern day is a matter for debate, though in the focus groups virtually all respondents were willing, after discussion, to subscribe to a term that was agreed to embrace aspects of collecting, ownership, and enjoyment of the material print object, while stressing that they loved the act of reading even more than the material object. Technophilia motivates only a small fraction of readers to choose digital. In having no claim on the affections of technophiles, it would appear that Kindles are perhaps now so humble and ubiquitous that a gadget lover finds little that is exciting, compelling, or new to tempt them. Book lovers, whether or not they embrace the label of bibliophile, can love e-reading devices, can love books they encounter on screen, and can, through avenues including digital audition, annotation and other forms of customisation, and patronage, deepen their relationships with beloved e-books. These strategies suggest ways in which the image and status of e-books can be further shaped by bibliophiles' needs, reverse engineering a role that continues to complement rather than undermine print culture.

E-books are only sometimes real, but it is their very flexibility that makes them so valuable to book lovers. They can be public or private, permanent or ephemeral, valuable or valueless, intimate or distant, depending on one's usage and settings but also on one's idea of what an e-book is; and, as demonstrated, that idea is highly adaptable and at least sometimes under one's conscious control. And in those instances where digital simply cannot provide the same experience as print, as with feeling paper under one's fingers or lifting a volume from a physical bookshop shelf, digital can be augmented with print, layering formats and forms of use. Shifting one's conception of the nature of an e-book to suit one's intended use, willing it to be the thing one desires (and then willing it to be something else when one's desires change), goes to the heart of how readers integrate e-books into their broader reading lives.

Coda

'It's the content that **counts** rather than the format.'

'I'm more interested in the writing than the format. Any format which conveys the author's expression **counts**.'

'Anything you can read that communicates the information **counts**.'

'Yes, books are the physical container. But what's inside is what **counts**.'

(All Survey 2022, free-text responses to 'Do you consider
e-books to be real books? Why?')

In October 2014, Simon & Schuster released the print edition of Anna Todd's first novel. That novel had already been read over a billion times.[1] Appearing as over a hundred serialised chapters on online storytelling platform Wattpad between Spring 2013 and Spring 2014, *After* began as fan fiction, but unlike *Fifty Shades of Grey* or *Twilight*, it achieved incredible prominence in its original, digital form, making Todd, and Wattpad, the subjects of extensive media attention long before the print book became available in shops.[2] In March 2014, David Streitfeld had written in the *New York Times* about Wattpad and the *After* phenomenon, using (as Todd, her readers, and Wattpad executives do), the terms *writer, novel,* and *chapter*.[3] Sven Birkerts, writing two years later, used Todd's success to illustrate an argument about the threat to the 'literary' posed by 'technology' (very much in the vein of his well-known 1994 *Gutenberg Elegies*, discussed in earlier chapters). He deployed the construction 'a woman named Anna Todd, who uses Wattpad to post episodes of a saga called "After"'.[4] (The 'named' is a further diminishment, as like 'called' it can serve as a signal to the reader that the writer under discussion is obscure, lacking in stature, or an outright pretender to professional status.)[5] The 'saga... "After"' is presented in quotation marks, while mainstream published novels mentioned in the essay appear in the typical italics. Other people who write things are named as 'authors': Mohsin Hamid in reference to his novels, but also journalist Matt McFarland, described as the 'author' of a *Washington Post* newspaper article. Birkerts demotes Todd to a 'woman' who 'posts'. In Birkerts' formulation, this 'saga' has readers but no author. Like a diplomat refusing to officially recognise a country, Birkerts elaborately excludes Todd and authors like her from any category that could suggest an earned place in the world of literature, and what she's written from any kind of bookness.

Do e-books count? The readers in my own study say yes – with conditions. They consider e-books real books specifically because 'any format which conveys the author's expression counts.' Or 'anything you can read that communicates the information counts.' Or 'it's the content that counts rather than the format.' Or 'what's inside is what counts.' But do e-books 'convey' reliably? Who decides whether they communicate 'the information' in the same way? And what are the boundaries of 'content' and 'inside'? The answer to the graduate student's excellent question, the query that opened this book, remains, unsatisfyingly, *sometimes*.

Bookness is a form of legitimacy that matters to at least some readers at least some of the time, but neither bookness nor realness is essential in every circumstance. Moreover, readers move between ideas of what an e-book is, typically conceptualising their e-books as real when realness is an asset, and unreal (*ersatz*, digital proxy, or incomplete) when any particular form of unrealness best suits their needs.

Reading Real Books

This book has followed readers through some stops on a (generalised and idealised) journey with an e-book. In Chapter 2, on first impressions, we saw e-books functioning as unreal: as *ersatz books* (perceived as lacking certification by the publishing industry, whether or not these perceptions are accurate) and as digital proxies. Readers demanding professionalism are ostensibly willing to consider the possibility of excellence appearing in e-books, but receptiveness in theory may not translate into receptiveness in practice. In evaluating individual e-books, readers transact with authors and publishers in some new and some familiar ways, continuing to draw on both peritextual and epitextual elements, demonstrating that the spatial dimension of paratext still exists for e-books even if it functions very differently than for books in print.

In Chapter 3, on transactions, we saw e-books functioning as real books, but alternatively as *ersatz books* or digital proxies. The deep-seated conviction, shared by many readers, that they have a natural right to own, keep, and give away e-books in the same way they do print books indicates a sense on a profound level that e-books are books. A sense of meaningful ownership can be seized, and reappropriated, via principled resistance, digital audition, or a conscious decision to change one's idea of what an e-book can be and accept a digital book collection as a personal library. However, pain-free book disposal and some forms of piracy favour, instead, a conception of the e-book as *ersatz book*, while the use of digital reading copies to meaningfully spend time with a distant or sacrosanct book collection calls for a digital proxy. This recasts e-books as integral to building a personal library, but not necessarily as components of that library; when an e-novel is used as a digital proxy, it operates more as a tool for reaching a book than as a book in its own right. In Chapter 4, on materiality and the act of reading, we saw that in terms of enjoyment, e-novels function sometimes as real, but more often as incomplete books. Aesthetic pleasure in the material object emerges as something effectively exclusive to print, and tactile and sensory pleasure in handling the material object nearly so. However, other forms of pleasure are preserved or even heightened. Many respondents describe reading as such a valued and integral part of their daily lives that it is essential to them to have a book, ready for reading, at every moment: the fear of being caught bookless is so real that having e-books available as emergency reading relieves anxiety as well as providing enjoyment. The 'backup book' eases painful 'abibliopho-bia' precisely because, in this light, the e-book is real: potentially an austere or unlovely book, but still a book. While some ceremonies of reading such as physical bookshop browsing and putting aside time to relax on the sofa with a fat hardcover may be muted or even lost, interacting with literature on one's own terms, choosing the available, adaptable, accommodating book, fosters a new kind of intimacy, and opens up new spaces for reading in participants' lives. For some participants, the incomplete book is some-thing that cannot thrive on its own – presenting barriers to immersion and being 'lost in a book' – but for others, it can deliver key reading pleasures just as well as print. In Chapter 5, on reading identities, we saw the e-book as again sometimes real, but more often unreal because it is incomplete. It can't contribute to readerly identity as fully as can a print book because its own identity is obscured: it is not only less visible to friends and to observers in the reader's physical environment but also less visible to the reader themself. While their e-books are to retailers uncomfortably and unprecedentedly visible, readers consider data gathered by retailers to be unrepresentative and misleading. Readers who object to retailer surveil-lance demonstrate particular concern about Amazon; the evidence that they avoid Amazon for e-book purchases but still use Amazon for print book purchases underscores the degree to which it is surveillance of page-by-page reading, not tracking of books purchased, that troubles them most intensely. Despite the image of e-reading devices as vital tools for furtive reading, the actual importance of furtive reading as a motivator for choosing digital appears very low, making the exaggerated, and gendered, image of the furtive reader a distorted and damaging stereotype.

And finally, when it comes to emotion, e-books can function not only as incomplete books but also as real books. Print inspires deep feelings and passionate loyalty for many: numerous qualitative responses highlight love, either for print books themselves or for print-specific activities such as browsing physical bookshops. That said, digital enthusiasts' love is no less true for being somewhat unusual. Loathing of e-books is rare, and the most common stance towards e-books among book lovers is tepid appreciation. E-reading is wholly compatible with a love of books, and with identification as a bibliophile. Participants qualified the bibliophile definition to stress that while they loved the material object, they loved reading and literature more, some describing themselves as 'readingophiles' or 'whatever the equivalent for stories is'. Book lovers, whether or not they embrace the label of bibliophile (and only a minority do embrace it), can experience love for e-books, and, through avenues including digital audition, annotation and other forms of personalisation, and patronage, can deepen their relationships with beloved e-books.

These four conceptions of what an e-book is – a real book, an *ersatz book*, a digital proxy, or an incomplete book – illuminate how the type of unrealness matters as much as the unrealness itself. Different conceptions further different agendas, and readers gain from being able to move between realness and unrealness, and back and forth between different forms of unrealness. The *ersatz book*, for example, is painless to discard and equally painless to steal. The digital proxy allows users to feel that they are spending time with their own cherished books without hefting, transporting, or damaging personal print copies. The incomplete book can give, at least for some, experiences of absorptive reading pleasure, intimacy, and connection shorn of all that draws attention, takes up space, or makes demands of the reader or those around them. Any one conception of an e-book has disadvantages, even the e-book as real book. But moving between conceptions, even in the same reading situation or for the same book, offers, on the face of it, the best of all worlds. Readers can have their books and read them, too. The price is a degree of instability, and evidence here indicates that readers are willing to accept that small price: to tolerate ambiguity, and to embrace contradiction rather than strive for tidiness. Given the rewards, it is easier to envision a future of continued flexible movement than it is to predict an outbreak of consistency.

But even if we have evidence that readers benefit from the instability – is that all readers? Subjective and conditional realness is one thing if, should you for any reason require realness (the experience or feeling of it for yourself, or the reliable appearance of it to others), you can simply revert to print. If you are among the many for whom print is not an option, having one's reading open to relegation is anything but trivial. Returning to the free-text comments of survey respondents explaining why they consider e-books to be real books, 'the argument about what constitutes real reading is very annoying for those of us with disabilities who have less choice of how we read', meaning that 'only classing physical books as "real books" feels outdated and ableist' and 'implying that [e-books] are somehow less valid is not okay'. If a person with visual impairment who uses text-to-speech or audiobooks, or whose dyslexia is helped by the low-glare screen and adjustable margins and line spacing of an e-ink reader, or indeed a person who presents as female and likes reading on a Kindle, but loses the cultural capital associated with reading because onlookers assume that she must be reading *Fifty Shades of Grey*, can have their reading 'unrealed', that is an erasure – one that is as unnecessary as it is unjust. If we accept a status quo of subjective and conditional realness, we must also accept authority and autonomy on the part of the reader. For literary communities to shrug our collective shoulders and say *I guess it's real to you* is complacent and insufficient. What would bring such readers in from the cold, and make our reading equal, would be *if it's real to you, that makes it real full stop.*

Creating Real Books

The present inability of e-books to consistently serve as real books presents creators with an immediate challenge and a longer term question. Just as moving between conceptions requires comfort with a degree of inconsistency, the idea that an e-book can attain bookness without first attaining realness requires a certain mental flexibility. But as Tea Uglow makes clear, it is possible to be an enthusiastic creator of e-books,[6] and a creator who regards e-books as books, without conceding that e-books are real.[7]

The challenge lies in generating capital – economic, social, or cultural – from e-books when not only their value but their nature is also in constant flux. If (as I hypothesised at the very start of this project) there were evidence of some distinct population of readers that believes e-books to be always real, always enjoying bookness, or always equal in value to print, shrewd marketers might locate and cater to an 'e-books are real books' camp, and work to expand that camp by understanding and promoting its motivations and beliefs. The fact that it is the same readers, sometimes when reading the same novel, who see an e-book as real or unreal, and enjoying or not enjoying bookness, as it suits their present needs, demands that any strategy address those present needs, and approach specific reading contexts and reading events, not just specific readers.

On the level of marketing, framing a given e-novel as a portable, unobtrusive part of a book (as contemporary Kindle marketing, with its iconography of park benches and beach totes, so often does) is not immediately compatible with framing it as real and whole, or indeed as a handy digital proxy or undemanding *ersatz book*. While major publishers or retailers may have the data and the resources to microtarget advertising based on reading context and reading event (a crude but immediately feasible example would be using location data to speak differently to a reader on a speeding commuter train, a reader outside her usual country of residence, and a reader sitting in her own home – after all, Amazon knows where you live), smaller operations may not. If so, independent publishers and retailers could be forced to choose, foregrounding one conception at the expense of others. On a deeper level, that of e-book and e-reading device design, the e-novel as product could be shaped to cater to certain needs, and hence conform to certain conceptions: either in committing to one path and accepting that readers will be fickle, or in attempting to create texts and devices capable of adaptation. Examples could include further advances in adaptable paratext, with changes controlled by the reader (as with customisable font) or controlled by the publisher (as with targeted advertisements overlaying a Kindle Original e-book on a basic-model Kindle). Chapter 4 explored reader customisation efforts such as hacking e-book files to embed favoured cover images, as with Penguin Classics-inspired cover art for the Harry Potter series.[8] Netflix's controversial practice of presenting the same film with different movie-poster visuals depending on customer viewing history and inferred demographics (e.g. sometimes showing Black supporting characters as if they were central characters, but only to customers whom Netflix thinks may be Black),[9] which will only be accelerated by increasing use of AI,[10] raises the possibility not only of targeted cover art but also other elements of peritext such as blurbs, scholarly prefaces, reading group guides, and preview chapters that influence reading of the text. A retailer like Amazon knows when a given customer reads the same e-novel twice, suggesting that it had become a rare 'reread novel'. Similarly, it knows (as long as all the purchases were with Amazon) when a given customer has bought an e-book followed by a print edition, suggesting either digital audition or gift, or print followed by an e-book edition, suggesting reading copy. The way that a retailer like Amazon could then tailor paratext to foreground a real book, *ersatz book*, incomplete book, or digital proxy conception opens up new possibilities for paratextual exchange – if authors and publishers are privy to the essential data.

The question facing creators is whether e-books represent a viable medium for their art. The idea that e-books can ever be real could be welcome news to writers previously leery of e-only or digital-first imprints. But the fact that any e-books they make will not be consistently real, and can at any moment lose their bookness, may not satisfy the author, editor, designer, or artist called to create books. Is the e-novel real enough, *book* enough, to be their life's work? A sense that they have created a functional part of a book (such as a text that fosters genuine narrative engagement and gives a true experience of being 'lost in a book' even if certain aspects of enjoyment of the physical object are, so to speak, out of reach) may be acceptable, but the sense that they have invested their hours and their identity into the making of an *ersatz book* may not. Whether contingent realness and unstable bookness can be enough may depend on a given creator's combination of personal motivations: for example, creating for the sake of profit, prestige, wide readership, professional recognition, what Lewis Hyde would recognise as a gift to the world,[11] or any proportion of these. But, as Uglow demonstrates, creators are not dependent on realness any more than bookness is dependent on realness. Creators may find the idea of parallel and coexisting conceptions of realness liberating and invigorating, opening up new creative possibilities for books that do not need to be real to be useful, valuable, important, meaningful, and loved.

The nature of authorship is, at the time this book goes to press, on the brink of complete transformation. Advances in AI made 2023 the year when routine use of natural language processing was placed in the hands of the general public, and when machine-authored literature passed from the domain of experimentation by an informed and technologically equipped minority (a long-standing tradition, as Henrickson documents)[12] into routine publishing workflows. As the rights of authors whose works have been used, without their consent, to train large language models[13] are thrashed out in the courts, the status of authors of any text, AI-assisted or not, remains uncertain. The scenario Eichhorn envisaged in 2022, asking 'could Harlequin Romance, which already publishes a massive amount of content each month (about 120 unique titles), lower its cost and increase its content production by handing over some or all of its writing to romance-writing bots?'[14] is now perfectly within reach – if one is comfortable with considering 'some' to include a human writing prompts, approving the cover, opening the Amazon CreateSpace account, and posting the output as a book, Kindle Unlimited is already teeming with examples (some of which parasitically pursue sales by appropriating the name of an established author).[15] But data from this study suggest that the technical means to replace human authors would not automatically translate to a commercial imperative, or a cultural shift, or even appetite for such a replacement. As we've seen, human effort constitutes a core argument for e-book realness: if to any reader 'a person wrote it, a person is reading it,' is the reason why 'it's a book', the author is not expendable.[16] Shot through the discourse of the 'e-book wars' is constant fear of diminishment: anxiety that moves towards digital will mean a loss of magic (as with respondents choosing print because 'the smell of old paper is magic' and headlines such as 'With Its New Kindles, Amazon Tries to Replicate the Magic of Paper'), and reaching backwards for a time when, as Howard explained, a rare, costly, imposing book could attain bookness through status as an 'object of veneration. . .a thing with dignity, magic, and the power to inspire awe'.[17] If human authors are one means of attaining bookness, and bookness holds magic we still desire, how is it in our interests to demote even a single magician?

For readers, implications include the degree to which experiences of realness are individual, contextualised, utilitarian, and specific. If creators need not strive in every case for realness as a necessary precondition for importance or meaning, readers need not grasp after it either. As consciously switching between conceptions allows readers to effectively make e-books real at will, the power appears to have shifted in this regard decisively from authors and publishers to readers. With digital audition, reading device choice, and paratextual customisation offering further opportunities to readers to consciously distance themselves from some texts and cultivate closer relationships to others, authors and publishers are more dependent than ever on negotiation with, rather than dictation to, the reader. But as the power of publishers wanes, the power of retailers may be increasing. If the act of purchase can indeed meaningfully foster feelings of connection to a given e-book (an important area for further research), exactly how Apple and Amazon and other major distributors frame the transaction – as purchase or (as with Kindle Unlimited) as loan – will have enormous influence on readers' relationships to books (much, perhaps, as Netflix and Amazon and Hulu exert influence on relationships not only to streaming television platforms but to the medium of television itself).

There are a multitude of reasons to defer study of e-book realness. Scholars are warned against research on the digital for fear of a rapidly changing topic and rapidly dating results.[18] Examination of the subjective and unstable is, as my student recognised, frustratingly short on firm conclusions. But learning more about reading, a vast swathe of which now takes place on screen, requires it. Understanding more about how we imagine the book, and what we want from it, requires it as well. Asking when, and how, and why e-books count is indivisible from the joint cultural project that is our evolving conception of the book. It is a vast and collective act of making in which no reader's experience can be ignored.

Definitions

As commonplace words used differently in different contexts, several key terms require a brief definition to clarify how they are used in this book.

The complexities of the term legitimacy are evident from the first elements of its Oxford English Dictionary definition of '1. Conformity to the law, to rules, or to some recognized principle; lawfulness. Also: conformity to sound reasoning; logicality; justifiability.'[1] The 'also' draws attention to the fact that there is more than one road to legitimacy. One route is that of conformity to laws or rules (as with a 'legitimate government'), but another is conformity to logic, in the sense of a position that can be soundly argued from first principles (as with a 'legitimate viewpoint'). The definition embraces respect for convention, yet also respect for the kind of critical reasoning that makes it possible to innovate, and in turn inaugurate new conventions. In this book, I use this conception of legitimacy as a destination that can be reached by more than one path, and acknowledge the role of communities as well as individuals in judging whether the destination has been reached or not. Explorations of legitimacy in social science frequently draw on Max Weber's 1924 argument that the legitimacy of a social order depends on whether 'action is approximately or on the average oriented to certain determinate "maxims" or rules'.[2] Johnson, Dowd, and Ridgeway, examining definitions of legitimacy from across social psychological and organisational literature, find differences in emphasis of various aspects, but identify some 'fundamental similarities', among them that '(b) Although legitimacy is mediated by the perceptions and behaviours of individuals, it is fundamentally a collective process. It comes about through and depends upon the implied presence of a social audience, those assumed to accept the encompassing framework of beliefs, norms, and values, and, therefore, the construal of the object as legitimate'.[3] In this book, I use the term legitimacy to describe such collective processes mediated by individuals, ones in which readers are neither all-powerful, passing judgement in a vacuum and unaffected by any implied social audience, nor powerless, passive observers of a process that does not involve them. (This differs from Bourdieu's use of the term in distinctions between 'legitimate', 'middle-brow', and 'popular' taste, where 'legitimate' still very much describes orientation towards rules and maxims, but specifically refers to categories more and less associated with elite audiences.)[4]

Reputation, in contrast, is frequently defined as a phenomenon in which the individual is less directly involved. Reputation is generally understood to be a meta-belief, a 'belief about beliefs'.[5] An individual may decide that a reputation is undeserved and choose to defy it (as with a customer buying a novel on Amazon despite one-star reviews), or attempt to ignore it, but that is not the same thing as denying that the reputation exists and matters. The Oxford English Dictionary definition of reputation further foregrounds the relative aspect of reputation – that it encompasses not merely esteem but also whether it is more or less esteem than enjoyed by others – and 'good name', or the role reputation plays in marking out an individual or organisation as suitable for future relations: '*1. a. The condition, quality, or fact of being highly regarded or esteemed; credit, fame, distinction; respectability, good report. b. The honour, credit, good name, or fame of a particular person or thing 2. The general opinion or estimate of a person's character or other qualities; the relative esteem in which a person or thing is held.*'[6] This also emphasises that reputation is a 'general opinion or estimate': it need not be a consensus view to have a meaningful effect. This conception of reputation is particularly visible in Publishing Studies, where one instance of suspected client poaching can cost a young agent her 'good name' or where Picador's 'reputation as a publisher of upmarket literary writing' does not mean that every novel on its list will automatically be seen as upmarket.[7] Management research, a field in which the study of reputation has increasing prominence, identifies a 'triad of identity, image and reputation' where 'these concepts are related to but still different from each other'.[8] In my usage of the term in this book, I similarly draw a distinction between identity, which implies authenticity and truth, and reputation, which only implies reasonably wide recognition. I also draw a distinction between image, which even when shared by many individuals, or actively communicated by an organisation, is construed directly,[9] and reputation, a meta-belief.

Credibility also involves belief, but in a much more direct way. *Credible* is defined by the Oxford English Dictionary as 'able to be believed' or 'believed in'.[10] As Rieh and Danielson point out in their examination of credibility in a multidimensional framework, researchers in different fields use diverse methodologies to study characteristics of source, comparisons between media, and evaluation of information (the latter typical of their own fields of Information Studies and Human–Computer Interaction) but ultimately there is an individual at the end of the process: a person who is convinced or not convinced.[11] While credibility can be a component of reputation,[12] and the judgement of the many is inarguably a factor in one person's ability to trust, the individual is directly involved. In this book, I use 'credible' and 'credibility' to indicate actors and objects that have convinced individuals or endeavour to convince individuals, whether as 'honest, principled or authentic' (as an author may be) or 'effective or operational' (as an app or device may be).

E-novel and *e-book* are, as discussed in the overview of prior research, contentious terms that have been applied at different times to many varieties of artefacts and humanistic knowledge objects.[13] In this book, I use the terms broadly and inclusively. Rather than attempt to police usage or to exclude any given artefact from the definition (e.g. if it were conspicuously short, or comprised video as well as text, or presented as a Microsoft Word file rather than PDF or .EPUB), if a survey, focus group, or interview participant chose to describe an artefact as an e-book, I have classed it as an e-book and included it in the analysis. Similarly, if a participant described an artefact as an e-novel, I have classed it as such, rather than vetting it for length, platform, and so on (or, indeed, applying an attempt at criteria of fiction versus non-fiction). This means that forms such as interactive literature and Wattpad- or AO3-distributed fan fiction are discussed by some participants alongside e-books that remain within bounds of what could be represented in a mainstream-published print novel, but by other participants held apart. Policies of breadth and inclusivity have the obvious effects on the results, making them more authentic to respondents' experience, but not automatically generalisable to e-books or e-novels when defined more narrowly in other studies.

Finally, this book defines *reader* broadly and inclusively. Rather than limit this to some variation of 'non-professional', in the sense of a person not employed in some manner in the publishing industry (a very problematic definition for an industry with porous borders) or impose criteria regarding frequency of reading, I use 'reader' to mean any person who reads, whatever their background, knowledge base, or experience.

Notes

Introduction

1 Survey 2020 in both cases.
2 Survey 2015.
3 Survey 2015.
4 Survey 2015.
5 Desktop publishing by such means was limited to those with coding expertise as well as access to the requisite equipment: as Bryan Dietz explains, 'I extracted the Fortran programs from the [*Software Tools*] tape and built a working version of NROFF. Since the H316 didn't have an upper/lower case printer, I plugged in a spare T1200 and wrote a driver to let the NROFF program print its output on the upper lower case T1200.' Bryan Dietz, 'E-mail message to author', 7 December 2022.
6 Brian W. Kernighan and P.J. Plauger, *Software Tools* (Boston, MA: Addison-Wesley, 1976).
7 To this day, I'm not sure how it came into my hands: the company wasn't focussed on personal electronics, and I didn't recall ever having been asked to look at a physical product of any kind before. My hope is that my excessive enthusiasm didn't cost anyone any money.
8 For more on the wedge and its supposed bookishness, please see Chapter 4.
9 NuvoMedia, the company that made the Rocket eBook, was acquired by Gemstar in 2000, and soon after the Rocket went down with the Gemstar ship. Famously, NuvoMedia founders Martin Eberhard and Marc Tarpenning first offered their technology to Jeff Bezos, but went into business for themselves rather than agree to Bezos's demand for exclusivity. For more, see Barbara A. Schreiber, 'Martin Eberhard and Marc Tarpenning: Tesla Co-Founders & American Entrepreneurs', in *Encyclopedia Britannica*, www.britannica.com/biography/Martin-Eberhard-and-Marc-Tarpenning; Brad Stone, *The Everything Store: Jeff Bezos and the Age of Amazon* (London: Little, Brown, 2014).
10 Matthew Rubery, *The Untold Story of the Talking Book* (Cambridge, MA: Harvard University Press, 2016), 2.

11 For which Douglas Adams is duly celebrated, the 1978 radio play of *The Hitchhiker's Guide to the Galaxy* representing one of the earliest known uses of 'electronic book'. See Simon Peter Rowberry, 'The Ebook Imagination', *Digital Humanities Quarterly* 16, no. 1 (18 February 2022): 11.

12 This was for the first six rounds the survey spontaneous and unprompted: from 2014 to 2017 and again in 2020–21, there were no questions on realness. In 2022, to investigate this directly, I added a final question, appearing after all the standard questions from previous years, which I'll discuss in detail in Chapter 1.

13 Survey 2022, 2015, 2014.

14 Survey 2015 in both cases.

15 Laura Dietz, Claire Warwick, and Samantha Rayner, 'Auditioning for Permanence', *Logos* 26, no. 4 (2015): 25, https://doi.org/10.1163/1878-4712-11112088.

16 Survey 2015.

17 Survey participants were adults aged 18+, with half (49.8 per cent) living in the UK and half living in other countries. The survey was released in English and gathered data from English speakers only. The survey has 1,732 respondents, of which 751 are March 2020 or later. For statistical tests, I used an alpha level of 0.05 and for effect size a threshold of Cramer's $V > 0.1$, where degrees of freedom (df) $= 1$. Focus groups (2014–17) were 'pre-acquainted' (see Rosaline Barbour, *Doing Focus Groups* (London: Sage, 2007), 66–7) naturally occurring groups of participants who gathered regularly to discuss fiction, including book groups and the editorial team of a student anthology. Interviews were with individuals who were regular members of such naturally occurring groups, such as book groups or creative writing courses. Qualitative data, including free-text responses, were analysed using Braun and Clark's thematic analysis approach (see Virginia Braun and Victoria Clarke, 'Using Thematic Analysis in Psychology', *Qualitative Research in Psychology* 3, no. 2 (1 January 2006): 77–101, https://doi.org/10.1191/1478088706qp063oa) and using Nvivo software. Data from 2014 to 2017 was previously published as part of a doctoral dissertation with University College London (UCL). The survey was approved by the ethics panels of the Faculty of Arts and Humanities at UCL (pre-2020) and the Faculty of Arts, Humanities and Social Sciences at Anglia Ruskin University (ARU, post-2020).

18 Tom Clark et al., *Bryman's Social Research Methods*, 6th ed. (Oxford: Oxford University Press, 2021), 271, 497–520.

19 Jussi Parrika, *What Is Media Archaeology?* (Cambridge: Polity, 2012); Nick Montfort and Ian Bogost, *Racing the Beam: The Atari Video Computer System* (Cambridge, MA: MIT Press, 2009).

20 Janice Radway, *Reading the Romance*, 2nd ed. (Chapel Hill, NC: University of North Carolina Press, 1991); READ-IT, 'About the Project', READ-IT Project, https://readit-project.eu/about-the-project/.

21 Johanna Drucker, *The Century of Artists' Books*, 2nd ed. (New York: Granary Books, 2004); Johanna Drucker, 'The Virtual Codex from Page Space to

E-Space', in *A Companion to Digital Literary Studies*, ed. Susan Schreibman and Ray Siemens (Oxford: Blackwell, 2007): 238–50; Paul Gooding, Melissa Terras, and Claire Warwick, 'The Myth of the New: Mass Digitization, Distant Reading, and the Future of the Book', *Literary and Linguistic Computing* 28, no. 4 (2013): 629–39, https://doi.org/10.1093/llc/fqt051; Rowberry, 'The Ebook Imagination'; Ted Striphas, *The Late Age of Print: Everyday Book Culture from Consumerism to Control* (New York: Columbia University Press, 2011); Matt Hayler, *Challenging the Phenomenology of Technology: Embodiment, Expertise and Evolved Knowledge* (Basingstoke: Palgrave Macmillan, 2015); Simone Murray, *The Digital Literary Sphere: Reading, Writing, and Selling Books in the Internet Era* (Baltimore, MD: Johns Hopkins University Press, 2018).

22 Nicholas Carr, 'Beyond Words: The Kindle Fire and the Book's Future', *Roughtype (blog)*, 28 September 2011, www.roughtype.com/?p=1534; Striphas, *The Late Age of Print*, 101–2; Mark McGurl, 'Everything and Less: Fiction in the Age of Amazon', *Modern Language Quarterly* 77, no. 3 (1 September 2016): 449, https://doi.org/10.1215/00267929-3570689; Murray, *The Digital Literary Sphere*, 54, 58–9; Alex Preston, 'How Real Books Have Trumped Ebooks', *The Observer*, 14 May 2017, sec. Books, www.theguardian.com/books/2017/may/14/how-real-books-trumped-ebooks-publishing-revival; Ivana Kottasová, 'Real Books Are Back. E-Book Sales Plunge Nearly 20%', *CNNMoney*, 27 April 2017, https://money.cnn.com/2017/04/27/media/ebooks-sales-real-books/index.html; Conor Pope, 'Rise and Fall of the Kindle: How Real Books Are Fighting Back', *The Irish Times*, 22 May 2017, www.irishtimes.com/news/consumer/rise-and-fall-of-the-kindle-how-real-books-are-fighting-back-1.3086282.

23 Anne Mangen, 'The Digitization of Literary Reading', *Orbis Litterarum* 71, no. 3 (2016): 244, https://doi.org/10.1111/oli.12095; Anne Mangen, Gérard Olivier, and Jean-Luc Velay, 'Comparing Comprehension of a Long Text Read in Print Book and on Kindle: Where in the Text and When in the Story?', *Frontiers in Psychology* 10 (2019), www.frontiersin.org/articles/10.3389/fpsyg.2019.00038.

24 Ben Davies, Christina Lupton, and Johanne Gormsen Schmidt, *Reading Novels During the Covid-19 Pandemic* (Oxford: Oxford University Press, 2022), 12.

25 Jonathan Rose, 'Rereading the English Common Reader: A Preface to the History of Audiences', in *The Book History Reader*, ed. David Finkelstein and Alistair McCleery, 2nd ed. (Abingdon: Routledge, 1992), 425; Christine Pawley, 'Seeking "Significance": Actual Readers, Specific Reading Communities', *Book History* 5 (2002): 148–49, 157, https://doi.org/10.1353/bh.2002.0013.

26 Danielle Fuller and DeNel Rehberg Sedo, '"Boring, Frustrating, Impossible": Tracing the Negative Affects of Reading from Interviews to Story Circles', *Participations* 16, no. 1 (2019): 625. Fuller and Rehberg Sedo's experiments with participatory methods move beyond critique to the difficult work of

piloting new approaches, and in so doing presenting a new standard for imaginative, provocative research.

27 While recognising that acknowledging the situatedness of research data doesn't by itself provide easy answers about how the inquiry process affects research data. See p. 99, Nick J. Fox and Pam Alldred, 'Applied Research, Diffractive Methodology, and the Research-Assemblage: Challenges and Opportunities', *Sociological Research Online* 28, no. 1 (1 March 2023): 99, https://doi.org/10.1177/13607804211029978.

28 John W. Creswell, *Research Design: Qualitative, Quantitative and Mixed Methods Approaches*, 4th ed. (London: Sage, 2014), 15, 20.

29 Follow-up studies focussed on participants such as agents or editors would be extremely valuable.

30 Danielle Fuller and DeNel Rehberg Sedo, 'Introduction: Read This! Why Reading about Readers in an Age of Digital Media Makes Sense', *Participations* 16, no. 1 (2019): 134; Robert Darnton, 'What Is the History of Books?', in *The Book History Reader*, ed. David Finkelstein and Alistair McCleery, 2nd ed. (Abingdon: Routledge, 1982), 9–26.

31 Padmini Ray Murray and Claire Squires, 'The Digital Publishing Communications Circuit', *Book 2.0* 3, no. 1 (2013): 3–24, https://doi.org/10.1386/btwo.3.1.3_1.

32 Ray Murray and Squires, 'The Digital Publishing Communications Circuit'.

33 Ray Siemens et al., 'HCI-Book? Perspectives on E-Book Research, 2006–2008 (Foundational to Implementing New Knowledge Environments)', *Papers of the Bibliographical Society of Canada / Cahiers de La Société Bibliographique Du Canada* 49, no. 1 (2011): 49, https://doi.org/10.33137/pbsc.v49i1.21941.

34 J. Tappuni, 'What Nielsen Bookscan Data Tells Us about Ebook Sales Cycles and the Ebook Plateau', *Publishing Technology* (blog), 16 February 2015, www.publishingtechnology.com/2015/01/what-nielsen-bookscan-data-tells-us-about-ebook-sales-cycles-the-ebook-plateau/.

35 Nielsen BookData, 'Making Sense of 2022 – Nielsenbook-UK', https://nielsenbook.co.uk/making-sense-of-2022/; Nielsen BookData, 'A Tale of Three Formats – Nielsenbook-UK', 21 November 2022, https://nielsenbook.co.uk/a-tale-of-three-formats/.

36 Ellen Duffer, 'Amazon E-Book Sales Grow in 2017 and 2018', *Forbes*, 27 July 2018, www.forbes.com/sites/ellenduffer/2018/07/27/amazon-e-book-sales-grow-in-2017-and-2018/; Oliver Beldham, 'Bookscan Training' (Anglia Ruskin University, UK, 1 November 2018).

37 Nielsen, 'Year in Books Review', 2016, www.nielsen.com/us/en/insights/reports/2016/2015-us-book-industry-year-end-review.html.

38 Beldham, 'Bookscan Training'.

39 Laura Dietz, 'Projection or Reflection? The Pandemic Bookshelf as a Mirror for Self-Image and Personal Identity', *English Studies* 103, no. 5 (4 July 2022): 675–89, https://doi.org/10.1080/0013838X.2022.2087034; Porter Anderson, 'Coronavirus Impact: A New Survey by Italian Publishers Sees "Abandonment of Reading"', *Publishing Perspectives*, 16 July 2020, https://

publishingperspectives.com/2020/07/coronavirus-impact-a-new-survey-by-italian-publishers-sees-reading-dropping/; Joumana Khatib, 'How the Pandemic Changed the Way We Read', *The New York Times*, 12 March 2021, sec. Books, www.nytimes.com/interactive/2021/03/12/books/reading-trends.html; Emmanuel Stip, Linda Östlundh, and Karim Abdel Aziz, 'Bibliotherapy: Reading OVID During COVID', *Frontiers in Psychiatry* 11 (2020), www.frontiersin.org/articles/10.3389/fpsyt.2020.567539; Davies, Lupton, and Gormsen Schmidt, *Reading Novels During the Covid-19 Pandemic*; Porter Anderson, 'Coronavirus Impact: Nielsen Book India on Readers in the Pandemic', *Publishing Perspectives*, 15 July 2020, https://publishingperspectives.com/2020/07/coronavirus-impact-india-publishing-industry-nielsen-book-impact-study-pandemic-covid19/; Alison Flood, '"This Is Revolutionary": New Online Bookshop Unites Indies to Rival Amazon', *The Guardian*, 2 November 2020, sec. Books, www.theguardian.com/books/2020/nov/02/this-is-revolutionary-new-online-bookshop-unites-indies-to-rival-amazon; Mark Chandler, 'ACE Makes £152,000 Grant for Library e-Books and Audio', *The Bookseller*, 21 January 2021, www.thebookseller.com/news/ace-awards-152000-grant-library-e-books-and-audio-1233873; 'World Book Night: One in Three Reading More during Lockdown', *BBC News*, 23 April 2020, sec. Entertainment & Arts, www.bbc.com/news/entertainment-arts-52379327; Elisabeth Egan and Tina Jordan, 'Celeste Ng, Ann Patchett, Min Jin Lee and Others on the Books That Bring Them Comfort', *The New York Times*, 18 March 2020, sec. Books, www.nytimes.com/2020/03/18/books/comfort-books-celeste-ng-ann-patchett-and-others-coronavirus.html.

40 Bronwen Thomas, 'Taking Stock: Understanding Readerly Practices under Lockdown (Keynote)', *Digital Practices: Reading, Writing and Evaluation on the Web Conference* (University of Basel, 2020).

41 A trajectory suggested by signs in late 2023 that UK e-book sales were already subsiding after the 'digital bonanza of the pandemic', at least for major mainstream publishers. See Tom Tivnan, 'E-Book Sales Stall for the Big Six as Collective Returns Second-Lowest Total', *The Bookseller*, 3 February 2023, www.thebookseller.com/spotlight/e-book-sales-stall-for-the-big-six-as-collect Ive-returns-second-lowest-total.

42 Extensive work has been done to examine the changing metaphor of the book, most often from a theoretical perspective. International teams such as those assembled by the Implementing New Knowledge Environments (INKE) project and UNESCO Crossing Media Boundaries: Adaptations and New Media Forms of the Book Project have been instrumental in gathering and synthesising research from different fields. In the UK, the Arts and Humanities Research Council (AHRC)-funded The Book Unbound project, based at the Stirling Centre for International Publishing and Communication, has provided some of the most targeted research into the changing status of the book as a cultural object, in the context of broader changes to publishing in the face of digital transformations. See also Lisa Gitelman, *Always Already New: Media, History and the Data of Culture* (Cambridge, MA: MIT Press,

2006); Matthew Kirschenbaum, *Mechanisms: New Media and the Forensic Imagination* (Cambridge, MA: MIT Press, 2012); N. Katherine Hayles, *How We Think: Digital Media and Contemporary Technogenesis* (Chicago, IL: University of Chicago Press, 2012); Alan Galey, 'The Enkindling Reciter: E-Books in the Bibliographical Imagination', *Book History* 15 (2012): 210–47; Johanna Drucker, 'Performative Materiality and Theoretical Approaches to Interface', *Digital Humanities Quarterly* 7, no. 1 (1 July 2013), www .digitalhumanities.org/dhq/vol/7/1/000143/000143.html; Hayler, *Challenging the Phenomenology of Technology*.

43 Jean Baudrillard, *Simulacra and Simulation* (Ann Arbor, MI: University of Michigan Press, 1994); Jay David Bolter and Richard A. Grusin, 'Remediation', *Configurations* 4, no. 3 (1996): 311–58; Drucker, 'The Virtual Codex from Page Space to E-Space'; Striphas, *The Late Age of Print*; Siemens et al., 'HCI-Book?'; Claire Squires, Padmini Ray Murray, and Paula Jane Kiri Morris, 'The Book Unbound: Disruption and Disintermediation in the Digital Age', *Digital Artefact* (University of Stirling, Scott Russell Publishing Services, and Electric Bookshop, 2012), www.stir.ac.uk/research/hub/publication/ 704346; Alexis Weedon, 'The Book as a Dynamic System for the Commodification of Ideas and Cultural Expressions', *Primerjalna Knjizevnost* 35 (1 June 2012): 177–88; Jonathan Westin, 'Loss of Culture: New Media Forms and the Translation from Analogue to Digital Books', *Convergence* 19, no. 2 (1 May 2013): 129–40, https://doi.org/10.1177/1354856512452398; Gooding, Terras, and Warwick, 'The Myth of the New'; Alexis Weedon et al., 'Crossing Media Boundaries: Adaptations and New Media Forms of the Book', *Convergence: The International Journal of Research into New Media Technologies* 20 (7 February 2014): 108–24, https://doi.org/10.1177/ 1354856513515968; Simon Peter Rowberry, 'Ebookness', *Convergence* 23, no. 3 (1 June 2017): 289–305, https://doi.org/10.1177/1354856515592509.

44 Gooding, Terras, and Warwick, 'The Myth of the New'; Shafquat Towheed, Rosalind Crone, and Katie Halsey, 'General Introduction', in *The History of Reading: A Reader*, ed. Shafquat Towheed, Rosalind Crone, and Katie Halsey (Abingdon: Routledge, 2011), 3.

45 While Brown and his collaborators had ambitions to produce a functional device, and there are some reports that a demo was exhibited in New York later in the 1930s, scholars have not to date found convincing evidence that a working prototype ever existed. See Craig Saper, 'Introduction and Notes on the Text:—Readies for Bob Brown's Machine—Machine Art—Conceptual Poetry—Political Engagement—e-Literacies—', in *Readies for Bob Brown's Machine: A Critical Facsimile*, ed. Craig Saper and Eric White (Edinburgh: Edinburgh University Press, 2019), xxii–iii, https://doi.org/10.1515/ 9781474455060-003.

46 Alan Galey, 'Reading the Book of Mozilla: Web Browsers and the Materiality of Digital Texts', in *The History of Reading, Volume 3: Methods, Strategies, Tactics*, ed. Shafquat Towheed and Rosalind Crone (Basingstoke: Palgrave Macmillan, 2011), 205.

Chapter 1

1 Murray, *The Digital Literary Sphere*; Jessica Pressman, *Bookishness: Loving Books in a Digital Age* (New York: Columbia University Press, 2020); Angus Phillips and Miha Kovač, *Is This a Book?* (Cambridge: Cambridge University Press, 2022).

2 John B. Thompson, *Book Wars: The Digital Revolution in Publishing* (Cambridge: Polity, 2021).

3 Simone Murray, '"Selling" Literature: The Cultivation of Book Buzz in the Digital Literary Sphere', *Logos* 27, no. 1 (7 June 2016): 12, https://doi.org/10.1163/1878-4712-11112094.

4 Westin, 'Loss of Culture', 130.

5 Caroline Koegler and Corinna Norrick-Rühl, *Are Books Still 'Different'?: Literature as Culture and Commodity in a Digital Age* (Cambridge: Cambridge University Press, 2023), 14.

6 Jean-Claude Carrière and Umberto Eco, *This Is Not the End of the Book* (London: Harvill Secker, 2011); Michael Bhaskar, *The Content Machine* (London: Anthem, 2013); Leslie Howsam, *Old Books and New Histories: An Orientation to Studies in Book and Print Culture* (Toronto: University of Toronto Press, 2006); Kathleen Fitzpatrick, *Planned Obsolescence: Publishing, Technology, and the Future of the Academy* (New York: New York University Press, 2011).

7 Weedon considered the value systems underpinning such metaphors (e.g. of the book as a hinge, a crystal goblet, or a rose) as she explored the book as 'a dynamic system to commodify ideas and cultural expressions'. See Weedon, 'The Book as a Dynamic System for the Commodification of Ideas and Cultural Expressions'; Weedon et al., 'Crossing Media Boundaries', 109, 120.

8 Siemens et al., 'HCI-Book?', 49.

9 Siemens et al., 'HCI-Book?', 49.

10 Striphas, *The Late Age of Print*; Galey, 'The Enkindling Reciter'; Ellen McCracken, 'Expanding Genette's Epitext/Peritext Model for Transitional Electronic Literature: Centrifugal and Centripetal Vectors on Kindles and IPads', *Narrative* 21, no. 1 (2013): 105–24.

11 Mangen, 'The Digitization of Literary Reading'; Mangen, Olivier, and Velay, 'Comparing Comprehension of a Long Text Read in Print Book and on Kindle'; Maryanne Wolf, *Reader, Come Home: The Reading Brain in a Digital World* (New York: HarperCollins, 2018).

12 Sven Birkerts, *The Gutenberg Elegies: The Fate of Reading in an Electronic Age*, 2nd ed. (New York: Fawcett Columbine, 2006).

13 Stephann Makri et al., 'A Library or Just Another Information Resource? A Case Study of Users' Mental Models of Traditional and Digital Libraries', *Journal of the American Society for Information Science and Technology* 58, no. 3 (2007): 433–45, https://doi.org/10.1002/asi.20510; George Buchanan, Dana McKay, and Joanna Levitt, 'Where My Books Go: Choice and Place in Digital Reading', in *Proceedings of the 15th ACM/IEEE-CS Joint Conference*

on Digital Libraries, JCDL '15 (New York: Association for Computing Machinery, 2015), 17–26, https://doi.org/10.1145/2756406.2756917.

14 Millicent Weber, 'Conceptualizing Audience Experience at the Literary Festival', *Continuum* 29, no. 1 (2 January 2015): 84–96, https://doi.org/10.1080/10304312.2014.986058; Murray, '"Selling" Literature'; Murray, *The Digital Literary Sphere*.

15 Yehuda E. Kalay, 'Introduction: Preserving Cultural Heritage through Digital Media', in *New Heritage: New Media and Cultural Heritage*, ed. Yehuda E. Kalay, Timothy Kvan, and Janice Affleck (London: Routledge, 2008).

16 De Hamel, quoted in Preston, 'How Real Books Have Trumped Ebooks'.

17 James Raven, 'The Industrial Revolution of the Book', in *The Cambridge Companion to the History of the Book*, ed. Leslie Howsam (Cambridge: Cambridge University Press, 2014), 143–61.

18 Striphas, *The Late Age of Print*; John B. Thompson, *Merchants of Culture: The Publishing Business in the Twenty-First Century*, 2nd ed. (Cambridge: Polity, 2012).

19 Westin, 'Loss of Culture', 129–34. Westin used Callon and Latour's Actor-Network Theory (ANT) perspectives to approach the limitations of given book formats (e.g. the limitations of a .MOBI file as read on a Kindle) as non-human actants that participate alongside human actors in the functions of society.

20 Rowberry, 'Ebookness', 302.

21 Philip Smith, 'The Whatness of Bookness, or What Is a Book', Text, *Book_Arts-L* (Peter D. Verheyen, 20 November 1996), www.philobiblon.com/bookness.shtml.

22 Smith, 'The Whatness of Bookness'; Emily-Jane Dawson, 'Is It a Book?', *Book Arts*, 1997, www.philobiblon.com/isitabook/bookarts/index.html.

23 Donald R. Howard, *The Idea of the Canterbury Tales* (Berkeley, CA: University of California Press, 1976), 63.

24 Howard, *The Idea of the Canterbury Tales*, 63.

25 Fitzpatrick, *Planned Obsolescence*, 91.

26 Naomi Baron, *Words Onscreen: The Fate of Reading in a Digital World* (New York: Oxford University Press, 2015), 38. It is a stance that many audiobook listeners would fiercely dispute; see Rubery, *The Untold Story of the Talking Book*, 59–61.

27 In essence as a vague synonym for bookishness, but bookishness in its vernacular usage of relating in some way to books rather than what Pressman explores in depth in *Bookishness: Loving Books in a Digital Age*. There, Pressman introduces the concept with 'this is what I describe as "bookishness": creative acts that engage the physicality of the book within a digital culture, in modes that may be sentimental, fetishistic, radical' (2020, p. 1).

28 Gwen Glazer, 'The 12 Days of Bookness', *The New York Public Library*, 11 December 2017, www.nypl.org/blog/2017/12/11/12-days-of-bookness; Gabriela Silva, 'Mind Your Own Bookness', *Behance*, February 2014, www.behance.net/gallery/13854543/Mind-Your-Own-Bookness.

29 Drucker, *The Century of Artists' Books*, 7.
30 Drucker, 'The Virtual Codex from Page Space to E-Space'; 'Performative Materiality and Theoretical Approaches to Interface'; 'Graphical Approaches to the Digital Humanities', in *A New Companion to Digital Humanities*, ed. Susan Schriebman, Ray Siemens, and John Unsworth (Hoboken, NJ: Wiley-Blackwell, 2016). This range was showcased by the 2015–16 *Bookness: 14 Observations* exhibitions linked to the Books & the Human: AHRC 10th Anniversary Debate.
31 N. Katherine Hayles, *Electronic Literature: New Horizons for the Literary* (Notre Dame: University of Notre Dame Press, 2008); Hayles, *How We Think*; Kirschenbaum, *Mechanisms*; Matthew Kirschenbaum and Sarah Werner, 'Digital Scholarship and Digital Studies: The State of the Discipline', *Book History* 17 (2014): 406–58; Matthew Kirschenbaum, *Track Changes: A Literary History of Word Processing* (Cambridge, MA: MIT Press, 2016); Matthew Kirschenbaum, *Bitstreams: The Future of Digital Literary Heritage* (Philadelphia, PA: University of Pennsylvania Press, 2021); Galey, 'Reading the Book of Mozilla'; Galey, 'The Enkindling Reciter'.
32 Amaranth Borsuk, *The Book* (Cambridge, MA: The MIT Press, 2018), 18.
33 Baudrillard, *Simulacra and Simulation*, 2; Bolter and Grusin, 'Remediation', 346.
34 Sydney J. Shep, 'Digital Materiality', in *A New Companion to Digital Humanities*, ed. Susan Schreibman, Ray Siemens, and John Unsworth (Chichester: John Wiley & Sons, Ltd, 2015), 323, https://doi.org/10.1002/9781118680605.ch22.
35 Kirschenbaum, *Mechanisms*, 2; Christiane Paul, 'The Myth of Immateriality: Presenting and Preserving New Media', in *MediaArtHistories*, ed. Oliver Grau (Cambridge, MA: MIT Press, 2007), https://direct.mit.edu/books/edited-volume/1981/chapter/54117/The-Myth-of-Immateriality-Presenting-and; Jean-François Blanchette, 'A Material History of Bits', *Journal of the American Society for Information Science and Technology* 62, no. 6 (2011): 1042–57, https://doi.org/10.1002/asi.21542.
36 Shep, 'Digital Materiality', 323.
37 Gitelman, *Always Already New*, 96.
38 Shep, 'Digital Materiality', 323.
39 Hayler, *Challenging the Phenomenology of Technology*, 232, 225–29.
40 Kirschenbaum, *Mechanisms*, 3.
41 Kirschenbaum, *Mechanisms*, 11.
42 Kirschenbaum, *Mechanisms*, 12, 13.
43 Drucker, 'Performative Materiality and Theoretical Approaches to Interface'.
44 Drucker, 'Performative Materiality and Theoretical Approaches to Interface'.
45 Drucker, 'Performative Materiality and Theoretical Approaches to Interface'.
46 Siemens et al., 'HCI-Book?'.
47 Siemens et al., 'HCI-Book?', 35.
48 Siemens et al., 'HCI-Book?', 50–1, 57.
49 Galey, 'The Enkindling Reciter', 240.

50 Galey, 'The Enkindling Reciter', 240.
51 Gooding, Terras, and Warwick, 'The Myth of the New'.
52 Franco Moretti, *Graphs, Maps, Trees: Abstract Models for a Literary History* (London: Verso, 2007); Franco Moretti, *Distant Reading* (London: Verso, 2013); Matthew Jockers, *Macroanalysis: Digital Methods and Literary History* (Champaign, IL: University of Illinois Press, 2013); Jodie Archer and Matthew Jockers, *The Bestseller Code* (London: Allen Lane, 2016).
53 Gooding, Terras, and Warwick, 'The Myth of the New', 636, 637.
54 Please see Gérard Genette, *Paratexts: Thresholds of Interpretation*, trans. Jane Lewin (Cambridge: Cambridge University Press, 1997).
55 Fredrik Åström, 'The Context of Paratext: A Bibliometric Study of the Citation Contexts of Gérard Genette's Texts', in *Examining Paratextual Theory and its Applications in Digital Culture*, ed. Nadine Desrochers and Daniel Apollon (Hershey, PA: IGI global, 2014), 8–9.
56 Georg Stanitzek, 'Texts and Paratexts in Media', *Critical Inquiry* 32, no. 1 (September 2005): 35, https://doi.org/10.1086/498002.
57 Leah Tether, 'A Digital Manuscript Case Study: How Publishing Theory Can Advance the Practice of Manuscript Digitization', *Book 2.0* 3, no. 1 (1 June 2013): 61–77, https://doi.org/10.1386/btwo.3.1.61_1; Charlotte E. Cooper, 'What Is Medieval Paratext?', *Marginalia* 19 (2015): 37–50; Nadine Desrochers and Patricia Tomaszek, 'Bridging the Unknown : An Interdisciplinary Case Study of Paratext in Electronic Literature', in *Examining Paratextual Theory and Its Applications in Digital Culture*, ed. Nadine Desrochers and Daniel Apollon (Hershey, PA: IGI Global, 2014), 163; Astrid Ensslin, *Pre-web Digital Publishing and the Lore of Electronic Literature* (Cambridge: Cambridge University Press, 2022).
58 Dorothee Birke and Birte Christ, 'Paratext and Digitised Narrative: Mapping the Field', *Narrative* 21, no. 1 (2013): 67, https://doi.org/10.1353/nar.2013.0003.
59 Birke and Christ, 'Paratext and Digitised Narrative'; Nadine Desrochers and Daniel Apollon, eds., *Examining Paratextual Theory and Its Applications in Digital Culture* (Hershey, PA: IGI Global, 2014); Ellen McCracken, *Paratexts and Performance in the Novels of Junot Díaz and Sandra Cisneros* (New York: Palgrave Macmillan, 2016).
60 Galey, 'The Enkindling Reciter'; Rowberry, 'Ebookness'. Had it not been published at virtually the same time (late 2012 vs early 2013) Galey's paper would surely have challenged Birke and Christ's assertion that there was effectively no literature to review.
61 Maria Lindgren Leavenworth, 'The Paratext of Fan Fiction', *Narrative* 23, no. 1 (2015): 40–60; T. Shanmugapriya, Nirmala Menon, and Andy Campbell, 'An Introduction to the Functioning Process of Embedded Paratext of Digital Literature: Technoeikon of Digital Poetry', *Digital Scholarship in the Humanities* 34, no. 3 (1 September 2019): 646–60, https://doi.org/10.1093/llc/fqy064; Roswitha Skare, 'The Paratext of Digital Documents', *Journal of Documentation* 77, no. 2 (1 January 2020): 449–60, https://doi

.org/10.1108/JD-06-2020-0106; Ensslin, *Pre-web Digital Publishing and the Lore of Electronic Literature*; Kathryn Batchelor, *Translation and Paratexts* (Abingdon: Routledge, 2018).

62 Pierre Bourdieu, *The Rules of Art: Genesis and Structure of the Literary Field*, trans. Susan Emanuel (Cambridge: Polity, 1996).

63 See D.F. McKenzie, *Bibliography and the Sociology of Texts: The Panizzi Lectures (1986)* (Cambridge: Cambridge University Press, 1999).

64 See Jerome McGann, *The Textual Condition* (Princeton, NJ: Princeton University Press, 1991).

65 Thompson, *Merchants of Culture*, 332–33.

66 James F. English, *The Economy of Prestige* (Boston, MA: Harvard University Press, 2005); Claire Squires, *Marketing Literature* (Basingstoke: Palgrave MacMillan, 2007), 32.

67 Amy Hungerford, *Making Literature Now* (Stanford, CA: Stanford University Press, 2016), 38, quoting English, *The Economy of Prestige*, 14.

68 See Murray, *The Digital Literary Sphere*.

69 See Beth Driscoll, *The New Literary Middlebrow: Tastemakers and Reading in the Twenty-First Century* (Basingstoke: Palgrave Macmillan, 2014); Weber, 'Conceptualizing Audience Experience at the Literary Festival'; Millicent Weber, *Literary Festivals and Contemporary Book Culture* (London: Palgrave, 2018).

70 See Melanie Ramdarshan Bold, 'The Return of the Social Author: Negotiating Authority and Influence on Wattpad', *Convergence* 24, no. 2 (1 April 2018): 117–36, https://doi.org/10.1177/1354856516654459.

71 See Kenna MacTavish, 'The Emerging Power of the Bookstagrammer', in *Post-digital Book Cultures Australian Perspectives*, ed. Alexandra Dane and Millicent Weber (Clayton: Monash University Publishing, 2021), 57–80.

72 See Beth Driscoll and DeNel Rehberg Sedo, 'Faraway, so Close: Seeing the Intimacy in Goodreads Reviews', *Qualitative Inquiry* 25, no. 3 (1 March 2019): 248–59, https://doi.org/10.1177/1077800418801375; Alexandra Dane, 'Goodreads Reviewers and Affective Fan Labour', in *Post-digital Book Cultures Australian Perspectives*, ed. Alexandra Dane and Millicent Weber (Clayton: Monash University Publishing, 2021), 57–80; Millicent Weber, 'Online Reading During the COVID-19 Pandemic', in *Post-Digital Book Cultures: Australian Perspectives*, ed. Alexandra Dane and Millicent Weber (Clayton: Monash University Publishing, 2021).

73 See Stevie Marsden, '"I Didn't Know You Could Read": Questioning the Legitimacy of Kim Kardashian-West's Status as a Cultural and Literary Intermediary', *Logos* 29, nos. 2–3 (17 November 2018): 64–79, https://doi.org/10.1163/18784712-02902008; Maxine Branagh-Miscampbell and Stevie Marsden, '"Eating, Sleeping, Breathing, Reading": The Zoella Book Club and the Young Woman Reader in the 21st Century', *Participations* 16, no. 1 (2019).

74 Jessica Pressman, *Digital Modernism: Making It New in New Media* (New York: Oxford University Press, 2014); Saper, 'Introduction and Notes on the Text'.

75 Matthew Rubery, 'Projected Books', *Bibliodiversity: A Book History Workshop*, (Queen Mary University of London, 2023).

76 Including a very different visual metaphor, that of 'a scholar's desk with multiple books open for simultaneous consultation', rather than a single page commanding the reader's undivided attention; see Borsuk, *The Book*, 211.

77 Dennis Yi Tenen, 'Reading Platforms: A Concise History of the Electronic Book', in *The Unfinished Book*, ed. Alexandra Gillespie and Diedre Lynch (Oxford: Oxford Academic, 2020), 318.

78 Marie Lebert, *Project Gutenberg (1971–2008)*, 2008, www.gutenberg.org/ebooks/27045; Striphas, *The Late Age of Print*; Kirschenbaum, *Track Changes*.

79 Borsuk, *The Book*, 231.

80 Kirschenbaum and Werner, 'Digital Scholarship and Digital Studies', 441–42.

81 Judy Malloy, *Uncle Roger* (The WELL, 1986), https://people.well.com/user/jmalloy/uncleroger/unclerog.html; Michael Joyce, *Afternoon, a Story* (Watertown, MA: Eastgate Systems, 1987); Robert Coover, 'The End of Books', *New York Times*, 21 June 1992, https://archive.nytimes.com/www.nytimes.com/books/98/09/27/specials/coover-end.html.

82 Kirschenbaum, *Track Changes*, 180.

83 Lebert, *Project Gutenberg (1971–2008)*.

84 Joshua Farringdon, 'Science Museum to Display James Novel', *The Bookseller*, 6 March 2014, www.thebookseller.com/news/science-museum-display-james-novel.

85 Alison Flood, 'Where Did the Story of Ebooks Begin?', *The Guardian*, 12 March 2014, sec. Books, www.theguardian.com/books/2014/mar/12/ebooks-begin-medium-reading-peter-james.

86 Laura Dietz, 'Many Gates with a Single Keeper: How Amazon Incentives Shape Novels in the Twenty-First Century', in *The Routledge Companion to Literary Media*, ed. Astrid Ensslin, Julia Round, and Bronwen Thomas (Basingstoke: Routledge, 2023): 371-384.

87 Coover, 'The End of Books'.

88 See Striphas, *The Late Age of Print*, xvi; Squires, *Marketing Literature*, 32; Thompson, *Merchants of Culture*, 314–15.

89 Striphas, *The Late Age of Print*, 19–20.

90 'Active Book – Computer – Computing History', Centre for Computing History, www.computinghistory.org.uk/det/53902/Active-Book/.

91 Tenen, *Reading Platforms*, 329.

92 Hayler, *Challenging the Phenomenology of Technology*, 3, 29.

93 Drucker, 'The Virtual Codex from Page Space to E-Space'.

94 Amazon, '2007 Letter to Shareholders', 2008, www.sec.gov/Archives/edgar/data/1018724/000119312508084145/dex991.htm.

95 See Amazon, '2007 Letter to Shareholders'; Amazon, 'Amazon Kindle Publishing Guidelines', 2018, https://kindlegen.s3.amazonaws.com/AmazonKindlePublishingGuidelines.pdf; Amazon, 'Kindle Scribe (16 GB), the First Kindle and Digital Notebook, All in One, with a 10.2" 300 Ppi Paperwhite Display, Includes Basic Pen: Amazon.Co.Uk: Everything Else', 2023, www.amazon.co.uk/gp/product/B09BS5XWNS.

96 Amazon, '2007 Letter to Shareholders'.

97 Carr, 'Beyond Words'; McGurl, 'Everything and Less'; Striphas, *The Late Age of Print*, 101–2.

98 Murray, *The Digital Literary Sphere*, 54.

99 Or service; see Rowberry, 'Ebookness'.

100 Coles Books, 'Homepage', *Coles Books*, https://coles-books.co.uk/; Forum Books, 'Welcome!', *Forum Books*, www.forumbooksshop.com; The Real Book Shop, 'How to Shop at The Real Book Shop', *The Real Book Shop*, www.therealbookshop.com/pages/frontpage.

101 Leah Price, *What We Talk about When We Talk about Books* (New York: Basic Books, 2019), 19.

102 Survey 2016, 2015, 2014.

103 Survey 2014, 2015, 2016, FG 1 participant 3.

104 Jila Ghomeshi et al., 'Contrastive Focus Reduplication in English (The Salad-Salad Paper)', *Natural Language & Linguistic Theory* 22, no. 2 (1 May 2004): 312, https://doi.org/10.1023/B:NALA.0000015789.98638.f9.

105 FG 1 participant 1, participant 5, participant 3.

106 FG 1 participant 3, Survey 2015, FG 4 participant 1, FGs 1 and 4.

107 Gitelman, *Always Already New*, 96.

108 '7: Spelling, Distinctive Treatment of Words, and Compounds, 7.57: "Scare Quotes"', in *Chicago Manual of Style Online,* 2023, www-chicagomanualof style-org.libproxy.ucl.ac.uk/book/ed17/part2/ch07/psec057.html.

109 Statista, 'Consumer Attitudes towards Books and E-Books in the United States as of April 2017, by Gender. [Online] 12th April', 2017, www.statista .com/statistics/707158/attitude-books-e-books-by-gender/.

110 Statista, 'Reasons for Choosing Print Books Instead of E-Books by Gender in the U.S. 2017', *Statista*, 2017, www.statista.com/statistics/706278/reasons-for-choosing-print-books-instead-of-e-books-by-gender/.

111 And of the two who skipped the question, one used the free-text box to explain why they skipped: 'Haven't really thought about it'.

112 Looking only at those respondents who read e-books ($n = 189$), the general pattern remains: 96.5% of those younger than 55 agreed versus 85.4% of those older than 55.

113 A total of 82.2% of women and 84.1% of men agreed, a virtual tie. This was a remarkable contrast to the 2017 US survey, where the only demographic information shared was on gender, and men were almost twice as likely as women (29% vs 16%) to say that e-books are not real books. However, all respondents in my own survey who identified as non-binary/gender fluid, whose gender was other than one listed in the survey, or declined to share this information agreed that they consider e-books to be real books. In this survey, the sample sizes for these groups ($n = 5$ in each case) were too small for confidence in the significance of the results, but the findings suggest that further investigation would be warranted.

114 A moderately strong effect X^2 $(1, n = 227) = 37.6$, $p < 0.001$, Cramer's $V = 0.41$. Nine out of ten audiobook listeners (90.5%) also agree

that they consider e-books to be real books, compared with 77.3% of non-listeners.

115 X^2 (1, $n = 228$) = 8.9, $p = 0.003$, Cramer's $V = 0.2$

116 X^2 (1, $n = 228$) = 14.7, $p < 0.001$, Cramer's $V = 0.25$

117 Drucker, 'Performative Materiality and Theoretical Approaches to Interface'.

118 Bolter and Grusin, 'Remediation'.

119 Rubery, *The Untold Story of the Talking Book*, 60.

120 Cathryn Johnson, Timothy J. Dowd, and Cecilia L. Ridgeway, 'Legitimacy as a Social Process', *Annual Review of Sociology* 32 (2006): 53–78. Please see Appendix for more on how the terms *legitimacy, reputation, credibility*, and *novel* are used in this book.

121 Drucker, 'Performative Materiality and Theoretical Approaches to Interface'.

122 See Drucker, 'Performative Materiality and Theoretical Approaches to Interface'; Kirschenbaum, *Mechanisms*.

123 Galey, 'The Enkindling Reciter', 240.

Chapter 2

1 Survey 2022 in both cases.

2 Westin, 'Loss of Culture', 131.

3 Genette, *Paratexts*, 1.

4 Genette, *Paratexts*, 1.

5 Genette, *Paratexts*, 1. Here, Genette is looking backwards to the pre-codex era, but his form of words fortuitously makes space for examination of a future with different norms.

6 Lejune, quoted in Genette, *Paratexts*, 2.

7 Genette, *Paratexts*, 20–1.

8 Gérard Genette, *Palimpsests: Literature in the Second Degree*, trans. Channa Newman and Laude Doubinsky, 8th ed. (Lincoln, NE: University of Nebraska Press, 1997). Many anglophone audiences encountered his para-textual theory for the first time after *New Literary History* published his 'Introduction to the Paratext', largely a translation of the introduction to *Seuils*, in 1991.

9 Melanie Ramdarshan Bold and Corinna Norrick-Rühl, 'Audience Building and the Three Per Cent Problem', in *By the Book Conference* (Villa Finaly, Florence, 2016).

10 Genette, *Paratexts*, 406.

11 Genette, *Paratexts*, 1–2.

12 Genette, *Paratexts*, 11.

13 Ensslin, *Pre-web Digital Publishing and the Lore of Electronic Literature*, 36, 25, 110–11, 37.

14 Dene Grigar, 'Rebooting Electronic Literature: Photos of Sarah Smith's "King of Space"', in *Rebooting Electronic Literature: Documenting Pre-web Born Digital Media* (Vancouver: Nouspace Publications, Washington State

University Vancouver, 2018), https://scalar.usc.edu/works/rebooting-elec
tronic-literature/photos-of-sarah-smiths-king-of-space.

15 FG 3 participant 5.

16 FG 1 participant 2.

17 Birke and Christ, 'Paratext and Digitised Narrative', 80.

18 Birke and Christ, 'Paratext and Digitised Narrative', 77.

19 Genette, *Paratexts*, 406.

20 McCracken, 'Expanding Genette's Epitext/Peritext Model for Transitional
   Electronic Literature', 105.

21 Genette, *Paratexts*, 1, 4–5.

22 Genette, *Paratexts*, 4–5.

23 Genette, *Paratexts*, 2.

24 Genette, *Paratexts*, 25. For more on McCracken's concern in 2013 that
   Amazon advertisements overlaying the text will influence readers because they
   effectively enter the text, but also her confidence that Kindle's habit of
   skipping over front matter necessarily affects reading, because the only parts
   of a book that can fail to influence on some level are parts of the book that
   have been excised or obscured, see McCracken, 'Expanding Genette's Epitext/
   Peritext Model for Transitional Electronic Literature'. McCracken also con-
   tends that when previously attached elements are 'migrated outside the
   electronic literary texts proper' they are 'functioning as expanded versions of
   what Genette terms epitexts' (110), and conversely that, when switched on,
   non-authorised elements such as Amazon's crowdsourced popular highlights
   become 'paratextual material because it is a new part of the authorized text'
   despite the fact that it is 'clear that the author did not add the underlining'
   because 'it becomes physically part of the digital edition of the text' (108).
   This depends, however, on readers agreeing with her view that Amazon here
   functions as 'the publisher, Amazon' (108), rather than the retailer, Amazon
   (as retailers do not generate true paratext on their own), a conclusion that
   must be revisited for the 2020s. Changes in Amazon's business model and
   public image, from a bookseller to an 'everything store', make it less likely that
   readers would regularly mistake the bookseller for the publisher where they are
   not one and the same. In addition, Amazon's move into the publishing space,
   offering its own products in competition with traditional publishers, foregrounds the fact that there are two categories. Findings from my survey, focus
   groups, and interviews indicate that readers have a strong grasp of Amazon's
   position as a retailer, and do not automatically attribute to it the powers, or
   the wisdom and cultural authority, of a publisher. But the differences in
   perceptions of traditional, mainstream-published books and self-published
   books are such that findings specific to one category may not be generalisable
   to the other.

25 Simone Murray, 'Is BookTube the Future of Literary Studies? Yes, Seriously',
   in *Books on Screen Conference* (University of Leeds and Anglia Ruskin
   University (online), 2022).

26 FG 1 participant 5.

27 McCracken, 'Expanding Genette's Epitext/Peritext Model for Transitional Electronic Literature', 109.

28 FG 1 participant 4.

29 Survey 2015; 'Pirate Bay' was a write-in source given in Surveys 2014, 2015, and 2017.

30 The bad publicity surrounding Amazon's *1984* debacle, where purchased copies vanished from customers' e-readers following a rights dispute, remaining a touchstone for scholars and sceptics of digital reading.

31 McCracken, 'Expanding Genette's Epitext/Peritext Model for Transitional Electronic Literature', 114.

32 Nicole Matthews, 'Introduction', in *Judging a Book by Its Cover: Fans, Publishers, Designers, and the Marketing of Fiction*, ed. Nicole Matthews and Nickianne Moody (Aldershot: Ashgate, 2007).

33 Early interfaces encouraged publishers to design differently for the screen, including simplifying covers and reducing design vocabulary for legibility on e-ink readers; Open Road publishing invested heavily in new cover designs for e-editions of already well-known novels, for consistency across an author's backlist but also because of a sense that what worked on a physical copy would not necessarily work on screen, see Thompson, *Merchants of Culture*, 74. If this trend had continued, readers could have come to rely less heavily on covers as a significant source of data. Similarly, professional-looking cover design is less of an indication of investment: since the 2010s, the self-publishing author services industry has offered a wide range of semi-custom cover design providers that more closely approximate a 'professional' cover for far lower prices than in the past; see Laura M. Holson, 'With Romance Novels Booming, Beefcake Sells, but It Doesn't Pay', *The New York Times*, 30 March 2016, sec. Business, www.nytimes.com/2016/04/03/business/media/with-romance-novels-booming-beefcake-sells-but-it-doesnt-pay.html. And in the 2020s, AI opens up additional routes. Finally, habits can change. Researchers studying the general information gathering tactics of students have noted the conservatism (not to say 'laziness') of reliance on familiar strategies over appropriate strategies , clinging to old tools until the tools break; see Makri et al., 'A Library or Just Another Information Resource?', 443, https://doi.org/10.1002/asi.20510. But it is also observed that when the tools do eventually break, information seekers move on.

34 Interview 1, FG 2 participant 1, Survey 2017.

35 FG 1 participant 1.

36 FG 3 participant 5, FG 4 participant 2.

37 Makri et al., 'A Library or Just Another Information Resource?', 436–43.

38 Genette, *Paratexts*, 403.

39 Galey, 'The Enkindling Reciter', 218.

40 Thompson, *Merchants of Culture*, 330.

41 McCracken, 'Expanding Genette's Epitext/Peritext Model for Transitional Electronic Literature', 109–10.

42 And in theory easily replaced, but his examples are of promotional materials of the type likely to be discarded by typical readers, and retained, or sought out

and reunited with the text afterwards, only by scholars, collectors, or fans, and then only for books and authors of special literary or personal significance.

43 Genette, *Paratexts*, 110.

44 John W. Maxwell et al., 'XML Production Workflows? Start with the Web', *Journal of Electronic Publishing* 13, no. 1 (1 March 2010), https://doi.org/10 .3998/3336451.0013.106.

45 Kirschenbaum, *Track Changes*, 226, though Price notes the shatter risk of stone tablets: see Price, *What We Talk about When We Talk about Books*, 85.

46 Galey, 'The Enkindling Reciter', 236.

47 Maxwell et al., 'XML Production Workflows?'.

48 Anne Mangen, Bente R. Walgermo, and Kolbjørn Brønnick, 'Reading Linear Texts on Paper versus Computer Screen: Effects on Reading Comprehension', *International Journal of Educational Research* 58 (1 January 2013): 66, https:// doi.org/10.1016/j.ijer.2012.12.002.

49 Kirschenbaum, *Track Changes*, 230.

50 Drucker, 'Performative Materiality and Theoretical Approaches to Interface'.

51 Genette, *Paratexts*, 356–67.

52 Galey, 'The Enkindling Reciter', 228–29. Further, by replacing Eric Gill's Joanna, a font that 'signified a rejection of industrial printing and the alienation it promulgated', with Microsoft's Georgia, Galey finds that this supposedly trivial bit of automated revision 'completely reverses the typographic politics of the print editions' (see 229). Not every font change is as momentous as this.

53 While it is technically possible to package a chosen font into the .EPUB file itself, guaranteeing initial display as the publisher intended, this is not in most cases legally possible for proprietary fonts, as such packaging effectively distributes that font, and hence violates typical terms of use. But an open source font or an author's own creation could be included, as long as the e-book is not then sold on Amazon; at time of press, Amazon's terms state that it will forcibly break any lock on font settings. While the technology is there to allow publishers to control e-book font, Amazon's promotion of customisable settings as a Kindle product feature, and power as the dominant retailer to force vendor compliance, make such control effectively impossible.

54 Survey 2022.

55 FG 4 participant 1.

56 Including fiction in niche microgenres (see Beth Driscoll, 'The Rise of the Microgenre', *Pursuit*, 13 May 2019, https://pursuit.unimelb.edu.au/articles/ the-rise-of-the-microgenre.) and books by LGBTQIA+ authors, authors of colour, and others for whom the mainstream publishing industry, an enduringly 'exclusive and exclusionary site of cultural production' (see Alexandra Dane, *White Literary Taste Production in Contemporary Book Culture* (Cambridge: Cambridge University Press, 2023), 1) is frequently a hostile environment (see Koegler and Norrick-Rühl, *Are Books Still 'Different'?*).

57 Simon Rowberry, *The Early Development of Project Gutenberg c.1970–2000* (Cambridge: Cambridge University Press, 2023), 5.

58 Rare holdouts, like Robert Caro, are often authors of notable backlist titles released before the e-book revolution, and for whom the role of e-book refusenik becomes part of their public persona. See Dana Rubinstein, 'Lights. Camera. Makeup. And a Carefully Placed 1,246-Page Book.', *The New York Times*, 28 May 2020, sec. New York, www.nytimes.com/2020/05/28/nyregion/power-broker-tv.html.

59 Survey 2016, 2017.

60 Interview 1, FG 3 participant 3.

61 The significant association closest to reasonable strength is to the extremely rare source of e-book gifts: those who choose e-books for reasons of selection are three times as likely to have received an e-book as a gift in the past 12 months, 14.8% vs 4.9% of others, X^2 (1, $n = 1,282$) $= 11.0$, $p < 0.001$, Cramer's $V = 0.093$.

62 FG 3 participant 2.

63 FG 3 participant 4.

64 FG 6 participant 5, FG 3 participant 2.

65 FG 5 participant 1, FG 1 participant 2.

66 FG 3 participant 1, participant 4.

67 FG 5 participant 4, FG 5 participants 4 and 3.

68 Thompson, *Merchants of Culture*, 11.

69 Survey 2015, FG 4 participant 2.

70 Survey 2016, 2017.

71 FG 6 participant 5.

72 Interview 1.

73 FG 1 participants, jointly; FG 3 participants 1, 2, and 3.

74 Survey 2015.

75 FG 5 participant 3.

76 FG 5 participant 3, participant 1.

77 FG 6 participant 5.

78 Survey 2015.

79 Lindsay Burokur, 'Should an Indie (Self-Published) Author Create an Imprint (i.e. Their Own "Press"?)', 11 December 2011, http://lindsayburoker.com/e-publishing/should-self-published-author-create-imprint-press/.

80 FG 1 participant 1.

81 FG 6 participant 3, Interview 1.

82 FG 6 participant 1, FG 3 participant 4.

83 FG 6 participant 4.

84 Interview 1, FG 3 participant 3.

85 FG 6 participant 3.

86 With, as of 2024, a rapidly withering presence on official Penguin Random House websites, likely presaging closure: some pages list the imprints as accepting submissions, but feature links that redirect to generic pages with no mention of the imprints. Other digital-first imprints such as HarperCollins's Avon Impulse, for romance fiction, have vanished. Evidence of such imprints is often most visible in writing and author-services

websites, particularly in out-of-date lists of publishers open to unsolicited submissions. See Penguin Random House, 'FAQs | Penguin Random House', *PenguinRandomhouse.com*, 2023, www.penguinrandomhouse.com/faqs/; Penguin Random House, 'Romance | Random House Group', *PenguinRandomhouse.com*, 2024, www.randomhousebooks.com/genres/romance/.

87 Ploughshares, 'About', Solos | Ploughshares, www.pshares.org/solos.

88 FG 1 participant 3.

89 FG 1 participant 1.

90 Survey 2022.

91 FG 1 participant 4.

92 Laura Dietz, 'Who Are You Calling an Author? Changing Definitions of Career Legitimacy for Novelists in the Digital Era', in *Literary Careers in the Modern Era*, ed. Guy Davidson and Nicola Evans (London: Palgrave Macmillan UK, 2015), 203–4, https://doi.org/10.1057/9781137478504_12.

93 Dietz, 'Who Are You Calling an Author?', 208–9.

94 Debbie Young, 'Should Self-Published Authors Create Their Own Publishing Imprints?', *The Self-Publishing Advice Center* (blog), 7 May 2015, https://selfpublishingadvice.org/should-self-published-authors-create-their-own-publishing-imprints/.

95 Burokur, 'Should an Indie (Self-Published)'.

96 Burokur, 'Should an Indie (Self-Published)'.

97 Lindsay Burokur, 'Why Self-Publish When You Have a Chance to Go Traditional?', 12 March 2012, http://lindsayburoker.com/ebook-news/why-self-publish-stay-indie/.

98 The project was more complex, more commercial, and more contentious than initial media coverage suggested, or all participating authors knew. See Alison Flood, 'Most Writers Earn Less than £600 a Year, Survey Reveals', *The Guardian*, 17 January 2014, sec. Books, www.theguardian.com/books/2014/jan/17/writers-earn-less-than-600-a-year; Porter Anderson, 'Author Earnings at DBW: Hostility Becomes a Handshake', *Publishing Perspectives*, 10 March 2016, https://publishingperspectives.com/2016/03/author-earnings-at-digital-book-world-conference/. Hugh Howey, 'The Reason for the Confusion', 29 July 2014, https://hughhowey.com/the-reason-for-the-confusion/. AuthorEarnings received data contributions from many thousands of authors before founding partner 'Data Guy' (later identifying himself as gaming industry analyst Paul Abbassi) reconstituted the effort as a private company, Bookstat, in 2018. Reports, once frequent and public, became exclusive to paying clients, prompting protests from some of the authors: 'the authors who gave Abbassi the sales data required to build and refine his models, who spread the word and brought him to the attention of the wider publishing industry, have little to show for it. Abbassi, on the other hand, has a business called BookStat. Caveat Emptor' (see Nate Hoffelder, 'The End of Author Earnings Report, Redux', *The Digital Reader* (blog), 29 March 2019, https://the-digital-reader.com/2019/03/29/the-end-of-author-earnings-report-redux/).

99 AuthorEarnings, 'Note on Methodology', 20 May 2014, http:// authorearnings.com/note-on-methodology/.

100 FG 2 participant 1.

101 FG 2 participant 3.

102 Stone, *The Everything Store*; Jason Heikenfeld et al., 'Review Paper: A Critical Review of the Present and Future Prospects for Electronic Paper', *Journal of the Society for Information Display* 19, no. 2 (2011): 129–56, https://doi.org/10.1889/JSID19.2.129.

103 Hayler, *Challenging the Phenomenology of Technology*; Rowberry, 'Ebookness'.

104 Drucker, 'The Virtual Codex from Page Space to E-Space'.

105 Coover, 'The End of Books'.

Chapter 3

1 Lynette Owen, *Selling Rights*, 7th ed. (London: Taylor & Francis, 2014), 392.

2 Robert McCrum, 'War Is Declared in the World of Ebooks', *The Guardian*, 14 December 2009, sec. Books, www.theguardian.com/books/booksblog/2009/dec/14/random-house-digital-rights.

3 Hugh Jones and Christopher Benson, *Publishing Law*, 5th ed. (London: Routledge, 2016), 110–11.

4 Jones and Benson, *Publishing Law*, 90.

5 Jones and Benson, *Publishing Law*, 90.

6 And an echo of earlier e-book and e-reading initiatives where industry had a louder voice than readers. The Open eBook Authoring Group that wrote early drafts of EPUB, the popular non-proprietary e-book format, was driven by Microsoft and included NuvoMedia and SoftBook, and was presented in 1999 to 'major publishers, eBook pioneers, and software and hardware manufacturers, as well as book distributors and retailers', including Barnes & Noble (see Microsoft, 1999). In The International Digital Publishing Forum that superseded the Open eBook Authoring Group (and now incorporated into the World Wide Web Consortium [W3C]), not-for-profit organisations such as the Open University, Norwegian Library of Talking Books and Braille, The American Library Association, and the educational charity Ithaka were outnumbered by corporate entities from Elsevier and Random House to Ingram Content Group to Apple, Google, Intel, and Sony (See International Digital Publishing Forum, 2017). Tenen argues that 'the trademark symbol in the title of the [EPUB] standard, along with the copyright notice on its front page, undermined the emphasis on the open, participatory nature of the endeavour' and 'from the moment of its founding, the "open" eBook format was embedded within the North American copyright regime, in a way that would later allow "content creators" and "persons or corporate bodies" to police access to the "reading device"'. See Tenen, *Reading Platforms*, 323–24; Microsoft, 'Microsoft's Call for an Open eBook

Standard Sees Major Milestone As Draft Specification Is Submitted for Final Approval', Stories, 25 May 1999, https://news.microsoft.com/1999/05/25/ microsofts-call-for-an-open-ebook-standard-sees-major-milestone-as-draft-spe cification-is-submitted-for-final-approval/; International Digital Publishing Forum, 'Member List', *International Digital Publishing Forum*, https://idpf .org/membership/members.

7 Natasha Singer, 'Tech's Ethical "Dark Side": Harvard, Stanford and Others Want to Address It', *The New York Times*, 12 February 2018, sec. Business, www.nytimes.com/2018/02/12/business/computer-science-ethics-courses .html. For more on Project Gutenberg and adoption of a more Silicon Valley than academic or archival ethos, see Rowberry, *The Early Development of Project Gutenberg c.1970–2000.*

8 Pamela Samuelson, 'Google Book Search and the Future of Books in Cyberspace. 94', *Minnesota Law Review*, 2009; Lebert, *Project Gutenberg (1971–2005)*; William Grimes, 'Michael Hart, a Pioneer of E-Books, Dies at 64', *The New York Times*, 9 September 2011, sec. Business, www.nytimes .com/2011/09/09/business/michael-hart-a-pioneer-of-e-books-dies-at-64 .html.

9 Lebert, *Project Gutenberg (1971–2008).*

10 Grimes, 'Michael Hart, a Pioneer of E-Books'.

11 Kirschenbaum, *Mechanisms*, 11.

12 Jack Schofield, 'Michael Hart Obituary', *The Guardian*, 13 September 2011, sec. Books, www.theguardian.com/books/2011/sep/13/michael-hart- obituary.

13 Grimes, 'Michael Hart, a Pioneer of E-Books'.

14 Borsuk, *The Book*, 224.

15 Samuelson, 'Google Book Search and the Future of Books in Cyberspace. 94', 4–5.

16 Lawrence Lessig, 'Creative Commons @ 5 Years', *Creative Commons*, 1 October 2007, https://creativecommons.org/2007/10/01/creative-com mons-5-years/.

17 Fanfic or fan fiction (both terms are in regular use by both practitioners and scholars, often interchangeably) is one branch of fan works, a broad category that can include visual art, music, performance, and so on. Defined by Hellekson and Busse as 'derivative amateur writing…texts based on another text, and not for professional publication', the term was for a brief period in the mid twentieth century used to describe fiction *about* fans, but now refers to 'imaginative interpolations and extrapolations by fans of existing literary worlds' (though much fan fiction draws on worlds originally created for film, television, games, etc.) (see Karen Hellekson and Kristina Busse, 'Introduction: Why a Fan Fiction Studies Reader Now?', in *The Fan Fiction Studies Reader*, ed. Karen Hellekson and Kristina Busse (Iowa City, IA: University of Iowa Press, 2014), 5–6). Though legal language focussed on questions of ownership and copyright infringement may stretch to describing fan work as 'any work by a fan, or indeed by anyone other than the content

owner(s), set in a fictional world or using such pre-existing fictional characters' (see Aaron Schwabach, *Fan Fiction and Copyright: Outsider Works and Intellectual Property Protection*, 2nd ed. (London: Taylor & Francis, 2016), 8), most definitions understand the fan to be not just 'anyone', but at the very least a committed and appreciative member of the audience for that fictional property, and often a member of an identifiable fandom or other fan community.

18 A controversial decision in some cases: Skains cites *Fifty Shades of Grey* as an instance where 'the fan community perceived James' "filing off the serial numbers" (deleting identifiable references to its source text) and pulling to publish as a betrayal of the community and an exploitation of community efforts to improve the work through feedback', see R. Lyle Skains, *Digital Authorship: Publishing in an Attention Economy* (Cambridge: Cambridge University Press, 2019), 68.

19 Henry Jenkins, 'Textual Poachers', in *The Fan Fiction Studies Reader*, ed. Karen Hellekson and Kristina Busse (Iowa City, IA: University of Iowa Press, 2014), 29; Nicola Humble, 'The Reader of Popular Fiction', ed. David Glover and Scott McCracken (Cambridge: Cambridge University Press, 2012), 96–7; Ramdarshan Bold, 'The Return of the Social Author'.

20 Schwabach, *Fan Fiction and Copyright*, 2.

21 FG 6 participant 3, participant 2.

22 UK Intellectual Property Office, 'Executive Summary Online Copyright Infringement Tracker Survey (12th Wave)', 3 February 2023, www.gov.uk/government/publications/online-copyright-infringement-tracker-survey-12th-wave/executive-summary-online-copyright-infringement-tracker-survey-12th-wave.

23 UK Intellectual Property Office, 'Executive Summary Online Copyright Infringement Tracker Survey'.

24 Rachel Noorda and Kathi Inman Berens, 'Immersive Media & Books 2020', *Panorama Project*, 2021, 38, www.panoramaproject.org/immersive-media-reading-2020.

25 Survey 2014, 2015, 2017.

26 Now AAAAARG.

27 Though not exclusively scholarly: as such repositories typically rely on volunteers to upload new material, many are willing to host what volunteers provide even where it falls outside their stated missions or original remits. LibGen (Surveys 2017, 2021, and 2022), for example, has millions of files of comics and prose fiction.

28 Alex Reisner, 'These 183,000 Books Are Fueling the Biggest Fight in Publishing and Tech', *The Atlantic*, 25 September 2023, www.theatlantic.com/technology/archive/2023/09/books3-database-generative-ai-training-copyright-infringement/675363/; Alex Reisner, 'Revealed: The Authors Whose Pirated Books Are Powering Generative AI', *The Atlantic*, 19 August 2023, www.theatlantic.com/technology/archive/2023/08/books3-ai-meta-llama-pirated-books/675063/.

29 Survey 2017.

30 FG 4 participant 2, participant 4. FG 4 participant 4 is describing a practice Noorda and Berens term robust sampling; they note how attitudes towards what might be described as a piracy preview are inevitably influenced by experience of film, TV, and music streaming subscriptions. See Noorda and Berens, 'Immersive Media & Books 2020', 69.

31 Piracy was not a purely digital phenomenon, either: FG 2 participant 3 reported that 'my friend who always used to work at Smiths...she used to get a copy [of new Harry Potter books] really early...she'd photocopy bits for me...', making her a strictly print-based privateer.

32 Alison Flood, '"We're Told to Be Grateful We Even Have Readers": Pirated Ebooks Threaten the Future of Book Series', *The Guardian*, 6 November 2017, sec. Books, www.theguardian.com/books/2017/nov/06/pirated-ebooks-threaten-future-of-serial-novels-warn-authors-maggie-stiefvater.

33 FG 1 participant 2.

34 Michael Heller and James Salzman, *Mine! How the Hidden Rules of Ownership Control Our Lives* (New York: Doubleday, 2021), 14, 240.

35 Heller and Salzman, *Mine! How the Hidden Rules of Ownership Control Our Lives*, 104.

36 Survey 2022.

37 Survey 2022, 2022, 2021. For more on special licensing terms during COVID-19, see Rachel Noorda and Kathi Inman Berens, 'Digital Public Library Ecosystem 2023' (American Library Association, 7 December 2023), www.ala.org/advocacy/sites/ala.org.advocacy/files/content/ebooks/Digital-PL-Ecosystem-Report%20(1).pdf.

38 Survey 2022.

39 Survey 2022 in both cases.

40 Aaron Perzanowski and Chris Jay Hoofnagle, 'What We Buy When We "Buy Now"', *University of Pennsylvania Law Review* 165, no. 2 (2017): 315–78. http://www.jstor.org/stable/26600431.

41 Perzanowski and Hoofnagle, 'What We Buy When We "Buy Now"', 22.

42 Heller and Salzman, *Mine! How the Hidden Rules of Ownership Control Our Lives*, 4, 16.

43 FG 1 participant 6, Survey 2020.

44 Survey 2014, 2015.

45 Perzanowski and Hoofnagle, 'What We Buy When We "Buy Now"', 7.

46 Perzanowski and Hoofnagle, 'What We Buy When We "Buy Now"', 8.

47 Leah Price, *How to Do Things with Books in Victorian Britain* (Princeton, NJ: Princeton University Press, 2013), 84.

48 Michel de Certeau, 'Reading as Poaching', in *The History of Reading: A Reader*, ed. Shafquat Towheed, Rosalind Crone, and Katie Halsey (Abingdon: Routledge, 1984), 136.

49 Heller and Salzman, *Mine! How the Hidden Rules of Ownership Control Our Lives*, 65.

50 Michel Foucault, *Language, Counter-Memory, Practice: Selected Essays and Interviews*, ed. Donald F. Bouchard (Ithaca, NY: Cornell University Press, 2019), 113–38, https://doi.org/10.1515/9781501741913.

51 Leah Henrickson, 'Natural Language Generation: Negotiating Text Production in Our Digital Humanity', *Proceedings of the Digital Humanities Congress 2018*, 2018, www.dhi.ac.uk/books/dhc2018/natural-language-generation/.

52 Survey 2022, FG 1 participant 2.

53 Just under half (45.7%) of men agreed, versus 58.2% of women, 55.6% of those who identify as non-binary/gender fluid, none of those whose gender identity was not listed, and 56.7% of those who declined to state, X^2 (4, $n = 1,636$) $= 21.8$, $p < 0.001$, Cramer's $V = 0.12$.

54 As with all questions about why they choose print over digital, for print-only readers the answers are, by definition, reasons for *always* choosing print. It describes a blanket policy, even, as discussed in greater detail in Chapter 5, a statement about personal identity. It is also informed by experience with print but not necessarily experience with digital: when someone who does not read e-books states that print is better for borrowing, their understanding of how digital book loans work may be entirely theoretical. In contrast, when those who read e-books (almost all of whom regularly read print books as well) state that print or digital is better, they are both comparing categories they know, though not necessarily specific options, as is the case for digital library loans, and describing not a policy but a book-by-book choice.

55 Survey 2015, 2014.

56 Those who agreed were more likely to have obtained a print book from a library and much more likely to have obtained one from a secondhand bookshop in the past twelve months. They were also more likely to have received a print book as a gift, another route that requires decoupling the owner and the original purchaser.

57 FG 5 participant 5, referring to a restriction specific to UK public libraries in the late 2010s; in the early 2020s, OverDrive's popular Libby library app allows for Kindle reading for many titles in the US and some other countries.

58 Survey 2014, 2015.

59 FG 6 participant 4.

60 FG 6 participant 5.

61 FG 2 participant 3.

62 Survey 2016, Interview 2.

63 Survey 2017.

64 Giles Clark and Angus Phillips, *Inside Book Publishing*, 5th ed. (Abingdon: Routledge, 2014), 74.

65 Stephen Nissenbaum, *The Battle for Christmas* (New York: Vintage, 1997), 132, 134.

66 Viv Groskop, 'The Kindle Christmas', *The Telegraph*, 30 January 2011, www.telegraph.co.uk/culture/books/bookreviews/8286090/The-Kindle-Christmas.html.

67 Pierre Bourdieu, *The Field of Cultural Production* (Cambridge: Polity, 1993), 49. For more on books and cultural capital, please see Chapter 5.

68 Natalie Zemon Davis, 'Beyond the Market: Books as Gifts in Sixteenth-Century France: The Prothero Lecture', *Transactions of the Royal Historical Society* 33 (1983): 69.

69 Allison Carruth and Amy Tigner, *Literature and Food Studies* (London: Routledge, 2018), 74.

70 Davis, 'Beyond the Market', 87.

71 Davis, 'Beyond the Market', 70.

72 Michael Bourne, 'How the Book Business Invented Modern Gift-Giving', *Literary Hub*, 8 December 2015, https://lithub.com/how-the-book-business-invented-modern-gift-giving/.

73 Nissenbaum, *The Battle for Christmas*, 150.

74 Nissenbaum also links book gifts and gift wrapping, arguing that 'Christmas presents had to obfuscate their commercial origins', and that books as sold in nineteenth-century America were effectively pre-obfuscated, perfect for placing under the tree in haste (1997, p. 173).

75 Steve Coll, review of *Citizen Bezos*, by Brad Stone, *The New York Review of Books*, 10 July 2014, www.nybooks.com/articles/2014/07/10/citizen-bezos-amazon/.

76 Survey 2017, 2014.

77 Survey 2016.

78 Davis, 'Beyond the Market', 73.

79 Genette, *Paratexts: Thresholds of Interpretation*, 136–37.

80 FG 5 participant 5.

81 Survey 2015, FG 6 participant 1.

82 FG 1 participant 5.

83 FG 1 participant 5, FG 2 participant 3.

84 FG 1 participant 6.

85 Survey 2022.

86 Survey 2022.

87 While book recommendations remain a source of enduring social pleasure in online environments, the interpersonal communication takes place, and satisfies, in different ways; see Danielle Fuller and DeNel Rehberg Sedo, *Reading Bestsellers: Recommendation Culture and the Multimodal Reader* (Cambridge: Cambridge University Press, 2023), 62.

88 FG 3 participant 2.

89 Neil M. Richards, 'The Perils of Social Reading', *Georgetown Law Journal* 101, no. 689 (2013) (29 March 2012): 714–15.

90 24.9% of men, vs 32.4% of women, 44.4% of those who identify as non-binary/gender fluid, none of those whose gender identity was not listed, and 43.3% of those who declined to state, X^2 (4, $n = 1,636$) $= 12.9$, $p = 0.12$, Cramer's $V = .089$.

91 Buchanan, McKay, and Levitt, 'Where My Books Go: Choice and Place in Digital Reading', 5–7.

92 Survey 2014.

93 Survey 2022.

94 Survey 2021, 2015, 2017, 2015.

95 Survey 2017.

96 Price, *What We Talk about When We Talk about Books*; Pressman, *Bookishness*.

97 David Hayes, '"Take Those Old Records off the Shelf": Youth and Music Consumption in the Postmodern Age', *Popular Music and Society* 29, no. 1 (1 February 2006): 51–68, https://doi.org/10.1080/03007760500167370; Markus Wohlfeil, 'Vinyl Records: The Future of Consuming Music?', *Australian–New Zealand Marketing Academy (ANZMAC) 2019 Conference* (Victoria University of Wellington, 2019), www.semanticscholar.org/paper/Vinyl-Records%3A-The-Future-of-Consuming-Music-Wohlfeil/d5b3db6c69fb61e57349a141f5278e468b7bba17.

98 Claire Warwick, 'Negotiating the Digital Dystopia: The Role of Emotion, Atmosphere and Social Contact in Making Decisions about Information Use in Physical and Digital Contexts', *New Review of Academic Librarianship* 27, no. 3 (3 July 2021): 259–79, https://doi.org/10.1080/13614533.2021.1964550; Tea Uglow, 'pBooks, eBooks, & dBooks: Why We Are Hooked on Books and Bookness.', *Medium* (blog), 5 January 2015, https://coffeedotfish.medium.com/pbooks-ebooks-dbooks-why-we-are-hooked-on-books-and-bookness-b24bbe506cd4; David Sax, *The Revenge of Analog: Real Things and Why They Matter* (New York: PublicAffairs, 2017). It remains true that, as Pressman observes, the book's unique power means that nostalgia for it is 'distinct from nostalgia for other kinds of older media like vinyl records, typewriters, fountain pens, or nearly anything else'; see Pressman, *Bookishness*, 33.

99 Pressman, *Bookishness*; Thomas, 'Taking Stock'; Murray, 'Is BookTube the Future of Literary Studies?'; MacTavish, 'The Emerging Power of the Bookstagrammer'; Fuller and Rehberg Sedo, *Reading Bestsellers*.

100 FG 1 participant 3, participant 2.

101 Survey 2021, 2016

102 Survey 2016, 2014.

103 FG 1 participant 4.

104 Dietz, Warwick, and Rayner, 'Auditioning for Permanence'.

105 Survey 2020.

106 Stip, Östlundh, and Abdel Aziz, 'Bibliotherapy: Reading OVID During COVID'; Dietz, 'Projection or Reflection?'.

107 FG 6 participant 5.

108 Survey 2015, 2017.

109 Intriguingly, choosing digital because it's better for keeping as part of a personal library is also linked to borrowing e-books from a non-Amazon service such as Scribd. However, non-Amazon subscription services remain a rare source, used by only 4.3% of respondents in the previous twelve months (for the 2020–22 surveys where this option was included). And half (52.2%) of those who used non-Amazon subscription services borrowed e-books from Amazon as well.

110 Survey 2017, 2016, 2016.
111 For example, the positive correlation between choosing e-books because they are 'better for keeping as part of a personal library' and because 'a reading device is more enjoyable to handle and use', X^2 (1, $n = 1,282$) $= 56.4$, $p < 0.001$, has a Cramer's V figure of 0.21. The positive correlation between choosing print books because they are 'better for keeping as part of a personal library' and because a print book is 'more enjoyable to handle and use', X^2 (1, $n = 1732$) $= 275.9$, $p < 0.001$, has a Cramer's V value of 0.4.
112 Thompson, *Book Wars*, 148.
113 One form of keeping and permanence of remarkably little concern to these survey participants is the permanence of one's reading history. Like other aspects of privacy, this is discussed further in Chapter 5
114 Dietz, Warwick, and Rayner, 'Auditioning for Permanence', 30.
115 Survey 2014, FG 5 participant 8, FG 5 participant 4, FG 6 participant 1, Noorda and Berens, 'Immersive Media & Books 2020', 73.
116 FGs 4, 5, 6.
117 FG 4 participant 2.
118 FG 1 participant 1.
119 Survey 2015, 2016.
120 Survey 2016, 2020, Interview 1.
121 Interview 1.
122 FG 4 participant 3.
123 Although thinking of the e-book file as a part of a book could potentially serve the same purpose, as in the manner of a weight-conscious long distance hiker ripping out chapters as they are finished, and carrying only what is needed for the remainder of the journey.
124 Dietz, Warwick, and Rayner, 'Auditioning for Permanence', 31.
125 Very much the kind of 'high-volume volume' Price identifies as a Morris-esque totem of luxurious 'conspicuous inconvenience', as discussed further in Chapter 4; see Price, *What We Talk about When We Talk about Books*, 108.

Chapter 4

1 Baron, *Words Onscreen*.
2 Jinghui Hou, Justin Rashid, and Kwan Min Lee, 'Cognitive Map or Medium Materiality? Reading on Paper and Screen', *Computers in Human Behavior 67*, no. C (1 February 2017), https://doi.org/10.1016/j.chb.2016.10.014.
3 Baron, *Words Onscreen*, 12.
4 For example, in January 2024, *Guardian* coverage of a new study indicating advantages for 'deep reading' in print – for fifty-nine school-age children wearing electrode caps in a Columbia Teachers' College lab – had to be hastily corrected to add that the study had not yet been peer reviewed, but not before the story had been widely shared on social media as proof of print

superiority. See Karen Froud et al., 'Middle-Schoolers' Reading and Processing Depth in Response to Digital and Print Media: An N400 Study' (bioRxiv, 1 September 2023), https://doi.org/10.1101/2023.08.30.553693; John R. MacArthur, 'A Groundbreaking Study Shows Kids Learn Better on Paper, Not Screens. Now What?', *The Guardian*, 17 January 2024, sec. Life and Style, www.theguardian.com/lifeandstyle/2024/jan/17/kids-reading-better-paper-vs-screen.

5 Angus Phillips, *Turning the Page: The Evolution of the Book* (Abingdon: Routledge, 2014); Pablo Delgado et al., 'Don't Throw Away Your Printed Books: A Meta-Analysis on the Effects of Reading Media on Reading Comprehension', *Educational Research Review* 25 (1 November 2018): , https://doi.org/10.1016/j.edurev.2018.09.003; Virginia Clinton, 'Reading from Paper Compared to Screens: A Systematic Review and Meta-Analysis', *Journal of Research in Reading* 42, no. 2 (2019), https://doi.org/10.1111/1467-9817.12269.

6 Survey 2014, Mangen, 'The Digitization of Literary Reading'; Terje Hillesund, Theresa Schilhab, and Anne Mangen, 'Text Materialities, Affordances, and the Embodied Turn in the Study of Reading', *Frontiers in Psychology* 13 (2022), www.frontiersin.org/articles/10.3389/fpsyg.2022.827058. For more on book smell and how readers express, and police, attitudes towards it, please see Chapter 5.

7 Survey 2014, 2015, 2014, 2021.

8 Survey 2020, 2020.

9 FG 1 participant 4. Participants' uses of the words 'hands' and 'hand' in accounts of their own reading remain quite distinct from display of images of single hands and pairs of hands on Bookstagram, BookTok, and other bookish social media, where an unseen hand may be holding up the camera; for more on hands in social media images, see Bronwen Thomas, 'The #bookstagram: Distributed Reading in the Social Media Age', *Language Sciences* 84 (1 March 2021), https://doi.org/10.1016/j.langsci.2021.101358.

10 Survey 2016, 2015.

11 Survey 2020.

12 Interview 1, Survey 2016, FG 4 participant 2.

13 Survey 2014.

14 Hungerford, *Making Literature Now*. This perhaps indicates that the attention to detail invested in iPhones and Samsung Galaxy devices by industrial design teams is not matched by Kindle developers or reading app software engineers. Alternatively, it could be that Amazon's decision to split its Kindle range into feature-laden high-end models such as the Scribe or Oasis and basic models, where customers must pay more just to avoid lockscreen ads, means that the image of Kindle is set by its cheapest, simplest examples, not the most expensive and best-designed.

15 Survey 2014.

16 Survey 2014, 2022.

17 FG 4 participant 2.

18 Survey 2022.
19 Beldham, 'Bookscan Training'.
20 Preston, 'How Real Books Have Trumped Ebooks'. While data from my study do not show increase over the survey period, the greater enthusiasm of young readers for print could signal a coming wave. That said, enjoyment of print books is already so widespread that there is limited opportunity for dramatic further increase.
21 X^2 (1, $n = 1,732$) $= 242.2$, $p < 0.001$, Cramer's $V = 0.37$.
22 X^2 (1, $n = 1,732$) $= 275.9$, $p < 0.001$, Cramer's $V = 0.4$.
23 X^2 (1, $n = 1,732$) $= 249.4$, $p < 0.001$, Cramer's $V = 0.38$.
24 Mangen, 'The Digitization of Literary Reading', 244.
25 FG 1 participant 6, Survey 2022, FG 1 participant 5, FG 4 participant 3, Survey 2016. 'Word document' status is explicitly linked to unrealness by some in the 2022 survey: as noted in Chapter 2, free-text responses on why they did not consider e-books to be real books included 'electronic materials feel like a copy, a pdf of the book' and 'an ebook is a shadow of a real book'.
26 Survey 2020.
27 This, of course, is no accident: e-reading interface designers are concerned with how to present texts legibly and attractively to current customers, and readers' near-universal experience with paper reading makes it pragmatic to, as Heikenfeld, Drzaic, Yeo, and Koch put it, 'aspire to reproduce the visual experience of conventional printed media' rather than pioneer new styles. See Heikenfeld et al., 'Review Paper', 133. Tenen, *Reading Platforms*.
28 Survey 2015 and Surveys 2014, 2015, 2016, 2017.
29 Gitelman, *Always Already New*, 96.
30 Kirschenbaum, *Mechanisms*, 74.
31 Gitelman, *Always Already New*, 95.
32 Thomas Frognall Dibdin, *Bibliomania; or Book-Madness; a Bibliographical Romance* (London: Henry G. Bohn, 1811). FG 4 participant 4, participant 2, FG 1 participant 5.
33 Survey 2015 in both cases.
34 X^2 (1, $n = 1,282$) $= 219.9$, $p < 0.001$, Cramer's $V = 0.41$.
35 Hou, Rashid, and Lee, 'Cognitive Map of Medium Materiality?', 84; Heikenfeld et al., 'Review Paper', 137.
36 Pew Research Centre, 'Mobile Fact Sheet', *Pew Research Center: Internet, Science & Tech* (blog), 7 April 2021, www.pewresearch.org/internet/fact-sheet/mobile/.
37 Pew Research Centre, 'Mobile Fact Sheet'.
38 Amazon, 'Kindle Voyage E-Reader, 6" High-Resolution Display (300 Ppi) with Adaptive Built-in Light, PagePress Sensors, Wi-Fi : Amazon.Co.Uk: Electronics & Photo', 2018, www.amazon.co.uk/gp/product/B00IOY524S/ref=fs_ice.
39 FG 3 participant 6.
40 Tim Moynihan, 'With Its New Kindles, Amazon Tries to Replicate the Magic of Paper', *Wired*, www.wired.com/2014/09/amazon-kindle-voyage/.

41 Amazon, 'Kindle Voyage E-Reader'.
42 For more on this history, see Dennis Duncan, *Index, a History of the: A Bookish Adventure* (London: Penguin, 2022).
43 FG 5 participant, 7, participant 3, participant 7.
44 McCracken, 'Expanding Genette's Epitext/Peritext Model for Transitional Electronic Literature', 117.
45 Survey 2015.
46 As of 2023, the Scribe is not waterproof.
47 Amazon, 'Kindle Scribe (16 GB)'.
48 Brad Stone, *Amazon Unbound: Jeff Bezos and the Invention of a Global Empire* (London: Simon and Schuster UK, 2021); Emma Simpson, 'Amazon Opens First UK Non-Food Store', *BBC News*, 5 October 2021, sec. Business, www.bbc.com/news/business-58806762.
49 Stone, *The Everything Store*, 295, 291.
50 Survey 2014.
51 Survey 2015, 2015, 2014, 2017.
52 X^2 (1, $n = 1,282$) = 206.3, $p < 0.001$, Cramer's $V = 0.4$.
53 Survey 2015 in all cases.
54 Buchanan, McKay, and Levitt, 'Where My Books Go', 8–9.
55 FG 2 participant 1.
56 Survey 2015, 2016, 2022, 2022.
57 An initiative closed in June 2020 after legal action by publishers, and presaging a sweeping judgement against the Internet Archive's controversial practice of controlled digital lending (CDL) in March 2023. At time of press, the Internet Archive has stated that it intended to pursue an appeal. See Andrew Albanese, 'Internet Archive to End "National Emergency Library" Initiative', *Publishers Weekly*, 12 June 2020, www.publishersweekly.com/pw/by-topic/digital/copyright/article/83584-internet-archive-to-end-national-emergency-library-initiative.html; Andrew Albanese, 'In a Swift Decision, Judge Eviscerates Internet Archive's Scanning and Lending Program', *Publishers Weekly*, 25 April 2023, www.publishersweekly.com/pw/by-topic/industry-news/libraries/article/91862-in-a-swift-decision-judge-eviscerates-internet-archive-s-scanning-and-lending-program.html.
58 Survey 2021 in all cases.
59 Survey 2014.
60 Those who choose digital because digital is easier to obtain were more likely to have used a laptop computer for reading an e-book in the past twelve months (44.2% vs 32.2% of others). They were more likely to have read e-book non-fiction, short fiction, and novels.
61 Survey 2015, 2014.
62 Survey 2015, FG 5 participant 8.
63 Survey 2020.
64 Survey 2015, 2015, 2017.
65 Survey 2017.
66 Survey 2015, 2015.

67 Survey 2015.
68 Survey 2015.
69 Survey 2014.
70 Survey 2015, 2015, 2014.
71 Survey 2014.
72 FG 2 participant 3.
73 FG 2 participant 3.
74 Survey 2016, 2014, 2017, 2014, 2022, 2021.
75 Survey 2014, 2015.
76 Survey 2015, 2016.
77 Survey 2015.
78 Price, *How to Do Things With Books in Victorian Britain*, 83.
79 Dennis T. Clark et al., 'A Qualitative Assessment of the Kindle E-book Reader: Results from Initial Focus Groups', *Performance Measurement and Metrics* 9, no. 2 (1 January 2008), https://doi.org/10.1108/14678040810906826.
80 Pew Research Centre, 'Mobile Fact Sheet'. Survey 2015. Gemma Walsh, 'Screen and Paper Reading Research – A Literature Review', *Australian Academic & Research Libraries* 47, no. 3 (2 July 2016), https://doi.org/10.1080/00048623.2016.1227661; Price, *How to Do Things With Books in Victorian Britain*, 57.
81 Price, *How to Do Things With Books in Victorian Britain*, 72.
82 Price, 51–53.
83 Kate Flint, *The Woman Reader 1837–1914* (Oxford: Oxford University Press, 1993).
84 Amazon, 'Kindle Oasis – Waterproof, 8GB Wi-Fi (Previous Generation – 9th) : Amazon.Co.Uk: Electronics & Photo', 2018, www.amazon.co.uk/dp/B06XDK92KS/ref=nav_shopall_k_dpcog.
85 Phillips, *Turning the Page*, 37–8.
86 Survey 2017.
87 A question added to the survey in 2020, so asked only of participants between 2020 and 2022 ($n = 751$).
88 Survey 2016 in all cases.
89 British Dyslexia Association, 'Visual Difficulties', *British Dyslexia Association*, www.bdadyslexia.org.uk/dyslexia/neurodiversity-and-co-occurring-differences/visual-difficulties.
90 Matthew H. Schneps et al., 'E-Readers Are More Effective than Paper for Some with Dyslexia', *PLOS ONE* 8, no. 9 (18 September 2013), https://doi.org/10.1371/journal.pone.0075634; Tjaša Krivec et al., 'Impact of Digital Text Variables on Legibility for Persons with Dyslexia', *Dyslexia* 26, no. 1 (2020), https://doi.org/10.1002/dys.1646.
91 Luz Rello and Ricardo Baeza-Yates, 'How to Present More Readable Text for People with Dyslexia', *Universal Access in the Information Society* 16, no. 1 (1 March 2017), https://doi.org/10.1007/s10209-015-0438-8.
92 Jessica Wery and Jennifer Diliberto, 'The Effect of a Specialized Dyslexia Font, OpenDyslexic, on Reading Rate and Accuracy', *Annals of Dyslexia* 67 (18 March 2016), https://doi.org/10.1007/s11881-016-0127-1.

93 Sanne M. Kuster et al., 'Dyslexie Font Does Not Benefit Reading in Children with or without Dyslexia', *Annals of Dyslexia* 68, no. 1 (April 2018), https://doi.org/10.1007/s11881-017-0154-6.

94 Survey 2014, 2014, 2014, FG 5 participant 8.

95 Survey 2014, 2017.

96 The participant showed samples on her personal iPad; see M. S. Corley, 'Harry Potter Series', *mscorley.com*, https://mscorley.com/Harry-Potter-Series.

97 Interview 1.

98 Survey 2014.

99 Survey 2015, FG 5 participant 5, Survey 2015, FG 1 participant 5. The importance of distinctiveness underscores the degree to which the myth of the identical copy persists in popular discourse, despite the impossibility of two digital artefacts being actually indistinguishable; see Kirschenbaum, *Mechanisms*.

100 FG 2 participant 3.

101 Survey 2022.

102 FG 2 participant 1.

103 Survey 2017, 2015.

104 Price, *What We Talk About When We Talk About Books*, 108.

105 Survey 2015, 2015, 2017.

106 Karen Hellekson and Kristina Busse, 'Fan Communities and Affect', in *The Fan Fiction Studies Reader*, ed. Karen Hellekson and Kristina Busse (Iowa City, IA: University of Iowa Press, 2014).

107 Jenkins, 'Textual Poachers', 20.

108 FG 3 participant 6.

109 Survey 2020.

110 Simon Frost, 'Readers and Retailed Literature: Findings from a UK Public High Street Survey of Purchasers' Expectations from Books', *Logos* 28, no. 2 (2017).

111 FG 5 participant 8.

112 FG 1 participant 5.

113 FG 5 participant 2, FG 3 participant 2.

114 Buchanan, McKay, and Levitt, 'Where My Books Go', 6.

115 FG 2 participant 3, FG 3 participants 5 and 6.

116 Survey 2014, 2015.

117 Tim Hutchings, 'E-Reading and the Christian Bible', *Studies in Religion/ Sciences Religieuses* 44, no. 4 (1 December 2015), https://doi.org/10.1177/0008429815610607.

118 Hutchings, 'E-Reading and the Christian Bible', 424.

119 Victor Nell, *Lost in a Book: The Psychology of Reading for Pleasure* (New Haven, CT: Yale University Press, 1998).

120 Baron, *Words Onscreen*, 88–92.

121 Mangen, 'The Digitization of Literary Reading', 248–57.

122 More often via theoretical than empirical means, or, in Birkert's case, via 'extrapolat[ion] from [his] own experience as a reader', see Birkerts, *The Gutenberg Elegies*. For more on fears regarding digital as a threat to literature and literary culture, please see Chapter 5.

123 Survey 2014 and 2015, 2020, 2015.

124 Survey 2020, 2021, 2021.

125 Survey 2015.

126 FG 2 participant 1.

127 FG 2 participant 2.

128 Antonio Tombolini, 'The Slow Reading Manifesto', *Slowreading.org*, www .slowreading.org/slow-reading-manifesto/.

129 Rick Busselle and Helena Bilandzic, 'Measuring Narrative Engagement', *Media Psychology* 12, no. 4 (23 November 2009), https://doi.org/10.1080/15213260903287259, 326. This is a distraction scenario most obviously relevant to one of Busselle and Bilandzic's undergraduates watching American television shows in a lecture hall, where a wandering mind means missing potentially crucial elements of the plot; the reader staring into space between pages may take a long time to finish a book, but the plot will be waiting for them when they return to it.

130 Ryan, quoted in Busselle and Bilandzic, 'Measuring Narrative Engagement', 323.

131 B. Wittmer and M. Singer, 'Measuring Presence in Virtual Environments: A Presence Questionnaire', *Presence: Teleoperators and Virtual Environments* 7, no. 3 (1998).

132 Hou, Rashid, and Lee, 'Cognitive Map or Medium Materiality?', 88.

133 Busselle and Bilandzic, 'Measuring Narrative Engagement', 324.

134 Green, 2004, quoted in Busselle and Bilandzic, 'Measuring Narrative Engagement', 324.

135 Busselle and Bilandzic, 'Measuring Narrative Engagement', 326.

136 Baron, *Words Onscreen*; Clinton, 'Reading from Paper Compared to Screens'; Hillesund, Schilhab, and Mangen, 'Text Materialities, Affordances, and the Embodied Turn in the Study of Reading'.

137 Mangen, 'The Digitization of Literary Reading', 257; Hou, Rashid, and Lee, 'Cognitive Map or Medium Materiality?', 85; Mangen, Olivier, and Velay, 'Comparing Comprehension of a Long Text Read in Print Book and on Kindle'.

138 Survey 2015, 2022, 2016.

139 Anne Mangen and Don Kuiken, 'Lost in an iPad: Narrative Engagement on Paper and Tablet', *Scientific Study of Literature* 4, no. 2 (1 January 2014), https://doi.org/10.1075/ssol.4.2.02man.

140 FG 1 participant 5, participant 3.

141 Jan M. Noyes and Kate J. Garland, 'VDT versus Paper-Based Text: Reply to Mayes, Sims and Koonce', *International Journal of Industrial Ergonomics* 31, no. 6 (1 June 2003), https://doi.org/10.1016/S0169–8141(03)00027-1; Judith Stoop, Paulien Kreutzer, and Joost G. Kircz, 'Reading and Learning

from Screens versus Print: A Study in Changing Habits: Part 2 – Comparing Different Text Structures on Paper and on Screen', *New Library World* 114, no. 9/10 (2013), https://doi.org/10.1108/NLW-04-2013-0034; Walsh, 'Screen and Paper Reading Research', 169.

142 It remains, however, critical to avoid assumptions that any gap is either natural or permanent: digital reading is in constant flux as technologies and reading practices change, and as cohorts of readers master successive generations of platforms and devices. While researchers like Chen, Cheng, Chang, Zheng, and Huang (2014) have found that comprehension gaps are greatest among novice users and small to negligible among experienced users, meta-analysis by Delgado, Vargas, Ackerman, and Salmerón (2018) found that across fifty-six studies between 2000 and 2017 effect sizes increased, suggesting that the print/digital reading gap (at least for the informational texts for which differences in comprehension were found) was growing, not shrinking. See Mangen, Walgermo, and Brønnick, 'Reading Linear Texts on Paper versus Computer Screen', 62–7; Guang Chen et al., 'A Comparison of Reading Comprehension across Paper, Computer Screens, and Tablets: Does Tablet Familiarity Matter?', *Journal of Computers in Education* 1, no. 2 (1 November 2014), https://doi.org/10.1007/s40692–014-0012-z; Delgado et al., 'Don't Throw Away Your Printed Books'.

143 Survey 2016, 2017, 2016.

144 Survey 2016.

145 Surveys 2014, 2015, 2016, 2017, 2020.

146 Survey 2016.

147 This avoidance of non-fiction aligned with data from surveys and focus groups, where some book components typical of non-fiction but not poetry or fiction, such as charts, tables, and footnotes, were frequently described as awkward or non-functional on screens, and cited as reasons to read particular book in print. Participants found that 'the footnotes get annoying [in e-books], because you always end up trying to find where the footnote's ended up' (FG 6 participant 3), 'some layout-heavy reference books aren't as useful as reflowable ebooks' (Survey 2016) and 'diagrams are not really usable in current state of e-books' (Survey 2014). The end result was that, as one respondent put it, 'print reading is much more usable for dipping in, skipping around, browsing etc. so I often prefer print books for non-fiction (Survey 2015)'. This preference for print for 'browse reading' appears to undermine one of the primary attractions of e-books, and stands in contrast to scholarly use as studied earlier in the twenty-first century, where large-scale surveys such as Nicholas, Rowlands, Clark, Huntington, Jamali, and Ollé's (2008) found that dipping in and out was far more prevalent than reading full e-books, or even full chapters of e-books. Despite the fact that male participants are more likely to read non-fiction and less likely to choose print for reasons of enjoyment, gender was not a significant factor. Some features described as awkward on screen, such as maps (FG 4 participant 2, FG 5 participant 5, Survey 1), were noted as items occasionally found in

novels, but sufficiently rarely that they did not constitute a reason to avoid novels on screen. See David Nicholas et al., 'UK Scholarly E-book Usage: A Landmark Survey', *Aslib Proceedings* 60, no. 4 (1 January 2008), https://doi.org/10.1108/00012530810887962.

148 Delgado et al., 'Don't Throw Away Your Printed Books'; Clinton, 'Reading from Paper Compared to Screens'.

149 Mangen and Kuiken, 'Lost in an iPad', 157, 162, 167.

150 In a later paper summarising the 2014 findings, Mangen argued that the booklet format was not a 'typical literary interface' (though it is clearly not a typical news interface either) and that it 'can be assumed to be more reminiscent of, say, article reading' (see Mangen, 'The Digitization of Literary Reading', 254), but this is a consequential assumption given conventions of English-language short story publishing, where publication in book-length print format is not the only or even the most typical presentation (see Adrian Hunter, *The Cambridge Introduction to the Short Story in English* (Cambridge: Cambridge University Press, 2007); Kasia Boddy, *The American Short Story Since 1950* (Edinburgh: Edinburgh University Press, 2010); Laura Dietz, 'The Short Story and Digital Media', in *The Edinburgh Companion to the Short Story in English*, ed. Paul Delaney and Adrian Hunter (Edinburgh: Edinburgh University Press, 2018), https://doi.org/10.1515/9781474400664-011; Ensslin, *Pre-web Digital Publishing and the Lore of Electronic Literature*.

151 Mangen and Kuiken, 'Lost in an iPad', 152.

152 Mangen, Olivier, and Velay, 'Comparing Comprehension of a Long Text Read in Print Book and on Kindle', 1.

153 Hou, Rashid, and Lee, 'Cognitive Map or Medium Materiality?'

154 Hou, Rashid, and Lee did not compare fiction with non-fiction, or work with purely textual material, and further experiments would be warranted before generalising their findings across genres and forms.

155 Survey 2014, 2016, 2015.

156 Survey 2015.

157 Survey 2015, 2015.

158 FG 1 participant 1.

159 FG 1 participant 3.

160 Hayler, *Challenging the Phenomenology of Technology*, 107–8, 117.

161 Clark et al., 'A Qualitative Assessment of the Kindle E-book Reader', 125.

162 Clark et al., 'A Qualitative Assessment of the Kindle E-book Reader', 125.

163 Clark et al., 'A Qualitative Assessment of the Kindle E-book Reader', 126.

164 Beatrice Warde, 1930, quoted in Helen Armstrong, *Graphic Design Theory: Readings from the Field* (New York: Princeton Architectural Press, 2009).

165 FG 1 participant 3.

166 Survey 2020.

167 Clark et al., 'A Qualitative Assessment of the Kindle E-book Reader', 125.

168 Amazon, '2007 Letter to Shareholders', 1.

169 Hayler, *Challenging the Phenomenology of Technology*, 96–7.

170 Drucker, 'Performative Materiality and Theoretical Approaches to Interface'.
171 Survey 2014; and very much the kind of subjective measure of reading performance that Mangen, Walgermo, and Bronnick propose for consideration alongside objective measures such as speed. See Mangen, Walgermo, and Brønnick, 'Reading Linear Texts on Paper versus Computer Screen', 66.
172 Survey 2015, 2017.
173 Survey 2014, FG 1 participant 6.
174 Levy, 2007, quoted in Hayler, *Challenging the Phenomenology of Technology*, 143.
175 Levy, 2007, quoted in Hayler, *Challenging the Phenomenology of Technology*, 143.
176 Survey 2022.
177 Survey 2022, Mangen, Olivier, and Velay, 'Comparing Comprehension of a Long Text Read in Print Book and on Kindle'; Hillesund, Schilhab, and Mangen, 'Text Materialities, Affordances, and the Embodied Turn in the Study of Reading'.
178 Dietz, 'Projection or Reflection?'
179 Survey 2015, FG 1 participant 1.
180 Survey 2015, 2016.
181 Survey 2015.
182 Survey 2014, 2015.
183 Michelle Faverio and Andrew Perrin, 'Three-in-Ten Americans Now Read E-books', *Pew Research Center* (blog), 6 January 2022, www.pewresearch .org/short-reads/2022/01/06/three-in-ten-americans-now-read-e-books/; Andrew Perrin, 'Slightly Fewer Americans Are Reading Print Books, New Survey Finds', *Pew Research Center* (blog), 19 October 2015, www .pewresearch.org/short-reads/2015/10/19/slightly-fewer-americans-are-read ing-print-books-new-survey-finds/; McCracken, 'Expanding Genette's Epitext/Peritext Model for Transitional Electronic Literature', 114.
184 Survey 2020.
185 Mangen, 'The Digitization of Literary Reading', 248.
186 David Comer Kidd and Emanuele Castano, 'Reading Literary Fiction Improves Theory of Mind', *Science* 342, no. 6156 (18 October 2013), https://doi.org/10.1126/science.1239918; Maria Eugenia Panero et al., 'Does Reading a Single Passage of Literary Fiction Really Improve Theory of Mind? An Attempt at Replication', *Journal of Personality and Social Psychology* 111, no. 5 (2016), https://doi.org/10.1037/pspa0000064; Colin F. Camerer et al., 'Evaluating the Replicability of Social Science Experiments in Nature and Science between 2010 and 2015', *Nature Human Behaviour* 2, no. 9 (September 2018), https://doi.org/10.1038/s41562-018-0399-z.
187 David Dodell-Feder and Diana I. Tamir, 'Fiction Reading Has a Small Positive Impact on Social Cognition: A Meta-Analysis', *Journal of Experimental Psychology. General* 147, no. 11 (November 2018), https://doi .org/10.1037/xge0000395.
188 Weber, 'Conceptualizing Audience Experience at the Literary Festival'.

Chapter 5

1 Richards, 'The Perils of Social Reading', 712.
2 And not always by choice, as with students or academics obliged to use course or library materials in digital form because that is what their institution provides.
3 Bourdieu, *The Field of Cultural Production*, 20, 35, 45–8.
4 Bourdieu, *The Field of Cultural Production*, 46, 49.
5 Bourdieu, *The Field of Cultural Production*, 48.
6 Bourdieu, *The Field of Cultural Production*, 48–9.
7 Balázs Kovács and Amanda J. Sharkey, 'The Paradox of Publicity: How Awards Can Negatively Affect the Evaluation of Quality', *Administrative Science Quarterly* 59, no. 1 (1 March 2014): 1–5, https://doi.org/10.1177/0001839214523602.
8 Unless they make a living via 'odd jobs' in journalism, publishing, or academia, which can confer a quasi-Bohemian status unavailable to the 'bourgeois' popular novelist supported by sales; see Bourdieu, *The Field of Cultural Production*, 59.
9 Squires, *Marketing Literature*, 57.
10 English, *The Economy of Prestige*, 208.
11 Davis, quoted in Fuller and Rehberg Sedo, *Reading Bestsellers*, 37.
12 Driscoll, *The New Literary Middlebrow*, 67; Humble, 'The Reader of Popular Fiction', 93.
13 FG 3 participant 1.
14 Dietz, Warwick, and Rayner, 'Auditioning for Permanence', 27.
15 RNIB, 'Readers Left Red-Faced Over Choice of Books: Press Release', *RNIB*, 23 September 2013, 1.
16 RNIB, 'Readers Left Red-Faced Over Choice of Books', 1.
17 8.4% of women versus 2.8% of men, 5.9% of those who identify as non-binary/gender fluid, none of those whose gender identity was not listed, and 4.0% of those who declined to state, X^2 (4, n = 1,209) = 11.8, p = 0.019, Cramer's V = 0.1.
18 At X^2 (6, n = 1,216) = 32.0, p < 0.001, Cramer's V = 0.16, a stronger effect than seen with gender.
19 Survey 2014.
20 For a small selection of representative examples, see Shannon Donnelly, 'Sex on the Kindle', *The Daily Beast*, 25 August 2009, www.thedailybeast.com/sex-on-the-kindle; Josh Catone, 'Why Printed Books Will Never Die', *MashableUK* (blog), 16 January 2013, https://mashable.com/2013/01/16/e-books-vs-print/#nfD5lEvgW8qP; Anita Singh, 'E-Book Readers' Guilty Pleasures Revealed', *The Telegraph*, 26 August 2015, www.telegraph.co.uk/culture/books/booknews/11824405/E-book-readers-guilty-pleasures-revealed.html; Andrew Levy, 'A Cover-up! Guilty Secret We Hide in Our Kindles: Quarter of Users Admit Using Device to Read Books They Wouldn't if Others Could See the Cover', *Mail Online*, 27 September 2013, sec. News,

www.dailymail.co.uk/news/article-2434613/A-cover-Guilty-secret-hide-Kindles-Quarter-users-admit-using-device-read-books-wouldnt-cover.html; James Parker and Charles McGrath, 'Is There Anything One Should Feel Ashamed of Reading?', *The New York Times*, 7 April 2015, sec. Books, www .nytimes.com/2015/04/12/books/review/is-there-anything-one-should-feel-ashamed-of-reading.html.

21 Though there was no meaningful link to the publication status of the last book read, underscoring the fact that enjoying a given genre does not translate into reading in that genre to the exclusion of others.

22 Romance is an exceptionally successful genre in digital format, and there are reports that self-published romance authors who have seen their sales drop dramatically since Kindle Unlimited was launched. See Romance Writers of America, 'About the Romance Genre', *rwa.org*, 2018, www.rwa.org/ Online/Romance_Genre/About_Romance_Genre.aspx; David Streitfeld, 'Amazon Offers All-You-Can-Eat Books. Authors Turn Up Noses.', *The New York Times*, 27 December 2014, sec. Technology, www.nytimes.com/ 2014/12/28/technology/amazon-offers-all-you-can-eat-books-authors-turn-up-noses.html.

23 While 'binge' is a term now closely associated with streaming television services, this and other forms of concentrated media consumption are increasingly examined as phenomena related to existing fiction reading practices; Jenner notes the 'consistent parallel to novels' in media theory surrounding Netflix. See Jennifer Keishin Armstrong, 'A Mostly Healthy Obsession: The Joy of Binge Reading', 21 October 2014, www.bbc.com/culture/article/ 20140317-the-joy-of-binge-reading; Mareike Jenner, *Netflix and the Reinvention of Television* (London: Palgrave, 2018), 169.

24 Carol Flynn, 'Samuel Richardson', in *The Cambridge History of the English Novel*, ed. Robert L. Caserio and Clement Hawes (Cambridge: Cambridge University Press, 2012), 97–112; Melissa Sodeman, *Sentimental Memorials: Women and the Novel in Literary History* (Stanford, CA: Stanford University Press, 2014), 3; Nancy Armstrong, *Desire and Domestic Fiction: A Political History of the Novel* (Oxford: Oxford University Press, 1987), 104–10.

25 Armstrong, *Desire and Domestic Fiction*, 105; Flint, *The Woman Reader 1837–1914*, 73.

26 Faverio and Perrin, 'Three-in-Ten Americans Now Read E-books'; Nielsen, 'Year in Books Review'; Perrin, 'Slightly Fewer Americans Are Reading Print Books'; Sian Cain, 'Marlon James: "Writers of Colour Pander to the White Woman"', *The Guardian*, 30 November 2015, www.theguardian.com/books/ 2015/nov/30/marlon-james-writers-of-colour-pander-white-woman-man-booker-event-brief-history-seven-killings.

27 Flint, *The Woman Reader 1837–1914*, 10; Belinda Jack, *The Woman Reader* (New Haven, CT: Yale University Press, 2012), 39, 43.

28 Huyssen, 1986, cited by Driscoll, *The New Literary Middlebrow*, 29.

29 Danuta Kean, 'Are Things Getting Worse for Women in Publishing?', *The Guardian*, 11 May 2017, sec. Books, www.theguardian.com/books/2017/

may/11/are-things-getting-worse-for-women-in-publishing; Alison Flood, 'Gender Pay Gap Figures Reveal Big Publishing's Great Divide', *The Guardian*, 23 March 2018, sec. Books, www.theguardian.com/books/2018/mar/23/gender-pay-gap-figures-reveal-big-publishings-great-divide; Lyndsey Claro, 'Women in the Gentleman's Career of Publishing', *Princeton University Press Ideas*, 6 March 2020, https://press.princeton.edu/ideas/women-in-the-gentlemans-career-of-publishing; Sarah Brouillette, 'Wattpad's Fictions of Care', *Post45: Peer Reviewed*, 13 July 2022, https://post45.org/2022/07/wattpads-fictions-of-care/.

30 The gender disparities in publishing sit alongside a general lack of diversity in terms of race, ethnicity, geography, and class; in particular, chronic under-representation of BAME (Black, Asian and Minority Ethnic) professionals. While my focus in this discussion is gender rather than intersecting factors, other dimensions inform this discussion and are incredibly important subjects for further data gathering. For more on lack of diversity in publishing, see Claire Squires's 2017 *Publishing's Diversity Deficit*. Amy King and Sarah Clark, 'The 2016 VIDA Count • VIDA: Women in Literary Arts', *VIDA: Women in Literary Arts* (blog), 17 October 2017, www.vidaweb.org/vida-count/the-2016-vida-count/; Koegler and Norrick-Rühl, *Are Books Still 'Different'?*; Claire Squires, *Publishing's Diversity Deficit*, vol. 2, CAMEo Cuts (Leicester: CAMEo Research Institute for Cultural and Media Economics, 2017).

31 C.I.L.I.P./A.R.A., 'A Study of the UK Information Workforce: Mapping the Library, Archives, Records, Information Management and Knowledge Management and Related Professions, Executive Summary' (Chartered Institute of Library and Information Professionals and Archive and Records Association, 2015), https://archive.cilip.org.uk/sites/default/files/documents/executive_summary_nov_2015-5_a4web_0.pdf.

32 Hungerford, *Making Literature Now*, 68.

33 Driscoll, *The New Literary Middlebrow*, 6.

34 Humble, 'The Reader of Popular Fiction', 92–3.

35 Maggie Brown, 'The Fifty Shades Effect: Women Dominate Self-Publishing', *The Observer*, 9 November 2014, sec. Books, www.theguardian.com/world/2014/nov/09/fifty-shades-of-grey-women-dominate-self-publishing; Alison Flood, 'Self-Publishing Lets Women Break Book Industry's Glass Ceiling, Survey Finds', *The Guardian*, 6 March 2015, sec. Books, www.theguardian.com/books/2015/mar/06/self-publishing-lets-women-break-book-industrys-glass-ceiling-survey-finds.

36 Murray, '"Selling" Literature', 17–8; Dietz, 'Who Are You Calling an Author?', 197–201.

37 FG 2 participant 3, Singh, 'E-Book Readers' Guilty Pleasures Revealed'; Archer and Jockers, *The Bestseller Code*, 83.

38 Humble, 'The Reader of Popular Fiction', 86.

39 For an excellent discussion of the ubiquity of food metaphors in eighteenth-to early twentieth-century discussions of reading, with novels in particular

likened to sugar and fancies, and the special concern for women as both exceptionally vulnerable to literary gluttony and particularly unsightly when succumbing, see Flint, *The Woman Reader 1837–1914*, 50–2; Armstrong, *Desire and Domestic Fiction*, 109–10.

40 Romance Writers of America, 'About the Romance Genre'; Driscoll, *The New Literary Middlebrow*.

41 Radway, *Reading the Romance*, 19–20.

42 David Glover and Scott McCracken, 'Introduction', in *The Cambridge Companion to Popular Fiction*, ed. David Glover and Scott McCracken (Cambridge: Cambridge University Press, 2012), 8.

43 Archer and Jockers, *The Bestseller Code*, 40.

44 FG 2 participant 3, Survey 2014.

45 The lack of such censure in the case of young adult (YA) reading underscores the degree to which this form of digital reading privacy is distinct from the early twenty-first-century fashion for simultaneously releasing children's and YA books with a significant adult readership (or books to which publishers hoped to attract a significant adult readership) with 'child' and 'adult' covers. While sometimes attributed to adults feeling embarrassment over covers, this trend never concealed the title or author, it merely altered paratext to present that visible title and author in a different light, as material targeted towards a different audience. The double-cover fashion is an element of a fascinating, and wholly separate, topic of the role of paratext in the Harry Potter phenomenon and the wider growth of adult readership of YA. For an example of attention to 'childish' covers, see Nigel Reynolds, 'Adult Fans Taking over Harry Potter', *The Telegraph*, 22 June 2007, www.telegraph.co.uk/culture/books/3666031/Adult-fans-taking-over-Harry-Potter.html.

46 Natasha Onwuemezi, 'New E L James Novel Coming in November', *The Bookseller*, 10 October 2017, www.thebookseller.com/news/new-50-shades-coming-november-649906.

47 Julie Bosman, 'Discreetly Digital, Erotic Novel Sets American Women Abuzz', *The New York Times*, 10 March 2012, sec. Business, www.nytimes.com/2012/03/10/business/media/an-erotic-novel-50-shades-of-grey-goes-viral-with-women.html.

48 Nicholas Carr, 'Never Mind E-books: Why Print Books Are Here to Stay', *Wall Street Journal*, 4 January 2013, sec. Life and Style, http://online.wsj.com/article/SB10001424127887323387420457821956335697002.html. Carr speaks long after Hoskins but does not refer to her earlier insight.

49 Terje Colbjørnsen, 'The Construction of a Bestseller: Theoretical and Empirical Approaches to the Case of the Fifty Shades Trilogy as an eBook Bestseller', *Media, Culture & Society* 36, no. 8 (2014): 1100–117, https://doi.org/10.1177/0163443714544999.

50 Bosman, 'Discreetly Digital, Erotic Novel Sets American Women Abuzz'; Emma Brockes, 'Stephen King: On Alcoholism and Returning to the Shining', 21 September 2013, www.theguardian.com/books/2013/sep/21/

stephen-king-shining-sequel-interview; Parker and McGrath, 'Is There Anything One Should Feel Ashamed of Reading?'
51 Archer and Jockers, *The Bestseller Code*, 89–90.
52 Goran Trajkovski and Samuel G. Collins, eds., *Handbook of Research on Agent-Based Societies: Social and Cultural Interactions* (Hershey, PA: IGI Global, 2009).
53 Parker and McGrath, 'Is There Anything One Should Feel Ashamed of Reading?'
54 FG 4 participant 4.
55 Levy, 'A Cover-up!'; Singh, 'E-Book Readers' Guilty Pleasures Revealed'.
56 Donnelly, 'Sex on the Kindle'.
57 Donnelly, 'Sex on the Kindle'.
58 Quite like E. L. James and her imitators in this respect.
59 Still very much in circulation, though some influential theories from the early twentieth century, such as Benedict's division between guilt as distress after having fallen short of one's personal standards and shame as distress after having violated societal norms, have been sharply critiqued; as Doi lays out in his analysis of Benedict's framework of Western 'guilt cultures' and Eastern 'shame cultures', this assigns higher value to both guilt and to the Westerners who supposedly hold a monopoly on guilt. See Ruth Benedict, *The Chrysanthemum and the Sword: Patterns of Japanese Culture*, Reprint 1947 (London: Secker and Warburg, 1946); Takeo Doi, *The Anatomy of Dependence*, trans. John Bester (Tokyo, 1976).
60 James Gilligan, *Violence: A Reflection on the National Epidemic* (New York: Pantheon, 1997).
61 Humble, 'The Reader of Popular Fiction', 86.
62 TED, 'Brené Brown: The Power of Vulnerability', *TED Talks*, June 2010, www.ted.com/talks/brene_brown_the_power_of_vulnerability/no-; Brené Brown, 'Brené Brown | Speaker | TED', *TED Talks*, www.ted.com/speakers/brene_brown. Reportage on Brown, a female academic whose massive popular audience is largely female, is fascinating in itself.
63 Brené Brown, 'Shame Resilience Theory: A Grounded Theory Study on Women and Shame', *Families in Society* 87, no. 1 (2006): 45.
64 FG 6 participant 4, FG 4 participant 4.
65 Survey 2015, Survey 2021, FG 2 participant 3.
66 FG 5 participants 1, 5, and 8.
67 Bourdieu, *The Field of Cultural Production*, 30.
68 Flint, *The Woman Reader 1837–1914*, 72.
69 And far from sui generis in either literary or technological terms. Saper points out that 'fascination with machine aesthetics was very much of the moment in June 1930' (see Saper, 'Introduction and Notes on the Text', xxv), and as Tenen observes, 'Brown's blueprints did not rise out of a vacuum—they were preceded by over a century of technological developments in micrographic print', with speculation on how photography might invite new forms of

circulation for micronised texts emerging by the mid nineteenth century (see Tenen, *Reading Platforms*, 316–17)

70 Robert Brown, *The Readies*, Reprint (Baltimore, MD: Roving Eye Press, 1930), 28.

71 Price, *What We Talk about When We Talk about Books*, 165–66.

72 Paul Duguid, 'Material Matters: The Past and Futurology of the Book', in *The Future of the Book*, ed. Geoffrey Nunberg (Berkeley, CA: University of California Press, 1996): 63–102; Pressman, *Bookishness*.

73 Baron, *Words Onscreen*.

74 Striphas, *The Late Age of Print*; Kirschenbaum, *Track Changes*; Price, *What We Talk about When We Talk about Books*.

75 Birkerts, *The Gutenberg Elegies*, 151.

76 Birkerts, *The Gutenberg Elegies*, 20.

77 Birkerts, *The Gutenberg Elegies*, 19, 28. Birkerts' confident but unsupported assertion that 'a change in procedure [of writing, to composition on screen] must be at least subtly reflected in the result. How could it not?' (19) is ably interrogated by Kirschenbaum. See Kirschenbaum, *Track Changes*.

78 Pressman, *Bookishness*, 26–7. Commentary was so extensive by the early 1990s that Birkerts had to start a special file for newspaper clippings and notes, which he titled 'the Reading Wars'. See Birkerts, *The Gutenberg Elegies*, 32.

79 Hayler, *Challenging the Phenomenology of Technology*, 4.

80 Price, *How to Do Things with Books in Victorian Britain*, 5; Robert Buderi, *Engines of Tomorrow: How the World's Best Companies Are Using Their Research Labs to Win the Future* (New York: Simon & Schuster, 2000), 360; Duguid, 'Material Matters'.

81 Duguid, 'Material Matters', 63.

82 Mar Hicks, 'Computer Love: Replicating Social Order Through Early Computer Dating Systems', *Ada: A Journal of Gender, New Media, and Technology*, no. 10 (2016), https://doi.org/10.7264/N3NP22QR.

83 Hicks, 'Computer Love'.

84 Striphas, *The Late Age of Print*, 109–10.

85 Amazon, '2007 Letter to Shareholders'. Amazon's initial e-book products competed more on price than on the promise of a revolutionary interface for accessing texts; see Coll, 'Citizen Bezos'.

86 Gooding, Terras, and Warwick, 'The Myth of the New', 631.

87 Alberto Manguel, *A Reader on Reading* (London: Yale University Press, 2010), 6.

88 Becky Chambers, *A Long Way to a Small and Angry Planet* (London: Hodder and Stoughton, 2015).

89 FG participant 6, participant 3.

90 Survey 2016, 2020, Beth Driscoll and Claire Squires, 'Oh Look, a Ferry'; Or 'The Smell of Paper Books', *TXT* 4 (2018): 64, https://hdl.handle.net/1887/. As Driscoll and Squires note, a sentiment often expressed as if it were rare, strange, or unexpected, as with 'weird one, but I like the smell of print books!' in my own 2022 survey.

91 FG 1 participant 2, participant 5.

92 FG 3 participant 5.

93 Adriaan van der Weel, 'E-Roads and i-Ways A Sociotechnical Look at User Acceptance of E-Books', *Logos* 21, nos. 3–4 (1 January 2010): 54, https://doi.org/10.1163/095796511X559945.

94 Richards, 'The Perils of Social Reading', 695.

95 A belief foregrounded by debate on bookshelves as pandemic-era Zoom backgrounds. For more on pandemic bookshelves, see Corinna Norrick-Rühl and Shafquat Towheed, 'Introduction', in *Bookshelves in the Age of the COVID-19 Pandemic*, ed. Corinna Norrick-Rühl and Shafquat Towheed (London: Palgrave Macmillan, 2022), 1–27; Sally Blackburn-Daniels and Edmund G. C. King, 'Bookshelves, Social Media and Gaming', *English Studies* 103, no. 5 (4 July 2022): 653–59, https://doi.org/10.1080/0013838X.2022.2094575.

96 FG 2 participant 2.

97 FG 2 participant 2.

98 Interview 1.

99 FG 1 participant 1, Survey 2015.

100 Survey 2014, 2022.

101 Survey 2015.

102 Interview 2.

103 FG 6 participant 5.

104 FG 6 participant 4, participant 3.

105 FG 1 participant 5, FG 2 participant 3.

106 FG 3 participant 6, participant 4.

107 FG 3 participant 1, participant 2.

108 FG 3 participant 2, participant 1.

109 FG 5 participant 5, participant 1.

110 X^2 (1, $n = 745$) = 2.1, $p = 0.146$, Cramer's $V = 9.05$.

111 X^2 (1, $n = 537$) = 5.1, $p = 0.023$, Cramer's $V = 0.1$.

112 Neil M. Richards, *Intellectual Privacy* (Oxford: Oxford University Press, 2015).

113 Richards, 'The Perils of Social Reading', 691, 704.

114 Richards, 'The Perils of Social Reading', 693, 704.

115 Richards, 'The Perils of Social Reading', 704, 712.

116 Joseph Turow et al., 'Divided We Feel: Partisan Politics Drive American's Emotions Regarding Surveillance of Low-Income Populations' (Annenberg School of Communication, University of Pennsylvania, 27 April 2018), https://ssrn.com/abstract=3609974, 3.

117 Price, *How to Do Things with Books in Victorian Britain*, 3; Ina Ferris, 'Bibliographic Romance: Bibliophilia and the Book-Object', *Romantic Circles*, 2004, www.rc.umd.edu/praxis/libraries/ferris/ferris.html.

118 David McKitterick, *Print, Manuscript and the Search for Order, 1450–1830* (Cambridge: Cambridge University Press, 2003), 20.

119 Ferris, 'Bibliographic Romance'.

120 Alberto Manguel, *A History of Reading* (London: London Flamingo, 1997), 244.
121 Steven Chen and Neil Granitz, 'Adoption, Rejection, or Convergence: Consumer Attitudes toward Book Digitization', *Journal of Business Research* 65, no. 8 (1 August 2012): 1224, https://doi.org/10.1016/j.jbusres.2011.06.038.
122 Survey 2014, FG 3 participant 5, FG 1 participant 3, FG 1 participant 3.
123 FG 4 participant 2.
124 Survey 2015 in both cases.
125 FG 4 participant 3, Survey 2014.
126 FG 6 participant 4.
127 Survey 2015, 2016, 2020, 2014.
128 FG 1 participant 1, Survey 2014, 2016.
129 Survey 2020, 2022.
130 Questions added for 2021 and 2022, as the 2020 survey launched in February, in those few weeks between the discovery of the virus and the declaration of a worldwide emergency.
131 Survey 2022, 2021, 2022, 2022.
132 Survey 2015, 2014.
133 Survey 2015, 2016, 2017.
134 Survey 2017.
135 Survey 2020, 2022, 2020, 2022.
136 FG 1 participant 1, FG 4 participant 4, both inflammatory statements that drew censure; please see earlier in this chapter for more on policing attitudes towards the material object of the print book.
137 Ferris, 'Bibliographic Romance'.
138 'Bibliophile, n. Meanings, Etymology and More', in *Oxford English Dictionary* (Oxford University Press), www.oed.com/dictionary/bibliophile_n#; Merriam-Webster, 'Definition of BIBLIOPHILIA', *Merriam-Webster Dictionary*, www.merriam-webster.com/dictionary/bibliophilia.
139 Dibdin, *Bibliomania*, 3; Ferris, 'Bibliographic Romance'.
140 Raven, 'The Industrial Revolution of the Book', 154.
141 Interview 2, FG 5, FG 5 participant 3.
142 FG 2 participant 3, participant 1.
143 FG 2 participant 2.
144 FG 1 participant 3, FG 2 participant 2.
145 FG 6 participant 2.
146 FG 3 participant 3.
147 FG 4 participant 1.
148 FG 4 participant 2.
149 FG 4 participant 4.
150 Now X. FG 4 participant 4.
151 FG 3 participant 3.
152 FG 3 participant 3, FG 1 participant 3.
153 FG 3 participant 2, FG 3.

154 Thomas Frognall Dibdin, *The Bibliomania; or Book-Madness* (London: Henry G. Bohn, 1809), 44.

155 FG 1 participant 6.

156 FG 1 participant 3, participant 1.

157 FG 6 participant 5.

158 Ferris, 'Bibliographic Romance'. Chesterfield, quoted by Price, *How to Do Things with Books in Victorian Britain*, 3.

159 Dibdin, *Bibliomania; or Book-Madness; a Bibliographical Romance*, 3–4.

160 Price, *How to Do Things with Books in Victorian Britain*, 3.

161 D'Israeli, quoted in Ferris, 'Bibliographic Romance'.

162 FG 6 participant 2.

163 Richard A. Peterson and Roger M. Kern, 'Changing Highbrow Taste: From Snob to Omnivore', *American Sociological Review* 61, no. 5 (1996): 905–6, https://doi.org/10.2307/2096460; Dietz, Warwick, and Rayner, 'Auditioning for Permanence', 28.

164 Michael Bhaskar, *The Content Machine* (London: Anthem, 2013), 87.

165 Bhaskar, 87.

166 Kate Eichhorn, *Content* (Cambridge, MA: The MIT Press, 2022), 20–1.

167 Tenen, *Reading Platforms*, 323.

168 Eichhorn, *Content*, 21.

169 Faverio and Perrin, 'Three-in-Ten Americans Now Read E-books'; Perrin, 'Slightly Fewer Americans Are Reading Print Books'; Nielsen, 'Year in Books Review'.

170 Survey 2020.

171 Murray, '"Selling" Literature', 12; Pressman, *Bookishness*, 26–7.

172 FG 3 participant 3.

173 Davies, Lupton, and Schmidt, *Reading Novels During the Covid-19 Pandemic*; Norrick-Rühl and Towheed, 'Introduction'; Dietz, 'Projection or Reflection?'; Dietz, 'Many Gates with a Single Keeper'.

174 29.8% of men versus 38.4% of women, 50.0% of those who identify as non-binary/gender fluid, none of those whose gender identity was not listed, and 40.0% of those declining to state, X^2 (4, $n = 1,632$) $= 12.8$, $p = 0.012$, Cramer's $V = 0.09$.

175 Lisa Otty, '"God-like and Immortal": Masculinity, Authority and the Cult of the Book, 1910–1930', in *Society for the History of Authorship, Reading and Publishing, Religions of the Book* (Society for the History of Authorship, Reading and Publishing, Religions of the Book, Antwerp, Belgium, 2014).

176 Driscoll, *The New Literary Middlebrow*, 29.

177 X^2 (1, $n = 1,732$) $= 19.8$, $p < 0.001$, Cramer's $V = 0.11$.

178 X^2 (1, $n = 1,732$) $= 167.4$, $p < 0.001$, Cramer's $V = 0.31$.

179 X^2 (1, $n = 1,732$) $= 205.8$, $p < 0.001$, Cramer's $V = 0.35$.

180 X^2 (1, $n = 1,732$) $= 231.0$, $p < 0.001$, Cramer's $V = 0.37$.

181 Survey 2016, 2017, 2021, 2022, 2014, 2014, 2014.

182 Suzanne Kean, *Empathy and the Novel* (Oxford: Oxford University Press, 2007), x; Archer and Jockers, *The Bestseller Code*, 52–5.

183 Anne Mangen et al., 'Empathy and Literary Style', *Orbis Litterarum* 73, no. 6 (2018): 2, https://doi.org/10.1111/oli.12193.

184 Kean, *Empathy and the Novel*, vii–viii, x.

185 Murray, 'Is BookTube the Future of Literary Studies?'.

186 Radway, *Reading the Romance*; Kean, *Empathy and the Novel*, x; Seth Studer and Ichiro Takayoshi, 'Franzen and the "Open-Minded but Essentially Untrained Fiction Reader"', *Post45: Peer Reviewed*, 8 July 2013, https://post45.org/2013/07/franzen-and-the-open-minded-but-essentially-untrained-fiction-reader/.

187 Studer and Takayoshi, 'Franzen and the "Open-Minded but Essentially Untrained Fiction Reader"'.

188 Studer and Takayoshi, 'Franzen and the "Open-Minded but Essentially Untrained Fiction Reader"'.

189 Flint, *The Woman Reader 1837–1914*, 30–1; Beth Driscoll, 'The Middlebrow Family Resemblance: Features of the Historical and Contemporary Middlebrow', *Post45: Peer Reviewed*, 1 July 2016, https://post45.org/2016/07/the-middlebrow-family-resemblance-features-of-the-historical-and-contemporary-middlebrow/.

190 Fuller and Rehberg Sedo, *Reading Bestsellers*, 42.

191 Hungerford, *Making Literature Now*, 30–1.

192 Survey 2021.

193 Survey 2022, 2014.

194 Survey 2014, 2022.

195 Survey 2022, 2014, 2021, 2022.

196 Survey 2016.

197 FG 3 participant 1, participant 2, FG 6 participant 5.

198 Duguid, 'Material Matters'. Vernacular use of 'technophile' does not perfectly harmonise with Hayler's distinction between obtrusive device and integrated technology, but does recognise a distinction between the humdrum everyday and exciting innovations. See Hayler, *Challenging the Phenomenology of Technology*.

199 12.2% of men versus 5.3% of all other respondents, X^2 (4, $n = 1,209$) = 23.9, $p < 0.001$, Cramer's $V = 0.14$.

200 Moynihan, 'With Its New Kindles'; Matt Reynolds, 'Kindle Oasis Review: The Ereader You'll Want, but Not One You Need', *Wired UK*, www.wired.co.uk/article/kindle-oasis-second-generation-review-price-specs-waterproof-ereader.

201 FG 4 participant 2, Survey 2017.

202 Kimberly Kennedy, 'Fan Binding as a Method of Fan Work Preservation', *Transformative Works and Cultures* 37 (13 March 2022): 9.2, https://doi.org/10.3983/twc.2022.2107.

203 Julia Alexander, 'Making Fanfiction Beautiful Enough for a Bookshelf', *The Verge [Online]*, 9 March 2021, www.theverge.com/22311788/fanfiction-bookbinding-tiktok-diy-star-wars-harry-potter-twitter-fandom.

204 Catherine Coker, 'The Margins of Print? Fan Fiction as Book History', *Transformative Works and Cultures* 25 (15 September 2017), https://doi.org/10.3983/twc.2017.01053.

205 The ownership of such bequests is open to question, as fan bindings represent gift economy rather than commercial exchanges. While many fan binders present a copy as a gift to the author, bound fic rarely changes hands for money: questions on the legality of selling fan fiction, even in the limited form of accepting payment for time and materials for layout and binding only, and harmony with community standards of gift exchange make it difficult for such bindings to circulate. See Shira Belén Buchsbaum, 'Binding Fan Fiction and Reexamining Book Production Models', *Transformative Works and Cultures* 37 (13 March 2022), https://doi.org/10.3983/twc.2022.2129; Kennedy, 'Fan Binding as a Method of Fan Work Preservation'.

206 Buchsbaum, 'Binding Fan Fiction and Reexamining Book Production Models', 8.1.

207 Buchsbaum, 'Binding Fan Fiction and Reexamining Book Production Models', 5.2.

208 Buchsbaum, 'Binding Fan Fiction and Reexamining Book Production Models', 7.6; Kennedy, 'Fan Binding as a Method of Fan Work Preservation', 2.3, 8.1.

209 FG 4.

210 Or presumably, for readers from late 2022, attaching sticky notes via a Kindle Scribe Basic Pen. FG 2 participant 3.

211 Survey 2014, FG 2 participant 3.

212 Patricia Meyer Spacks, *On Rereading* (Cambridge, MA: Belknap Press, 2013), 9. Given the extreme youth of the mass e-reading era, at present the notes some participants describe (annotations by great grandparents, what Spacks refers to as messages from one's younger self, etc.) have no direct counterpart in e-books. But the stunning durability of personal information online, and determination of tech companies to monetise memories (as with Facebook or Google Photos pushing algorithm-generated 'remember this day' albums to users) indicate how easily a digital notation could be saved, repurposed, and inserted into an individual's digital future.

213 FG 1 participant 5, Survey 2017. The ultimate in writing out of feeling is perhaps fan fiction: not only binding beloved fics, as discussed earlier in this chapter, but also writing new fics based on beloved original texts, or commenting on or otherwise publicly textually augmenting existing fics. But much more research is needed to understand how feeling for a particular fandom interacts with feeling for print, and whether anything like the same rules apply to transmedia fandoms.

214 FG 3 participant 1, participant 2.

215 Lewis Hyde, *The Gift: Creativity and the Artist in the Modern World* (New York: Vintage Books USA, 1983), xiv, FG 4.

216 Hyde, *The Gift*, xiv–xv.

217 Though Kickstarter is better known for games and devices than books, in 2022 fantasy author Brandon Sanderson's 'Surprise! 4 Secret Novels' raised more than $20 million in 72 hours to become the most-funded project in the platform's history (Atwell). As of December 2023, the project had raised over $41 million (Dragonsteel). While Brandon's success demonstrates what independent authors can develop with sufficient resources, expertise, and established audience, and makes him another author who, like Colleen Hoover, needs neither a Big Five publisher nor Amazon to reach their readership (Harris), Kickstarter's observations on the existing assets Sanderson brought to the table, including award-winning and bestselling prior novels, a passionate fan base engaged via constant interaction, 'credibility', 'visibility', and 'clout' from a long-term relationship with traditional publisher Tor, and professional production, marketing, promotion, and algorithm management from a team of thirty (Atwell), do not suggest this as a pathway open to the typical emerging author. See Margot Atwell, 'How Brandon Sanderson's Kickstarter Project Broke the Bookish Internet', *Kickstarter*, 3 December 2022, www.kickstarter.com/articles/how-brandon-sanderson-s-kickstarter-project-broke-the-bookish-internet; Dragonsteel Entertainment, 'Surprise! Four Secret Novels by Brandon Sanderson', *Kickstarter*, 19 December 2023, www.kickstarter.com/projects/dragonsteel/surprise-four-secret-novels-by-brandon-sanderson; Elizabeth A. Harris, 'Fantasy Author Raises $15.4 Million in 24 Hours to Self-Publish', *The New York Times*, 3 March 2022, sec. Books, www.nytimes.com/2022/03/03/books/brandon-sanderson-kickstarter.html.

218 Unbound, 'Work with Us', *Unbound*, 2024, https://unbound.com/authors/work-with-us.

219 Humble Bundle, 'What Is Humble Bundle?', *Humble Bundle*, www.humblebundle.com/about.

220 Hugh Howey, *Promises of London: A Short Story* (Broad Reach Publishing, 2014).

221 Howey, *Promises of London*.

222 Sarah Crown, 'Kindles Make Reading People Harder', *The Guardian*, 16 August 2011, sec. Books, www.theguardian.com/books/booksblog/2011/aug/16/e-readers-make-reading-people-harder.

Coda

1 Wattpad Brand Partnerships, 'The Story of After from Wattpad to Hollywood', *Brands Wattpad*, https://brands.wattpad.com/insights/the-story-of-after-from-wattpad-to-hollywood. Wattpad's measures of a 'read' are opaque, but the sheer number, and the benefits to the company and author of calculating the highest, most newsworthy figure, suggest that they include partial and re-reads in this count.

2 Also, unlike *Fifty Shades of Grey* and many other works of fan fiction, the free online version of *After* was never taken down. Its continuing availability on Wattpad did not prevent the print version selling tens of millions of copies across thirty-five languages. See Skains, *Digital Authorship*; Wattpad Brand Partnerships, 'The Story of After from Wattpad to Hollywood'.

3 David Streitfeld, 'Web Fiction, Serialized and Social', *The New York Times*, 24 March 2014, sec. Technology, www.nytimes.com/2014/03/24/ technology/web-fiction-serialized-and-social.html. It is worth noting that Streitfeld, whose article Birkerts cites for details of the deal, in one instance uses the word 'episode' as well, but interchangeably with 'chapter' to describe a section of Todd's serialised work. Fellow *New York Times* journalist Alexandra Alter similarly used 'novel' and 'chapter' to describe the work, and 'novelist' to describe Todd. See Alexandra Alter, 'Fantasizing on the Famous', *The New York Times*, 21 October 2014, sec. Business, www .nytimes.com/2014/10/22/business/media/harry-styles-of-one-direction-stars-in-anna-todds-novel.html.

4 Sven Birkerts, 'Can the "Literary" Survive Technology?', *Literary Hub*, 8 April 2016, https://lithub.com/can-the-literary-survive-technology/.

5 Jon Ronson, *So You've Been Publicly Shamed* (London: Picador, 2016), 46.

6 Including the blockchain artefact *A Universe Explodes*.

7 Uglow, 'pBooks, eBooks, & dBooks'.

8 An exercise that bears some resemblance to audiobook listeners customising by selecting their preferred reader voice, recorded or synthesised. See Rubery, *The Untold Story of the Talking Book*, 275.

9 Nosheen Iqbal, 'Film Fans See Red over Netflix "Targeted" Posters for Black Viewers', *The Observer*, 20 October 2018, sec. Media, www.theguardian.com/ media/2018/oct/20/netflix-film-black-viewers-personalised-marketing-target.

10 Eichhorn, *Content*.

11 Hyde, *The Gift*.

12 Leah Henrickson, *Reading Computer-Generated Texts* (Cambridge: Cambridge University Press, 2021).

13 Reisner, 'These 183,000 Books Are Fueling the Biggest Fight in Publishing and Tech'; Reisner, 'Revealed'.

14 Eichhorn, *Content*, 137.

15 Ella Creamer, 'Amazon Removes Books "Generated by AI" for Sale under Author's Name', *The Guardian*, 9 August 2023, sec. Books, www.theguardian .com/books/2023/aug/09/amazon-removes-books-generated-by-ai-for-sale-under-authors-name.

16 Survey 2022.

17 Survey 2020, Moynihan, 'With Its New Kindles, Amazon Tries to Replicate the Magic of Paper'; Howard, *The Idea of the Canterbury Tales*, 63.

18 Murray, *The Digital Literary Sphere*; Alexandra Dane and Millicent Weber, 'Post-Digital Book Cultures: An Introduction', in *Post-Digital Book Cultures: Australian Perspectives*, ed. Alexandra Dane and Millicent Weber (Clayton: Monash University Publishing, 2021).

Appendix

1 'Legitimacy, n. Meanings, Etymology and More | Oxford English Dictionary', www.oed.com/dictionary/legitimacy_n?tab=meaning_and_use.

2 Max Weber, *Economy and Society: An Outline of Interpretive Sociology*, vol. 1 (Berkeley, CA: University of California Press, 1978), 31.

3 Cathryn Johnson, Timothy J. Dowd, and Cecilia L. Ridgeway, 'Legitimacy as a Social Process', *Annual Review of Sociology* 32 (2006): 57.

4 Pierre Bourdieu, *Distinction: A Social Critique of the Judgement of Taste* (London: Routledge, 1986), 8.

5 Trajkovski and Collins, *Handbook of Research on Agent-Based Societies*, 246.

6 'Reputation, n. Meanings, Etymology and More | Oxford English Dictionary', www.oed.com/dictionary/reputation_n?tab=meaning_and_use#25891645.

7 John B. Thompson, *Merchants of Culture: The Publishing Business in the Twenty-First Century*, 2nd ed. (Cambridge: Polity, 2012), 81–2; Squires, *Marketing Literature*, 150.

8 Annika Veh, Markus Göbel, and Rick Vogel, 'Corporate Reputation in Management Research: A Review of the Literature and Assessment of the Concept', *Business Research* 12, no. 2 (1 December 2019): 1, 13, https://doi.org/10.1007/s40685-018-0080-4.

9 Tom J. Brown et al., 'Identity, Intended Image, Construed Image, and Reputation: An Interdisciplinary Framework and Suggested Terminology', *Journal of the Academy of Marketing Science* 34, no. 2 (1 March 2006): 99–106, https://doi.org/10.1177/0092070305284969.

10 As in '1. A. Able to be believed in, justifying confidence; convincingly honest, principled, or authentic and often, as a corollary, accurate (passing into sense A.1b); trustworthy, reliable. (a) Of information, evidence, etc. (b) Of a person, source of information, etc. B. Able to be believed; convincingly true or accurate. (a) Of an assertion, account, etc. (b) Of a matter of fact: with anticipatory *it*. (c) Able to be believed in as effective or operational. Originally of a nuclear weapon: considered likely to be used" See 'Credible, Adj. & n. Meanings, Etymology and More | Oxford English Dictionary', www.oed.com/dictionary/credible_adj?tab=meaning_and_use#8019519.

11 Soo Young Rieh and David R. Danielson, 'Credibility: A Multidisciplinary Framework', *Annual Review of Information Science and Technology* 41, no. 1 (2007): 307–64, https://doi.org/10.1002/aris.2007.1440410114.

12 Veh, Göbel, and Vogel, 'Corporate Reputation in Management Research', 16.

13 Ray Siemens et al., 'HCI-Book? Perspectives on E-Book Research, 2006–2008 (Foundational to Implementing New Knowledge Environments)', *Papers of the Bibliographical Society of Canada / Cahiers de La Société Bibliographique Du Canada* 49, no. 1 (2011): 49, https://doi.org/10.33137/pbsc.v49i1.21941; Rowberry, 'Ebookness'.

Index

CSS stylesheet, 46
24symbols, 76

A Prayer for Owen Meany, 90–91
AAAAARG, 218
AAARG. *See* AAAAARG
abibliophobia, 109, 132
  'backup book', 187
ableism, 31, 33–34, 189
accommodating book, 113, 116, 132
  demanding book, 129, 150
accommodating reader, 150
Active Book, 24
Adams, Douglas. *See Hitchhiker's Guide to the Galaxy*
ADHD, 115
Afternoon, a story, 19, 23
Agrippa. See Gibson, William
Amazon, 9, 53, 92, 98, 108, 192
  '1 click', 70
  47North, 57
  Amazon Prime Video, 104
  as 'judging' readers, 146, 156
  book recommendations, 155–56
  boycott of, 174
  conditional use licence, 61, 70, 180
  and contradictory narratives of realness, 64
  CreateSpace, 192
  as e-book retailer, 6, 23
  'ethos of bookishness', 26, 130, 148
  Kindle, 2, 6, 9, 25–26, 41, 112
  Kindle and immersion, 126–27
  Kindle app, 44, 47, 103, 125
  Kindle as 'library in my bag', 85
  'Kindle Christmas', 77
  Kindle device development, 3, 23–24, 130
  Kindle Direct Publishing, 9, 57, 138, 140
  Kindle Oasis, 104–5, 160, 176
  Kindle Paperwhite, 105
  Kindle Popular Highlights, 117, 178–79
  Kindle Scribe, 105, 176
  Kindle Singles, 180
  Kindle Store, 3
  Kindle Unlimited, 9, 76, 85, 137, 192
  Kindle Unlimited and novels, 8
  Kindle Unlimited and self-publishing, 1, 138
  Kindle Voyage, 104–5
  Kindle, sharing books on, 79
  PagePress, 104
  Prime, 105
  Prime Reading, 76, 85, 137
  and privacy, 157
  reader feelings regarding, 72, 161, 174–75
  terms and conditions, 5, 68
  Timeline, 104
  trust or lack of trust in, 86–87
  Whispernet, 41
  X-ray, 104, 122
American Library Association, 65, 216
Annotation, 177–78
Apple, 2, 9, 86, 180, 192, 216
  as e-book retailer, 6
  iBooks, 23
  iPad, 23, 125
  iPhone, 23
  iPod Touch, 23
  trust or lack of trust in, 87
Archer, Jodie, 143
Armstrong, Nancy, 236
artificial intelligence, 42
  AI authorship, 74
  and author status, 191–92
  Large Language Models, 66
Avon Impulse, 54

Barnes & Noble, 176, 216
Baron, Naomi, 93
Baudrillard, Jean, 17
Berens, Kathi Inman, 65, 88

Bezos, Jeffrey P., 26, 78, 105, 130, 148, 197
  reader feelings regarding, 161, 174
Bhaskar, Michael, 165
Bible, 23, 120
bibliophilia, 12, 134, 148, 168–72, 188
  and bookshops, 172
  and feelings about Amazon, 174
  and gender, 170, 173
  bibliomania, 162, 164
  compatibility with digital reading, 172
  negotiating definitions of the term, 162
  'readingophile', 164, 173
  and reading devices, 84, 174
Big Five, 54, 56
Bilandzic, Helena, 123
Birke, Dorothee, 20, 39
Birkerts, Sven, 147, 185–86
BitTorrent, 67, 72
Bolter, Jay David, 17, 33
book gifts, 41–42, 77–79, 81, 90, 98, 177
book history, 5–6, 14, 18, 40
Book Industry Study Group, 65
Bookman, 23
book rental, 71
bookshops, 35, 44
  and bibliophilia, 171
  physical bookshops, 8, 84
Bookstagram, 22, 41
BookTok, 41
Borsuk, Amaranth, 17, 208
Bourdieu, Pierre, 21, 134–35, 143
Brown, Bob, 10, 22, 147
Brown, Brené, 145
Buchsbaum, Shira, 177
Bush, Vannevar, 10, 22
Busselle, Rick, 123
Byliner, 56

Caro, Robert, 214
CD ROM, 2, 23
censorship, 24
certainty, 31–33
childcare, 95, 111–13
Christ, Birte, 20, 39
Chronicles of Narnia, 3
Colbjørnsen, Terje, 143
comic books, 91
  digital comics, 180
communications circuit, 7, 12
content, 165–66
  book as 'container', 167
Coover, Robert, 24, 59
Copyright Term Extension Act, 63
cover design, 35, 42–43

COVID-19, 8, 78, 84, 107
  and access to personal book collections, 130
  and book piracy, 65
  and feelings towards e-books, 160
  and library usage, 69, 75
Creative Commons, 64
Csikszentmihalyi, Mihaly, 123
cultural capital, 133, 151
  position-takings, 147
customisation, 117

Darnton, Robert, 7
Data Discman, 24
Daunt, James, 97
Davis, Natalie Zemon, 78
de Certeau, Michel, 72
debates on 'death of the book', 14, 148, 168
Dibdin, Thomas Frognall, 100, 164
digital audition, 87, 92, 187, 192
digital distraction, 121–22
digital fiction, 23
digital humanities, 5, 11, 14
digital proxy, 11, 36, 47, 91, 105, 186–87
digital reading copy, 90
Digital Rights Management, 45
disability, 114
display, 133, 153
Driscoll, Beth, 139
Drucker, Johanna, 5, 17–19, 25, 32, 34, 46, 128
dyslexia, 114
  Open Dyslexia font, 116

Eastgate, 37
Eberhard, Martin, 197
Eichhorn, Kate, 166, 191
electronic book, 22
elitism, 31, 33
Elsevier, 216
empathy, 131, 172–73
engagement, 121–31, 191
  'lost in a book', 93, 120–27, 191
  ludic, 48
English, James, 21, 135
Ensslin, Astrid, 21
equivalence, 36, 58
ersatz book, 11, 36, 59–60, 91, 105, 186–87

Facebook, 80
fan fiction, 64, 142–43, 217
  fan binding, 177
Ferris, Ina, 165
Fifty Shades of Grey, 65, 138, 142–43, 185
Flint, Kate, 147, 236
Franklin Electronics, 23

Franzen, Jonathan, 136, 173
Friedman, Jane, 62
front matter, 57
Fuller, Danielle, 6

Galey, Alan, 10, 17, 19, 21, 34, 43, 46–47
games, 23
gatekeeping, 54, 134
GE TermiNet 1200, 2
Gemstar, 197
Genette, Gérard, 20, 36–37, 39
Gibson, William, 19
Gitelman, Lisa, 5, 18, 27, 100
Gooding, Paul, 20
Goodreads, 22, 104, 179
Google, 62, 86, 216
    Google Books, 50, 63–64
Green, Melanie, 123, 125
Grigar, Dene, 39
Grusin, Richard, 17, 33
The Gutenberg Elegies, 147

Hachette, 9
Harlequin Romance, 192
HarperCollins, 9
Hart, Michael, 63
Hayler, Matt, 18, 126–27, 148
Hayles, N. Katherine, 17–18
Heller, Michael, 67, 70, 74
Henrickson, Leah, 74, 191
Hicks, Mar, 148
Hitchhiker's Guide to the Galaxy, 3
Hoofnagle, Chris Jay, 70–72, 77
Hoskins, Valerie, 142
Hou, Jinghui, 123, 125
Howey, Hugh, 180
Hulu, 193
Humble Bundle, 180
Humble, Nicola, 139
Hungerford, Amy, 21
Hutchings, Tim, 120
Hyde, Lewis, 191
HyperCard, 23
Hypertext fiction, 23

IBM Selectric, 147
IMDb (Internet Movie Database), 104
immersion. *See* engagement
Immersive Media and Books 2020, 65
incomplete book, 11, 106, 113, 132, 151,
    186–87
Independent Book Publishers Association, 65
Ingram Content Group, 216
inheritance of books, 71, 74

INKE project, 19–20, 201
insomnia, 111
Intel, 216
Intellectual property
    Digital Millennium Copyright Act, 24
    intellectual property law, 62
intermedia, 23
International Digital Publishing Forum, 216
Internet Archive, 226
ISBN, 8
Ithaka, 216

James, E. L., 142
Jenner, Mareike, 234
Jockers, Matthew, 143
Joyce, Michael, 19, 23

Kennedy, Kimberly, 177
Kickstarter, 180
Kindle. *See* Amazon
King, Stephen, 24
Kirschenbaum, Matthew, 5, 17–18, 23, 45, 63
Kobo, 160
Koegler, Caroline, 15
Kuiken, Don, 124–25

Leavis, Q. R., 135
legitimacy, 14
Lendle, 79
Lessig, Lawrence, 63–64
libraries, 42, 62, 69, 75, 98
    culling books from personal library, 84, 89,
        130
    e-books as part of personal libraries,
        84–86
    New York Public Library, 26
    personal libraries, 5, 82–84
    public libraries, 108
    storage space, 84
Library Genesis, 66
literary festivals, 22
literary prizes, 3
literary status, 21–22
    discredit, 134, 143, 146
    'highbrow', 78, 136, 165
    'middlebrow', 136, 139, 173
    status and gender, 139
    women as 'incompetent readers', 135, 138–40,
        151
Lulu, 176

Macmillan, 9
Malloy, Judy, 23, 208
Mangen, Anne, 6, 94, 124–25, 131

The Martian, 53
materiality, 10, 14, 18–19, 97
    appreciation for the 'insides' of books, 165
    book flavour, 100
    book smell, 4, 96, 100, 150, 152, 160, 192
    contingent materiality, 34
    'intangibility' of digital books, 100
    materiality scepticism, 150
McCracken, Ellen, 20, 39, 42, 104
McGann, Jerome, 18, 118
McLuhan, Marshall, 147
media archaeology, 5
Memex, 10, 22
memory, 124, 130, 153, 159, 179
Microsoft, 216
Mindwheel, 23
Morris, William, 118
Murray, Simone, 5, 21, 26, 172

Netflix, 190, 193
Netgalley, 85
Nissenbaum, Stephen, 77
Nook, 24, 129
Noorda, Rachel, 65, 88
Norrick-Rühl, Corinna, 15, 37
Norwegian Library of Talking Books and Braille, 216
novel, 8–9, 22–24, 112, 135
    graphic novels, 95, 125
    and rereading, 159
NuvoMedia, 130, 197, 216

Open eBook Authoring Group, 166, 216
Open Road Publishing, 212
Open University, 216
Oprah's Book Club, 136, 173
    other celebrity book clubs, 22
OverDrive, 65
    Libby, 220
Oyster, 87

PalmPilot, 2
pandemic. *See* COVID-19
paratext, 11, 20–21, 36–48, 146
    discerning authorial intention, 36–48
    durable peritext, 44
    epitext, 40, 56
    event paratext, 47
    peritext, 40, 79
    precarious peritext, 44
Patreon, 180
Penguin. *See* Penguin Random House
Penguin Random House, 9
    Alibi, 54
    Hydra, 54

Perzanowski, Aaron, 70–72, 77
photoshop, 35, 43
physical weight, 96, 99, 149, 161
piracy, 65–67
Pirate Bay, 42, 66
platform studies, 5, 15
PLATO, 22
Ploughshares Solos, 54
Pressman, Jessica, 147, 204
Price, Leah, 5, 26, 92, 118, 165
principled resistance, 72, 92, 187
Print-On-Demand, 54, 176
privacy
    and reading of low-status books, 140
    'binge reading', 138
    concern for print privacy as a bookish trait, 158
    'furtive reading', 137
    intellectual privacy, 158
    reading in print to evade tracking, 156–59, 182
    women as 'furtive readers', 138, 182
progress narratives, 148
Project Gutenberg, 23, 42, 49–50, 63, 98, 108
    and novels, 23
    development of, 63
    and Silicon Valley ethos, 62
    source for 'classics', 141
    terms and conditions, 67
    and tracking, 157
publishing studies, 5

Radway, Janice, 5, 172
Random House. *See* Penguin Random House
Ray Murray, Padmini, 7
Readies, 10, 22, 147
reading comprehension, 94
Rehberg Sedo, DeNel, 6
relocation
    forced relocation/loss of home, 90
    moving house, 82, 88, 130
Renegade Bindery, 177
Repurchasing, 154
Richards, Neil, 81, 158
Rocket eBook, 2–3, 23–24, 130
Rowberry, Simon, 16, 21
Royal National Institute of Blind People (RNIB), 136
Rubery, Matthew, 22

Salzman, James, 67, 70, 74
Schwabach, Aaron, 65
Sci-Hub, 66
Scribd, 76, 98, 137

self-publishing, 36, 42, 52–56, 60, 134, 143
  single-author imprint, 57
Shep, Sydney, 18
Sieghart Review, 62
Simon and Schuster, 9
Skains, R. Lyle, 218
snobbery, 4, 14, 33, 53
SoftBook, 216
Sony, 216
Sony Reader, 24
Squires, Claire, 7, 21, 135
Storyspace, 23
Streitfeld, David, 185
Striphas, Ted, 26
Studer, Seth, 173
Styron, William, 62

Takayoshi, Ichiro, 173
Tarpenning, Marc, 197
Technophilia, 86, 134, 148, 167, 175
  and Kindle, 175
Tenen, Dennis Yi, 22, 24, 166
terms and conditions, 70–71
Terras, Melissa, 20
Tether, Leah, 20
The WELL, 23

Thibodeau, Kenneth, 18
Thomas, Bronwen, 9, 224
Thompson, John B., 21, 87
Todd, Anna, 65, 185
travel, 1, 75, 90, 109, 111, 121
  commuting, 88, 109, 120, 136, 140, 144, 174, 190

Uglow, Tea, 189
UK Intellectual Property Office, 65
Uncle Roger, 23

van der Weel, Adriaan, 131

Warde, Beatrice, 127
Warwick, Claire, 20
Waterstones, 97
Wattpad, 8, 22, 65, 140, 185
Wendell, Sarah, 144
Werner, Sarah, 23
Wired, 176
Woolf, Virginia, 36
World Wide Web Consortium (W3C), 216

YouTube, 24, 41
YouVersion, 120
Zoom, 121

Printed in the United States
by Baker & Taylor Publisher Services